LAWS AND LEGISLATION

FIREARMS IN AMERICA

SELECTED ISSUES AND ANALYSES

LAWS AND LEGISLATION

Additional books in this series can be found on Nova's website
under the Series tab.

Additional e-books in this series can be found on Nova's website
under the e-book tab.

LAWS AND LEGISLATION

FIREARMS IN AMERICA

SELECTED ISSUES AND ANALYSES

ALFONSO D. SUTTON
EDITOR

New York

Library of Congress Cataloging-in-Publication Data

ISBN: 978-1-63117-823-8

Published by Nova Science Publishers, Inc. † New York

CONTENTS

PREFACE

Congress has broad authority pursuant to the Commerce Clause to enact laws in areas that may overlap with traditional state jurisdiction. As such, Congress has passed complex statutory provisions that regulate the possession, receipt, transfer, and manufacture of firearms and ammunition. Generally, courts have upheld the validity of firearms laws pursuant to Congress's commerce power. However, courts have been confronted with the question of whether federal laws can be applied to intrastate possession and intrastate transfers of firearms, or whether such application exceeds the authority of Congress. This book explores these cases and how courts have analyzed these as-applied challenges under the Supreme Court's Commerce Clause jurisprudence primarily set forth in *United States v. Lopez.*

Chapter 1 – The U.S. Constitution specifies the enumerated powers of the federal government. These powers, however, have been interpreted broadly so as to create a large potential overlap with state authority. States may generally legislate on all matters within their territorial jurisdiction. Indeed, criminal law, family law, property, and contract and tort law, among others, are typical areas of law that are regulated at the state level. Accordingly, states have enacted their own laws regarding the unlawful possession and disposition of firearms, as well as the manner in which firearms may be carried.

Congress, too, has enacted legislation related to firearms control. It includes, among others, the National Firearms Act of 1934, the Gun Control Act of 1968, the Firearm Owners' Protection Act of 1986, and the Brady Handgun Violence Prevention Act of 1993. Generally, Congress has relied on its authority under the Commerce Clause to enact such statutes. The Commerce Clause states: "The Congress shall have Power ... To regulate

Commerce with foreign Nationals, and among the several States, and with Indian Tribes."

Chapter 2 – The U.S. Supreme Court in *District of Columbia v. Heller* held that the Second Amendment to the U.S. Constitution protects an individual right to possess a firearm, unconnected with service in a militia, and the use of that firearm for traditionally lawful purposes, such as self-defense within the home. It also held that the Second Amendment applies to the states in *McDonald v. City of Chicago*. Since then, federal and state firearms laws have been challenged under the Second Amendment. Lower courts have been disputed in determining how to evaluate these provisions, given that the *Heller* decision was not an exhaustive analysis of the scope of the Second Amendment.

This report first discusses the two-step inquiry fashioned by the lower courts to analyze provisions under the Second Amendment. It proceeds to highlight how this test has been employed on a select number of firearms laws—namely, the federal age requirement and prohibition on possession by those convicted of a misdemeanor crime of domestic violence; and state requirements to obtain a concealed carry permit and a state assault weapons ban. How courts have applied the test to these categories may provide some indication as to how future firearms regulations may be considered by the Supreme Court. The report concludes with a discussion on how varied interpretations by the lower courts of the *Heller* decision may affect the burden upon the federal government to defend firearms provisions, as well as new analytical frameworks that have been suggested.

Chapter 3 – In the 113th Congress, there has been renewed congressional interest in gun control legislation. On January 16, 2013, President Obama announced his support for legislation on gun control, including a ban on certain semiautomatic assault firearms and large capacity ammunition feeding devices. Senator Dianne Feinstein introduced S. 150, the Assault Weapons Ban of 2013, which would prohibit, subject to certain exceptions, the sale, transfer, possession, manufacturing, and importation of specifically named firearms and other firearms that have certain features, as well as the transfer and possession of large capacity ammunition feeding devices. Representative Carolyn McCarthy introduced a companion measure, H.R. 437, in the House of Representatives. S. 150 is similar to the Assault Weapons Ban of 1994 (P.L. 103-322) that was in effect through September 13, 2004.

The Assault Weapons Ban of 1994 was challenged in the courts for violating, among other things, the Equal Protection Clause and the Commerce Clause. This report reviews the disposition of these challenges. It also discusses Second Amendment jurisprudence in light of the Supreme Court's decision in *District of Columbia v. Heller* and how lower courts have evaluated state and local assault weapons bans post-*Heller*.

Chapter 4 – Questions about the scope and efficacy of the background checks required during certain firearm purchases have gained prominence following recent mass shootings. These background checks are intended to identify whether potential purchasers are prohibited from purchasing or possessing firearms due to one or more "prohibiting factors," such as a prior felony conviction or a prior involuntary commitment for mental health reasons. Operationally, such background checks primarily use information contained within the National Instant Criminal Background Check System (NICS) and a particular focus of the debate in Congress has been whether federal privacy standards promulgated under the Health Insurance Portability and Accountability Act (i.e., the HIPAA privacy rule) or state privacy laws are an obstacle to the submission of mental health records to NICS.

Under the Gun Control Act of 1968 (GCA), as amended, persons adjudicated to be mentally defective or who have been committed to a mental institution are prohibited from possessing, shipping, transporting, and receiving firearms and ammunition. Neither a diagnosis of a mental illness nor treatment for a mental illness is sufficient to qualify a person as "adjudicated as a mental defective." Rather, an individual's "adjudication as a mental defective" relies upon a determination or decision by a court, board, commission, or other lawful authority. The definition of "committed to a mental institution" may apply only to inpatient settings. At least one federal court has held that the Supreme Court's recent recognition of an individual right to possess a firearm suggests that some emergency hospitalization or commitment procedures, that may not have as many procedural safeguards as formal commitment, should not be included within the meaning of "involuntary commitment" for purposes of the GCA. In 2007, Congress passed the NICS Improvement Amendments Act (NIAA), which authorizes the Attorney General to make additional grants to states to improve electronic access to records as well as to incentivize states to turn over records of persons who would be prohibited from possessing or receiving firearms.

In 2012, the Government Accountability Office (GAO) reported that a variety of technological, coordination, and legal (i.e., privacy) challenges limit the states' ability to report mental health records to NICS. The HIPAA privacy rule, which applies to most health care providers, regulates the use or disclosure of protected health information. On February 14, 2013, HHS announced that it will seek to amend the HIPAA privacy rule to remove any potential impediments to state reporting of mental health records to NICS. The privacy rule is most relevant as a potential obstacle where information used to generate mental health records on individuals prohibited from gun possession under the GCA is held by health care providers in states that do not expressly require disclosure of such records to NICS. Courts and health care providers that generate such prohibiting mental health records may also be subject to state health privacy laws that may be more restrictive than the HIPAA privacy rule.

Chapter 5 – As the Internet has become a significant venue for facilitating commercial transactions, concerns have arisen regarding the use of this medium to transfer firearms. This report discusses the sale of firearms and ammunition over the Internet, with a focus on the extent to which federal law regulates such activity. A review of the relevant factors indicates Internet-based firearm transactions are subject to the same regulatory scheme governing traditional firearm transactions. Over the years, this has raised concern about the possibility of increased violation of federal firearm laws, as well as challenges that law enforcement may face when attempting to investigate violations of these laws. A review of the relevant factors also indicates that the sale and transfer of ammunition are not as strictly regulated as firearms, and that these changes came into effect in 1986. Lastly, this report highlights recent legislative proposals, S. 3458 and H.R. 6241, companion measures introduced by Senator Frank Lautenberg and Representative Carolyn McCarthy in the 112th Congress that would affect online ammunition transactions.

Chapter 6 – The Protection of Lawful Commerce in Arms Act (PLCAA, P.L. 109-92) was passed in 2005. The PLCAA generally shields licensed manufacturers, dealers, and sellers of firearms or ammunition, as well as trade associations, from any civil action "resulting from the criminal or unlawful misuse" of a firearm or ammunition, but lists six exceptions where civil suits may be maintained. This act was introduced in response to litigation brought by municipalities and victims of shooting incidents against federally licensed firearms manufacturers and dealers, some of whom were located outside the state where the injuries occurred. Consequently, most lawsuits brought after the enactment of this law have been dismissed notwithstanding the exceptions that would permit a civil suit to proceed against a federal firearms licensee. This report provides an overview of the PLCAA and its exceptions, and discusses recent judicial developments.

Chapter 7 – In 2011, a total of 478,400 fatal and nonfatal violent crimes were committed with a firearm (table 1). Homicides made up about 2% of all firearm-related crimes. There were 11,101 firearm homicides in 2011, down by 39% from a high of 18,253 in 1993 (figure 1). The majority of the decline in firearm-related homicides occurred between 1993 and 1998. Since 1999, the number of firearm homicides increased from 10,828 to 12,791 in 2006 before declining to 11,101 in 2011.

Nonfatal firearm-related violent victimizations against persons age 12 or older declined 70%, from 1.5 million in 1993 to 456,500 in 2004 (figure 2). The number then fluctuated between about 400,000 to 600,000 through 2011.[1] While the number of firearm crimes declined over time, the percentage of all violence that involved a firearm did not change substantively, fluctuating between 6% and 9% over the same period. In 1993, 9% of all violence was committed with a firearm, compared to 8% in 2011.

In: Firearms in America
Editor: Alfonso D. Sutton

ISBN: 978-1-63117-823-8
© 2014 Nova Science Publishers, Inc.

Chapter 1

CONGRESSIONAL AUTHORITY TO REGULATE FIREARMS: A LEGAL OVERVIEW[*]

Vivian S. Chu

SUMMARY

Congress has broad authority pursuant to the Commerce Clause to enact laws in areas that may overlap with traditional state jurisdiction. As such, Congress has passed complex statutory provisions that regulate the possession, receipt, transfer, and manufacture of firearms and ammunition. Generally, courts have upheld the validity of firearms laws pursuant to Congress's commerce power. However, courts have been confronted with the question of whether federal laws can be applied to intrastate possession and intrastate transfers of firearms, or whether such application exceeds the authority of Congress. This report explores these cases and how courts have analyzed these as-applied challenges under the Supreme Court's Commerce Clause jurisprudence primarily set forth in *United States v. Lopez*.

---

[*] This is an edited, reformatted and augmented version of Congressional Research Service Publication, No. R43033, dated April 5, 2013.

OVERVIEW OF COMMERCE CLAUSE

The U.S. Constitution specifies the enumerated powers of the federal government.[1] These powers, however, have been interpreted broadly so as to create a large potential overlap with state authority. States may generally legislate on all matters within their territorial jurisdiction.[2] Indeed, criminal law, family law, property, and contract and tort law, among others, are typical areas of law that are regulated at the state level.[3] Accordingly, states have enacted their own laws regarding the unlawful possession and disposition of firearms, as well as the manner in which firearms may be carried.

Congress, too, has enacted legislation related to firearms control. It includes, among others, the National Firearms Act of 1934,[4] the Gun Control Act of 1968,[5] the Firearm Owners' Protection Act of 1986,[6] and the Brady Handgun Violence Prevention Act of 1993.[7] Generally, Congress has relied on its authority under the Commerce Clause to enact such statutes.[8] The Commerce Clause states: "The Congress shall have Power ... To regulate Commerce with foreign Nationals, and among the several States, and with Indian Tribes."[9]

Although a plain reading of the text might suggest that Congress has only a limited power to regulate commercial trade between persons in one state and persons of another state, the Clause has not been construed quite so narrowly, particularly in the modern era.[10] Since the 1930s, the U.S. Supreme Court has held that Congress has the ability to protect interstate commerce from burdens and obstructions "no matter what the source of the dangers which threaten it."[11] Over time, the Court concluded that Congress had considerable discretion in determining which commercial activities, including intrastate commercial activities, "affect" interstate commerce, as long as the legislation was "reasonably" related to achieving its goals of regulating interstate commerce.[12] Furthermore, the Court in *Wickard v. Filburn* also held that an activity, "though it may not be regarded as commerce, it may still, whatever its nature," be regulated by Congress if, in the aggregate, "it exerts a substantial economic effect on interstate commerce."[13] Under this prevailing interpretation of the Commerce Clause, the Supreme Court has upheld a variety of federal laws, including those regulating the production of wheat on farms,[14] racial discrimination by businesses,[15] and loan-sharking.[16]

United States v. Lopez and Progeny

However, in 1995, the Supreme Court revisited the scope of the Commerce Clause in *United States v. Lopez*.[17] In *Lopez*, the Supreme Court held that Congress had exceeded its constitutional authority when it passed the Gun-Free School Zones Act of 1990[18] (School Zones Act). The Court, clarifying the judiciary's traditional approach to Commerce Clause analysis, identified three broad categories of activity that Congress may regulate under its commerce power. These are

1) the channels of commerce;
2) the instrumentalities of commerce in interstate commerce, or persons or things in interstate commerce, even though the threat may come only from intrastate activities; and
3) activities which "substantially affect" interstate commerce.[19]

Under the first two categories, *Lopez* endorses Congress's "power to regulate all activities, persons or products that cross state boundaries. So long as a federal regulation relates to interstate transactions or interstate transportation, the federal regulation would be justified under the first two branches.... "[20] However, in examining the School Zones Act, the Court concluded that possession of a gun in a school zone was neither a regulation of the channels nor the instrumentalities of interstate commerce.[21] Because the conduct regulated was considered to be a wholly intrastate activity, the Court concluded that Congress could only regulate the activity if it fell within the third category and "substantially affects" interstate commerce. The Court indicated that intrastate activities have been, and could be, regulated by Congress where the activities "arise out of or are connected with a commercial transaction" and which are "part of a larger regulation of economic activity, in which the regulatory scheme could be undercut unless the intrastate activity were regulated."[22] The Court struck down the School Zones Act, declaring that the intrastate activity—possession of a handgun near a school—was not part of a larger economic firearms regulatory scheme.[23] Moreover, the act did not require that interstate commerce be affected, such as by requiring the gun to be transported in interstate commerce.[24]

For the same reasons identified in *Lopez*, the Supreme Court subsequently invalidated a part of the Violence Against Women Act (VAWA) in *United States v. Morrison*.[25] The Court in *Morrison* concluded that the activity regulated—a federal civil remedy for gender-motivated crimes—did not fall within the first two commerce categories, or the third category, because it was not an "economic activity"; furthermore, the provision contained no "jurisdictional element establishing that the federal cause of action [was] in pursuance of Congress's power to regulate interstate commerce."[26] In both *Lopez* and *Morrison*, the Court rejected the government's reasoning in establishing a connection between the regulated activity and its purported effect on interstate commerce, because the Court would have been required to "pile inference upon inference in a manner that would bid fair to convert congressional authority under the Commerce Clause to a general police power of the sort retained by the States."[27]

Although finding that Congress had exceeded its authority under the Commerce Clause with respect to the laws in *Lopez* and *Morrison*, the Court in *Gonzales v. Raich* subsequently clarified that Congress still has considerable authority under the "substantially affects" doctrine to regulate activity that is "quintessentially economic" on the intrastate level, even though the activity itself is not a part of interstate commerce.[28] The Court stated it did not need to determine for itself whether the activities, taken in the aggregate, substantially affect interstate commerce or undercut the larger regulatory scheme. Instead, it needed only to determine whether Congress had a rational basis to make such a conclusion.[29] Justice Scalia, in his concurring opinion, also emphasized the role of the Necessary and Proper Clause.[30] He opined that the Clause has been inherently relied on to regulate (1) economic intrastate activities that substantially affect interstate commerce, and (2) noneconomic intrastate activities that do not themselves substantially affect interstate commerce but that are a "necessary part of a more general regulation of interstate commerce."[31] The latter category, however, is limited by *Lopez* and *Morrison*, where the Court rejected arguments that "Congress may regulate *noneconomic* activity based solely on the effect that it may have on interstate commerce through a remote chain of inferences."[32]

Constitutional Limitations on Congress's Authority to Regulate Firearms

Although the Commerce Clause gives Congress broad authority to enact laws, there may be other constitutional constraints on its ability to regulate firearms. One constitutional limitation may be the Tenth Amendment to the U.S. Constitution, which provides: "The powers not delegated to the United States by the Constitution, nor prohibited by it to the States, are reserved to the

States respectively, or to the people."[33] Although the Tenth Amendment may limit the type of legislation Congress can pass, "a valid exercise of Congress' Commerce Clause power is not a violation of the Tenth Amendment."[34] Generally, the Supreme Court has ruled that the federal government's power over interstate commerce does not authorize it to require, or commandeer, state or local governments to take legislative acts or certain executive actions. For example, in *New York v. United States*, the Supreme Court held that federal legislation cannot require states to develop legislation on how to dispose of all low-level radioactive waste generated within the state, nor can it order states to take title to such waste.[35] Although the Court held that Congress had authority under the Commerce Clause to regulate low-level radioactive waste directly, such power did not authorize them to order states to enact laws.[36] The Court subsequently held in *Printz v. United States* that Congress cannot commandeer state executive branch officials from carrying out a federal program, as such an act is outside Congress's power and inconsistent with the Tenth Amendment.[37] However, the Court has upheld federal legislation that regulated state activities with respect to information obtained from drivers' license applications, because the law at issue "does not require the states in their sovereign capacity to regulate their own citizens ... [and it] does not require [the state] legislature to enact any laws or regulations, and it does not require state officials to assist in the enforcement of federal statutes regulating private individuals."[38]

The Second Amendment to the U.S. Constitution is another constitutional provision that may limit the type of legislation Congress may pass related to firearms. The Second Amendment provides: "A well regulated Militia, being necessary to the security of a free State, the right of the people to keep and bear Arms, shall not be infringed." The Supreme Court in *District of Columbia v. Heller* held that the Second Amendment protects an individual right to keep a firearm, unconnected with service to the militia, and to use that firearm for lawful purposes such as self-defense in the home.[39] Although Congress has the authority to regulate firearms under its commerce authority, it may not do so in a way that infringes upon the right guaranteed by the Second Amendment. Since *Heller*, several federal firearms laws have been challenged under the Second Amendment, though all have been upheld.

In sum, Congress has the general authority to enact regulations under its Commerce Clause authority, so long as the activities or conduct regulated fall within one of the three categories established by *Lopez*. However, even where Congress may have direct authority to regulate, it cannot do so in a manner that would be inconsistent with other constitutional principles, such as those under the Tenth or Second Amendments to the U.S. Constitution.

COMMERCE CLAUSE CHALLENGES TO FEDERAL FIREARMS LAWS

Federal firearms laws have been challenged periodically on grounds that Congress did not have authority under the Commerce Clause to pass them. This section examines lower courts' decisions regarding the constitutional validity of certain federal firearms laws, particularly the application of these laws to intrastate possession and intrastate transfer of firearms.

As described above, Congress's authority under the Commerce Clause extends to regulating items that move through interstate commerce and commercial activities that affect interstate commerce. It is therefore relatively settled that Congress may regulate the manufacture and transfer of firearms. For example, the constitutionality of a federal semiautomatic assault weapons ban, which was in effect for ten years, was challenged under the Commerce Clause. In 1994, Congress passed the Violent Crime Control and Law Enforcement Act, which included a provision making it unlawful to possess, manufacture, or transfer certain types of semiautomatic pistols, rifles, and shotguns (i.e., "assault weapons").[40] The U.S. Court of Appeals for the District of Columbia Circuit (D.C. Circuit), in *Navegar, Inc. v. United States*, addressed the question of whether the activities regulated under this act fell within one of the three categories of activity identified in *Lopez*.[41] Like the Court in *Lopez*, the D.C. Circuit determined that it was not required to analyze the act under the first or second categories because the "[it] readily falls within category 3 as a regulation of activities having a substantial [e]ffect on interstate commerce."[42] The court analyzed individually the act's prohibitions on manufacture, transfer, and possession.

Regarding the manufacturing prohibition, the D.C. Circuit declared that "[t]he Supreme Court has repeatedly held that the manufacture of goods which may ultimately never leave the state can still be activity which substantially affects interstate commerce."[43] Regarding the prohibition on transfers, the court similarly remarked that "the Supreme Court precedent makes clear that the transfer of goods, even as part of an intrastate transaction, can be an activity which substantially affects interstate commerce."[44] Based on these maxims, the court held that "it is not even arguable that the manufacture and transfer of 'semiautomatic assault weapons' for a national market cannot be regulated as activity substantially affecting interstate commerce."[45]

However, with respect to the possession of a semiautomatic assault weapon, the court in *Navegar* noted that the *Lopez* decision raised a question of whether "mere possession" can substantially affect interstate commerce. The court proceeded to analyze the purposes behind the act to determine whether "it was aimed at regulating activities which substantially affect interstate commerce."[46] Analyzing the congressional hearings, the court determined that the ban on possession was "conceived to control and restrict the interstate commerce in 'semiautomatic assault weapons,'" and that the "ban on possession is a measure intended to reduce the demand for such weapons."[47] The D.C. Circuit stated that the ban on possession was "necessary to allow law enforcement to effectively regulate the manufacture and transfers where the product comes to rest, in the possession of the receiver."[48] Based on these factors, the court concluded that the "purpose of the ban on possession has an 'evident commercial nexus.'"[49] Accordingly, the court held that the federal semiautomatic assault weapons ban was valid under Congress's commerce power.

Intrastate Possession

The Gun Control Act includes several provisions that criminalize possession of a firearm. For instance, 18 U.S.C. §922(o) makes it unlawful for any person to "possess a machinegun" and 18 U.S.C. §922(g) makes it unlawful for certain categories of persons to "possess in or affecting commerce, any firearm or ammunition,"[50] As demonstrated above, however, whether Congress actually has authority to regulate "mere possession" of firearms has been questioned by the courts.[51] In particular, courts have confronted the issue of whether these provisions as applied to intrastate possession are a proper exercise of Congress's power under the Commerce Clause. Analysis regarding the validity of these federal possession provisions has varied slightly, given the development of the Supreme Court's jurisprudence on the Commerce Clause.

Possession without a Jurisdictional Hook

Prior to and post-*Lopez*, federal courts generally upheld §922(o) as a valid exercise of Congress's commerce power, despite the absence of jurisdictional language requiring that the machinegun travel in or substantially affect interstate commerce.[52] However, once *Lopez* was decided, at least one federal court of appeals held §922(o) to be unconstitutional as applied to a defendant who was convicted of possessing machineguns that had been home assembled through parts kits. In *United States v. Stewart (Stewart I)*, the U.S. Court of Appeals for the Ninth Circuit (Ninth Circuit) held that there were limits in applying §922(o).[53] The court rejected the argument that the statute was constitutional under either of the first two categories in *Lopez*, even though some of the parts of the machineguns had, at some point, moved in interstate commerce.[54] It also found that the defendant's simple possession of homemade machineguns did not substantially affect interstate commerce as recognized by *Lopez*. In particular, the Ninth Circuit determined that possession of a machinegun is not, without more, economic in nature and that nothing in the legislative history indicates that the regulation itself has an economic purpose.[55] Therefore, the court held that, as applied to the defendant's possession of homemade machineguns, §922(o) was an unlawful extension of Congress's commerce power. *Stewart I*, however, was decided prior to the Supreme Court's decision in *Gonzales v. Raich*.

Upon remand, the Ninth Circuit in *Stewart II* held that §922(o) can be constitutionally applied to the defendant's possession of homemade machineguns in light of the Supreme Court's analysis in *Raich*.[56] The statute at issue, as well as the actions and claims of the defendant, were "nearly identical" to the claims and statute at issue in *Raich*, where the Court rejected the argument that the federal provision criminalizing possession of marijuana could not be applied to the intrastate possession of medical marijuana. As discussed *supra*, the Court in *Raich* reaffirmed its prior holdings that Congress may regulate "purely intrastate activity that is not itself 'commercial' ... if it concludes that failure to regulate that activity would undercut the regulation of the interstate market in that commodity."[57] Under this reasoning, the defendant in *Raich* was not successful in his attempt to carve out a class of intrastate activities as beyond the reach of Congress's commerce power. Relying on this analysis, the Ninth Circuit in *Stewart II* concluded that, like the regulation on possessing drugs in the Controlled Substances Act, the machinegun possession ban fits within a larger scheme for the regulation of interstate commerce of firearms.[58] The court's new focus under the substantially affects doctrine post-*Raich* was "not [the defendant] and his homemade machine guns, but all homemade machineguns manufactured intrastate. Moreover, [the court] does not require the government to prove that those activities *actually* affected interstate commerce; we merely inquire whether Congress had a rational basis for so concluding."[59] Thus, under this lens, machineguns, whether they are homemade or commercially made, are fungible commodities like marijuana,[60] and Congress had a rational basis for concluding that "in the aggregate, possession of homemade machineguns could substantially affect interstate commerce in machineguns."[61]

The analysis in *Raich*, followed by the Ninth Circuit in *Stewart II*, has been relied upon by other courts in evaluating state legislation that purports to exempt from federal law the intrastate manufacture and sale of firearms, firearms accessories, and ammunition. This type of law is known as a Firearms Freedom Act.[62] The United States District Court for the District of Montana, echoing the concerns in *Raich* and *Stewart II*, declared that "Montana's attempt to... excise a discrete local activity from the comprehensive regulatory framework provided by federal firearms laws cannot stand."[63] In upholding the validity of the National Firearms Act and Gun Control Act as applied to the intrastate manufacture and sale of firearms and firearms accessories, the district court stated that Congress had a rational basis, without the need to have particularized findings, to conclude that failure to regulate intrastate manufacture and sale of firearms would leave a "gaping hole" in the federal scheme regulating firearms.[64]

Possession with a Jurisdictional Hook

Individuals, who have been convicted under §922(g) for being a felon, or other prohibited person, in possession of a firearm, also have challenged whether such a provision is constitutionally valid under Congress's commerce power. For instance, the Ninth Circuit in *United States v. Jones* addressed the constitutional validity of §922(g)(8), which makes it unlawful for a person who is "subject to a court order that ... [meets specific requirements] ... to ... possess in or affecting commerce, any firearm or ammunition ."[65] The Ninth Circuit distinguished §922(g)(8) from the School Zones Act in *Lopez* on the basis that this statute contains "a jurisdictional element explicitly requiring a nexus between the possession of firearms and interstate commerce."[66] The court affirmed that this provision constitutes a valid exercise of Congress's power to regulate activity under the second and third categories identified under the *Lopez* framework.[67]

However, the jurisdictional hook—"in or affecting commerce"—relating to possession under §922(g), may not be "a talisman that wards off constitutional challenges."[68] One reason a jurisdictional hook is employed is to make facial constitutional challenges unlikely or impossible, "and to direct litigation toward the statutory question of whether, in the particular case, the regulated conduct possesses the requisite connection to interstate commerce."[69] Notwithstanding the jurisdictional hook that distinguishes it from the School Zones Act in *Lopez*, an argument could be made that a felon-in-possession statute does not fall within any of the categories identified in *Lopez*.

The U.S. Court of Appeals for the Tenth Circuit (Tenth Circuit) examined this issue in *United States v. Patton*, within the context of another federal statute similar to the felon-in-possession statute.[70] In *Patton*, the court analyzed whether Congress had authority to prohibit the intrastate possession by a felon of a bulletproof vest, in the absence of any commercial transaction or evidence of a connection to commercial activity other than the fact that, prior to the defendant's lawful purchase, the vest had been sold across a state line.[71] The Tenth Circuit concluded that such a provision did not fit within any of the three categories of *Lopez*, as clarified and affirmed by *Raich*, but the court nonetheless upheld the provision under a pre-*Lopez* precedent from the Supreme Court. After dismissing the three categories of commerce,[72] the Tenth Circuit turned to the Supreme Court decision *Scarborough v. United States*, which had analyzed the pre-Gun Control Act felon-in-possession statute.[73]

Because "in or affecting commerce" applies to the word "possess,"[74] the government, in cases of pure possession, must prove that possession of a firearm has some nexus to commerce in order to validly regulate the activity. Thus, in *Scarborough* the Court had to determine what proof is necessary for the government to satisfy the nexus between possession and interstate commerce.[75] The court rejected the argument that possession of the gun have some "contemporaneous connection with commerce at the time of the offense."[76] Instead, the Court concluded that the sensible reading, supported by the legislative history, demonstrated that "Congress intended no more than a minimal nexus requirement," which may be satisfied by proving that the firearm possessed had, at some time, traveled in interstate commerce.[77] Applying the principles from *Scarborough,* the Tenth Circuit in *Patton* upheld the constitutional validity of the body armor statute as applied to the defendant's intrastate possession, because the item, at some point, had moved across state lines and therefore such activity could be regulated under Congress's commerce power.[78]

As discussed above, a firearms possession statute, like §922(g), may be considered a proper exercise of Congress's commerce authority under the *Lopez* categories.[79] However, a reviewing court that conducts a thorough analysis of §922(g), like the Tenth Circuit in *Patton* did with similar regulation, could find that mere intrastate possession of a firearm, or any firearms accessory, does not fit under any of the three *Lopez* categories. If so, *Scarborough*, which appears to have been left intact by *Lopez*, seems to be the controlling precedent under which the federal firearms possession statute may be enforced against prohibited intrastate possessors. One court has noted that "nothing in *Lopez* suggests that the 'minimal nexus' test should be changed."[80] Notably, while courts have continued to follow *Scarborough*, they have also expressed doubts about its continuing validity. For example, in upholding the validity of §922(g), the United States Court of Appeals for the Fifth Circuit opined:

> If the matter were res nova, one might well wonder how it could rationally be concluded that mere possession of a firearm in any meaningful way concerns interstate commerce simply because the firearm had, perhaps decades previously before the charged possessor was even born, fortuitously traveled in interstate commerce. It is also difficult to understand how a statute construed never to require any but such a per se nexus could "ensure, through caseby-case inquiry, that the firearm possession in question affects interstate commerce." [citation omitted][81]

Several federal courts of appeals have noted the tension between *Scarborough* and the three-category approach later adopted by the Supreme Court.[82] Should the Supreme Court revisit the potential doctrinal inconsistency between *Lopez* and *Scarborough*, it is conceivable that regulation of intrastate possession of a firearm or any other firearms accessory may be found to be beyond the reach of Congress. Alternatively, if the jurisdictional hook were interpreted so that the intrastate possession must have some contemporaneous connection with interstate commerce- e.g., the defendant is engaging in commerce at the time of the offense or possessing the gun at an interstate facility,[83] then it would not be beyond Congress's commerce power to regulate some intrastate possession. The consequence of such an interpretation, however, would be that a subset of individuals would not be captured under Congress's commerce power (e.g., those who fall within a prohibited possessor category but who only maintain a firearm at home and never carry or possess it elsewhere). Another option could be to bring the wording of the current felon-inpossession statute in line with §922(o), which lacks a jurisdictional hook. In such case, to the extent that the Supreme Court would agree with the Ninth Circuit's application of *Raich* in its *Stewart II* decision, a felon-in-possession statute without a jurisdictional hook could constitutionally apply to intrastate possession, and would appear to remove the burden on the government to satisfy the nexus requirement between possession and interstate commerce.

Intrastate Transfer of Firearms

Section 922(d)(1) of title 18 of the U.S. Code makes it unlawful for any person to dispose or transfer a firearm to another individual knowing or having reasonable cause to believe that such person is under indictment for, or has been convicted in any court of, a crime punishable by more than one years' imprisonment.[84] Individuals who have been convicted under this provision for making unlawful transfers intrastate have contended that Congress exceeded its authority under the Commerce Clause by enacting this provision. Such challenges have proven unsuccessful. For instance, the U.S. Court of Appeals for the Sixth Circuit (Sixth Circuit) in *United States v. Rose* held that this contention "lacks merit inasmuch as the Supreme Court precedent leaves no doubt regarding the constitutionality of §922(d)(1)."[85] The Sixth Circuit analyzed this provision under the third *Lopez* category—the substantially affects doctrine—and concluded that the *Raich* analysis leads to the conclusion that §922(d)(1) is proper use of Congress's commerce power.[86]

The Sixth Circuit stated that guns, similar to marijuana, are a "fungible commodity" for which there is an established interstate market and that the provision at issue is a part of the larger regulatory framework.[87] The court concluded that the relevant "legislative history supports the logical connection between the intrastate sale and disposition of firearms and interstate market in firearms."[88]

Background Checks

As part of the regulatory framework for ensuring that firearms are not transferred to those persons deemed to be prohibited under federal law, Congress passed the Brady Handgun Violence Prevention Act of 1993 (Brady Act), which requires federal firearms licensees (FFLs) to conduct a background check on prospective firearms purchasers through the National Instant Criminal Background Check System (NICS).[89] However, prior to the establishment of NICS, the Brady Act's interim provisions required the chief law enforcement officers within a state to conduct a background check on a prospective firearms purchaser within five business days.[90] This portion of the act was invalidated on Tenth Amendment grounds in *Printz v. United States* under the theory that Congress was without authority to order or "commandeer" state executive branch officials.[91]

The holding in *Printz* indicates that although the Tenth Amendment limits the way in which Congress can implement background checks, it is not beyond its commerce power to require such checks as part of transferring a firearm. Under the current scheme, FFLs are required to conduct a background check through NICS before transferring a firearm to any non-FFL, including those who reside within the state in which the FFL is located.[92] Currently, Congress is considering legislation that would impose a background check on transactions between non-FFLs that occur within a state.[93] Just as Congress's authority to regulate intrastate transfers has been challenged, one might question whether Congress has the authority to require, or impose a requirement, that FFLs or non-FFLs conduct a background check on intrastate firearms transactions. Based on the Court's holdings in *Lopez* and *Raich*, discussed above, it seems that requiring a background check on intrastate firearms transactions is unlike regulating simple possession of firearms in a school zone.[94] Although the act of conducting a background check may not be itself "commercial," it is a condition on the commercial transfer of a firearm. Therefore, if such a measure were enacted, it seems that there would be a substantial basis upon which a court could regard it as a provision supporting the larger regulatory scheme—the Gun Control Act—that Congress enacted to "keep firearms out of the hands of those not legally entitled to possess them because of age, criminal background, or incompetency, and to assist law enforcement authorities in the states and their subdivisions in combating the increasing prevalence of crime in the United States."[95]

CONCLUSION

Congress has broad authority pursuant to the Commerce Clause to enact laws in areas that may overlap with traditional state jurisdiction. As such, Congress has passed complex statutory provisions that regulate the possession, receipt, transfer, and manufacture of firearms and ammunition. Notwithstanding this broad authority, Congress may not exceed other constitutional provisions or doctrines, such as the Tenth or Second Amendments to the U.S. Constitution. Thus, Congress may not pass legislation that infringes on the right guaranteed by the Second Amendment, nor may it pass legislation that orders state legislatures or its officials to implement and perform a federal law or program. Outside these types of limitations, exercise of Congress's commerce power appears to be proper as long as the regulated activity or conduct falls within one of the three categories established by the Supreme Court in *United States v. Lopez*, that is, (1) the channels of interstate commerce; (2) the instrumentalities of interstate commerce, including persons and things; and (3) activities that substantially affect interstate commerce. As explored in this report, courts have been confronted with the question of whether federal laws can be applied to intrastate possession and intrastate transfers of firearms, or whether such application exceeds the authority of Congress under its commerce power. Generally, the courts have upheld such laws under these as-applied challenges. With respect to intrastate possession, there remains noticeable tension between the Commerce Clause analysis set forth in *Lopez* and the pre-*Lopez* Supreme Court precedent that is still relied on by lower courts to uphold regulations on the possession of firearms. It is unclear how Congress's authority to regulate firearms possession would be affected should the Supreme Court resolve any perceived doctrinal inconsistency. Furthermore, the Supreme Court's analysis in *Gonzales v. Raich* has also buttressed the reasoning by which lower courts have concluded that Congress's authority to regulate firearms extends to intrastate manufacture and intrastate transfers and, as such, states cannot exempt themselves from federal regulation.

End Notes

[1] U.S. Const., art. I, §1("All legislative power herein granted shall be vested in a Congress of the United States.").

[2] The states' authority, or "police power," to enact such legislation does not arise from the U.S. Constitution. Rather, it is an inherent attribute of states' territorial sovereignty. *See* Alden v. Maine, 527 U.S. 706 (1999). The Supreme Court in *Alden* affirmed that states retain a "residuary and inviolable sovereignty" and that "our federalism requires that Congress treat the States in a manner consistent with their status as residuary sovereigns and joint participants in the governance of the Nation." *Id.* at 748.

[3] *See, e.g.*, Screws v. United States, 325 U.S. 91, 109 (1945) plurality opinion ("Our national government is one of delegated powers alone. Under our federal system the administration of justice rests with the States except as Congress, acting within the scope of those delegated powers, has created offenses against the United States."). The states have retained "inherent police power," *Newberry v. United States*, 256 U.S. 232 (1921), meaning the power to legislate for the "health, safety, and morals" of the citizenry. Barnes v. Glen Theatre, Inc., 501 U.S. 560, 569 (1991).

[4] P.L. 73-474 (1934), *codified at* 26 U.S.C. ch.53.

[5] P.L. 90-618 (1968), *codified at* 18 U.S.C. §§921 *et seq.*

[6] P.L. 99-308 (1986).

[7] P.L. 104-159 (1994).

[8] The National Firearms Act of 1934 levies taxes regarding the manufacture and transfer of certain firearms and other weapons. Therefore, it could be argued that Congress is also relying on its authority under the Taxing Clause to enact this statute. U.S. Const., art. I, §8, cl. 1.

[9] U.S. Const., art. I, §8, cl. 3.

[10] For a historical overview and early jurisprudence regarding the Commerce Clause, *see* CRS Report RL32844, *The Power to Regulate Commerce: Limits on Congressional Power*, by Kenneth R. Thomas. In the early 20th century, the U.S. Supreme Court generally declared various federal statutes, which regulated the movement of goods or persons, constitutional under the Commerce Clause. However, the Court struck down a series of federal statutes which attempted to extend commerce regulation to activities such as "production," "manufacturing," or "mining." *See, e.g.*, United States v. E.C. Knight Co., 156 U.S. 1 (1895); Carter v. Carter Coal Co., 298 U.S. 238 (1936).

[11] NLRB v. Jones & Laughlin Steel Corporation, 301 U.S. 1, 36 (1937) ("The fundamental principle is that the power to regulate commerce is the power to enact 'all appropriate legislation' [citation omitted] for 'its protection and advancement' [citation omitted]; to adopt measures 'to promote its growth and insure its safety' [citation omitted]; 'to foster, protect, control and restrain.' [citation omitted] ... Although activities may be intrastate in character when separately considered, if they have such a close and substantial relation to interstate commerce that their control is essential or appropriate to protect that commerce from burdens and obstructions, Congress cannot be denied the power to exercise that control." *Id.* at 37).

[12] United States v. Darby, 312 U.S. 100 (1941) (approving legislation relating to working conditions).

[13] Wickard v. Filburn, 317 U.S. 111, 125 (1942) (upholding constitutionality of the Agricultural Adjustment Act of 1938, which regulated national production of wheat, as applied to consumption of homegrown wheat).

[14] *Id.*

[15] Heart of Atlanta Motel v. United States, 379 U.S. 241, 256(1964) (upholding Title II of Civil Rights Act of 1964 as applied to hotels and stating "[T]he authority of Congress to keep the channels of interstate commerce free from immoral and injurious uses has been frequently sustained, and is no longer open to question."); Katzenbach v. McClung, 379 U.S. 294, 302 (1964) (upholding Title II of Civil Rights Act of 1964 as applied to restaurants and stating "the power to regulate [interstate commerce] extends to activities of retail establishments, including restaurants, which directly or indirectly burden or obstruct interstate commerce").

[16] Perez v. United States, 402 U.S. 146 (1971).

[17] 514 U.S. 549 (1995).

[18] P.L. 101-647 (1990). The School Zones Act had made it a federal offense for "any individual to knowingly possess a firearm at a place the individual knows, or has reasonable cause to believe, is a school zone." 18 U.S.C. §922(q) (1988 ed. Supp. V). The *Lopez* decision is significant in that it was the first time since 1937 that the Supreme Court struck down a federal statute purely based on a finding that Congress had exceeded its powers under the Commerce Clause.

[19] *Lopez*, 514 U.S. at 558-59.

[20] Erwin Chemerinsky, *Constitutional Law: Policies and Principles*, at §4.6 (3d ed. 2006).

[21] *Lopez*, 514 U.S. at 559-60. Interestingly, the Court in *Lopez* did not discuss that the three categories are intertwined to a certain degree. For example, the first category—the

regulation of "streams" or "channels" of commerce, which allows for the regulation of the creation, movement, sale, and consumption of merchandise or services—was justified in *NLRB v. Jones & Laughlin* by the "effect" of these activities on commerce. *See NLRB*, 301 U.S. at 31. Similarly, the second category—the regulation of the instrumentalities of commerce, such as planes, trains or trucks—is also based on the theory that a threat to these instrumentalities "affects" commerce, even if the effect is local in nature. *See* Southern Railway Co. v. United States, 222 U.S. 21, 26-27 (1911) (regulation of intrastate rail traffic has a substantial effect on interstate rail traffic). The third category arguably acts as a "catch-all" for all other activities that "substantially affect" interstate commerce.

[22] *Lopez*, 514 U.S. at 561 (referencing *Wickard v. Filburn*, 317 U.S. 111 (1942)).

[23] *Id.*

[24] *Id.* at 561-62. The Court found it significant that that the act "contains no jurisdictional element which would ensure, through a case-by-case inquiry, that the firearm possession in questions affects interstate commerce." A jurisdictional element would also "limit [the statute's] reach to a discrete set of firearms possessions that additionally have an explicit connection with or effect on interstate commerce." *Id.* at 562.

In 1996, Congress passed a new version of the Gun-Free School Zones Act (P.L. 104-208) that added a jurisdictional hook. The provision reads: "It shall be unlawful for any individual to knowingly possess a firearm that has moved in or otherwise affects interstate or foreign commerce at ... a school zone." The revised School Zones Act was challenged again in lower courts, but has been since upheld. *See, e.g.*, United States V. Dorsey, 418 F.3d 1038, 1046 (9th Cir. 2005) (holding that the new §922(q) "resolves the shortcomings that the *Lopez* Court found in the prior version of this statute because it incorporates a 'jurisdictional element which would ensure, through case-by-case inquiry, that the firearm in possession in question affects interstate commerce'").

[25] 528 U.S. 598 (2000).

[26] *Id.* at 613. Because the regulated activities in both *Lopez* and *Morrison* were considered noneconomic, the Court did not defer to Congress's conclusion that the regulated activities at issue substantially affected interstate commerce. Although the Court in *Lopez* stated that congressional findings could assist it in evaluating the legislature's judgment that the activity in question substantially affected interstate commerce, it noted that "[s]imply because Congress may conclude that a particular activity substantially affects interstate commerce does not necessarily make it so." *Lopez*, 514 U.S. at 557 n.2.

[27] Lopez, 514 U.S. at 567 (The Court in *Lopez* rejected the argument that possession of guns in school zones affected the national economy by its negative impact on education. *Id.* at 564.). In *Morrison*, the Court stated that if it accepted the government's argument, Congress would be allowed to regulate "any crime as long as the nationwide, aggregated impact of that crime has substantial effects on employment, production, transit, or consumption." *Morrison*, 529 U.S. at 616.

[28] Gonzales v. Raich, 545 U.S. 1 (2005). The Court held that the application of the Controlled Substances Act (CSA), which prohibited the possession of marijuana, to California users of homegrown marijuana for medical purposes was a proper use of Congress's Commerce Clause powers. The Court declared that "Congress can regulate purely intrastate activity that is not itself 'commercial,' in that it is not produced for sale, if it concludes that failure to regulate that class of activity would undercut the regulation of the interstate market in that commodity." *Id.* at 18.

[29] *Id.* at 21. The Court rejected the argument that the statute was unconstitutional because Congress did not make specific findings regarding the effect of intrastate cultivation and possession of marijuana on the larger interstate marijuana market.

[30] U.S. Const., Art. I, §8, cl. 18.

[31] *Raich*, 545 U.S. at 36-7 (Scalia, J., concurring) ("[U]nlike the channels, instrumentalities, and agents of interstate commerce, activities that substantially affect interstate commerce are not themselves part of interstate commerce and thus the power to regulate them cannot come from the Commerce Clause alone." *Id.* at 34.).

[32] *Id.* at 36 ("*Lopez* and *Morrison* affirm that Congress may not regulate certain 'purely local' activity within the States based solely on the attenuated effect that such activity may have in the interstate market. But those decisions do not declare noneconomic intrastate activities to be categorically beyond the reach of the Federal Government." *Id.* at 38-9.).

[33] U.S. Const., amend. X.

[34] Montana Shooting Sports Ass'n. v. Holder, 2010 U.S. Dist. LEXIS 104301, at *73 (D. Mont. 2010).

[35] New York v. United States, 505 U.S. 144 (1992).

[36] *Id.* at 159-60 (neither the text nor structure of the Constitution empowers Congress to commandeer the legislative process of the states).

[37] Printz v. United States, 521 U.S. 898, 926 (1997) (holding that Congress did not have the authority to pass part of the Brady Handgun Violence Prevention Act, which required state law enforcement officers to conduct background checks on prospective handgun purchasers within five days of an attempted purchase).

[38] Reno v. Condon, 528 U.S. 141, 151 (2000) (upholding the Driver's Protection Privacy Act of 1994, which imposed limitations on state governments' and private persons' ability to disclose information received through drivers' license applications).

[39] 554 U.S. 570 (2008).

[40] P.L. 103-322 (1994). For discussion on the federal assault weapon ban and legislative proposals, *see* CRS Report R42957, *Federal Assault Weapons Ban: Legal Issues*, by Vivian S. Chu and CRS Report R42987, *Gun Control Proposals in the 113ᵗʰ Congress: Universal Background Checks, Gun Trafficking, and Military Style Firearms*, by William J. Krouse.

[41] 192 F.3d 1050, 1066-68 (D.C. Cir. 1999), rehearing *en banc* denied, 200 F.3d, 868 (D.C. Cir. 2000), *cert. denied* 531 U.S. 816 (2000).

[42] *Id.* at 1055.

[43] *Id.* at 1057 (citing *United States v. Darby*, 312 U.S. 100, 118-19 (1941); *NLRB v. Jones & Laughlin Steel*, 301 U.S. 1, 37 (1937)).

[44] *Id.* at 1058 (citing *Lopez*, 514 U.S. at 560-61 (citing *Wickard v. Filburn*, 317 U.S. 111, 127-28 (1942) (noting that farmer's home consumption of wheat substantially affected interstate commerce and that farmer's selling of homegrown wheat and local marketing substantially affects interstate commerce)).

[45] *Id.*

[46] To determine whether an activity that does not have an clear connection with interstate commerce, the Court in *Lopez* stated that it would consider legislative findings and even congressional committee findings to determine if there were a rational basis for congressional action. *Lopez*, 514 U.S. at 562.

[47] *Navegar*, 192 F.3d at 1058-59 (citing other cases such as *United States v. Rybar*, 103 F.3d 273 (3d. Cir 1996) (holding that the Firearm Owners Protection Act of 1986 targets the mere intrastate possession of machine guns as a "demand-side measure to lessen the stimulus that prospective acquisition would have on the commerce of machine guns"); United States v.

Rambo, 74 F.3d 948 (9th Cir. 1995) (holding that the ban on possession is in effect "an attempt to control the interstate market ... by creating criminal liability for the demand-side of the market, i.e., those who would facilitate illegal transfer out of the desire to acquire mere possession" [citation omitted])).

[48] *Id.* at 1059.

[49] *Id.* (citing *Lopez*, 514 U.S. at 580 (Kennedy, J., concurring)). Although the Supreme Court further clarified its Commerce Clause jurisprudence in later decisions, as discussed above, it appears that the Commerce Clause analysis applicable to the ability of Congress to regulate or ban certain semiautomatic assault weapons would not be fundamentally altered by these later developments.

[50] 18 U.S.C. §922(o). Other similar provisions include 18 U.S.C. §§922(j), (k), (p), and (x).

[51] *See, e.g.*, Dean Strang, *Felons, Guns, and the Limits of Federal Power*, 39 Marshall L. Rev. 386 (2006); Joseph Luppino-Esposito, *Four Shots at the Commerce Clause: The Firearms Freedom Act and the Unarticulated Products Category of the Commerce Power*, 7 Seaton Hall Cir. Rev. 229 (2010).

[52] *See, e.g.*, United States v. Evans, 712 F. Supp. 1435 (D. Mont. 1989); United States v. Pearson, 8 F.3d 631 (8th Cir. 1993); United States v. Rambo, 74 F.3d 948 (9th Cir. 1996); United States v. Beuckelaere, 91 F.3d 781 (6th Cir. 1996); United States v. Haney, 264 F. 3d 1161 (10th Cir. 2001).

[53] United States v. Stewart (Stewart I), 348 F.3d 1132 (9th Cir. 2003), *vacated by, remanded by,* 545 U.S. 1112 (2005).

[54] *Id* ("At some level, of course, everything we own is composed of something that once traveled in commerce. This cannot mean that *everything* is subject to federal regulation under the Commerce Clause, else that constitutional limitation would be entirely meaningless." (emphasis in the original)).

[55] *Id.* at 1136-40. The Ninth Circuit applied a four-prong test articulated by the Supreme Court in *Morrison* to determine if the activity substantially affected commerce. The four factors are (1) whether the regulated activity is commercial or economic in nature; (2) whether an express jurisdictional element is provided in the statute to limit its reach; (3) whether Congress made express findings about the effects of the proscribed activity on interstate commerce; and (4) whether the link between the prohibited activity and the effect on interstate commerce is attenuated. *Morrison*, 529 U.S. at 610-12.

[56] United States v. Stewart (Stewart II), 451 F.3d 1071 (9th Cir. 2006).

[57] *Id.* at 1075 (citing *Raich*, 545 U.S. at 18).

[58] The Ninth Circuit noted §922(o), unlike the possession ban in the CSA, was enacted 20 years after the statute establishing the current federal firearms regulatory scheme. However, it stated that *Raich* did not require it to consider §922(o) as a standalone provision, "[t]hat Congress took a wait-and-see approach when it created the regime doesn't matter. The Commerce Clause does not prevent Congress from correcting deficiencies in its regulatory scheme in piecemeal fashion." *Id.* at 1076-77.

[59] *Id.* at 1077 (emphasis in the original).

[60] *Id.* at 1078 (Like seekers of unlawful drugs, "those seeking machineguns care only whether the guns work effectively-whether they discharge large amounts of ammunition with a single trigger pull. To the extent that homemade machineguns function like commercial machineguns, it doesn't matter whether they do so in a unique way; as economic substitutes, they are interchangeable." *Id.*).

[61] *Id.* at 1077. Observing that "the market for machineguns is established and lucrative, like the market for marijuana," the Ninth Circuit had no doubt that there was a rational basis for

Congress to conclude "that federal regulation of intrastate incidents of transfer and possession is essential to effective control of the interstate incidents of such traffic." *Id.* (citing United States v. Rambo, 74 F.3d 948, 952 (9th Cir. 1996)).

[62] Montana Shooting Sports Ass'n v. Holder, 2010 U.S. Dist. LEXIS 104301, at *1 (D. Mont. Aug. 31, 2010).

[63] *Id.* at *52.

[64] *Id.* ("The size of the 'gaping hole' that would be left in the federal regulatory scheme were Montana able to exempt the intrastate activities contemplated by the Act is of particular concern when taking into account the fact that, as of this writing, virtually identical Firearms Freedom Act legislation has been enacted in six more states and proposed in twenty-two others." *Id.* at *54-5.).

[65] United States v. Jones, 231 F.3d 508 (9th Cir. 2000).

[66] *Id.* at 514 (noting that the Ninth Circuit's post-*Lopez* decisions have upheld the constitutionality of §922(g)(1) on the same basis and that several other federal courts of appeals have also concluded that §922(g)(8) is a valid exercise of Congress's power under the Commerce Clause). *See also* United States v. Baker, 197 F.3d 211 (6th Cir. 1999); United States v. Bostic, 168 F.3d 718 (4th Cir. 1999); United States v. Cunningham, 161 F.3d 1343 (11th Cir. 1998).

[67] *Jones,* 231 F.3d at 514 ("[W]e observed that §922(g) can 'rationally be seen as regulating the interstate transportation of firearms and ammunition' and so constitutes a valid exercise of Congress's power to regulate activity" under the second category, which relates to the "the instrumentalities of interstate commerce, or persons or things in interstate commerce, even though the threat may come only from intrastate activities." *Id.*).

[68] *See* United States v. Rodia, 194 F.3d 465, 472-73 (3d Cir. 1999) (rejecting a "hard and fast rule that the presence of a jurisdictional element automatically ensures the constitutionality of a statute").

[69] United States v. Patton, 451 F.3d 615, 632 (10th Cir. 2006).

[70] *Id.* at 618 (examining 18 U.S.C. §931).

[71] In this case, the defendant was convicted of possession, all instances of which occurred entirely within the borders of the State of Kansas. According to the court, the only connection between the defendant's possession and interstate commerce was the fact that the bullet proof vest, prior to his purchase, had been manufactured in another state and moved across state lines. *Id.* at 620.

[72] *Id.* at 620-634. First, the court stated the provision prohibiting mere possession of body armor does not fit within the first category—channels of commerce—because "it is not directed at the movement of body armor through the channels of interstate commerce." *Id.* at 620-21. Second, the court stated that the provision does not fit within the second category—instrumentalities—because body armor is not an "an instrumentality, or means, of interstate commerce, and the statute does not protect it while moving in interstate shipment. Nor is the statute directed at the use of body armor in ways that threaten or injure the instrumentalities of interstate commerce." *Id.* at 621-22. Finally, the court concluded that the provision does not fit within the third category—substantially affects—because possession of body armor is not an activity that is commercial in nature, which is regulated as an essential part of "comprehensive legislation to regulate the interstate market in a fungible commodity as in *Raich.*" Furthermore, the court could not pinpoint any legislative history to suggest that regulating possession of body armor substantially affects the market for or movement of body armor. *Id.* at 622-34.

[73] 431 U.S. 563 (1977) (examining former 18 U.S.C. App. §§1201-1203, which made it unlawful for any person who had been convicted of a felony to "receive[], possess[], or transport[] in commerce or affecting commerce ... any firearm.").

[74] An earlier Supreme Court decision, *United States v. Bass*, 404 U.S. 336 (1971), examined the pre-Gun Control Act felon-in-possession statute, described *supra*; the Court had to determine if the statutory phrase "in commerce or affecting commerce" applied to "possess[]" or whether the statute "reaches the mere possession of guns without any showing of an interstate commerce nexus" in individual cases. *Id.* at 345-46. It adopted the narrower reading that the phrase "in commerce or affecting commerce" modified all three offenses, that is, unlawful receipt, possession, and transport of a firearm. *Id.* at 348-51. Notably, the Court in *Bass* had left open the question of the nexus of interstate commerce that must be shown in individual ways. *Id.* at 351.

[75] *Scarborough*, 431 U.S. at 564.

[76] *Id.* at 568-69. In other words, the defendant suggested that "at the time of the offense the possessor must be engaging in commerce or must be carrying the gun at an interstate facility." The defendant also suggested that one may be "convicted for possession without any proof of a present connection with commerce so long as the firearm was acquired after conviction." *Id.* The Court in *Scarborough* commented that the defendant's last theory creates "serious loopholes" because it would allow, for example, "an individual to go out in the period between his arrest and conviction and purchase and stockpile weapons with impunity." *Id.* at 576.

[77] *Id.* at 575.

[78] *Patton*, 451 F.3d at 635-36. *See also* 2A Fed. Jury Prac. & Instr. §39:14 (6th ed. updated Westlaw 2013). This model jury instruction for the federal courts on proving the element "in or affecting commerce" for §922(g)(1) offense states that the "government may meet its burden of proof on the question of being ["in or affecting commerce"] ... by proving to you, beyond a reasonable doubt, that the firearm identified in the indictment had traveled across a state boundary line."

[79] *See, e.g.*, United States v. Luna, 165 F.3d 316 (5th Cir. 1999) (upholding applicability of §922(j) which makes it unlawful to possess stolen firearms).

[80] United States v. Morris, 457 Fed. Appx. 900 (11th Cir. 2012).

[81] United States v. Rawl, 85 F.3d 240, 243 (5th Cir. 1996) (Garwood, J., concurring).

[82] *Patton*, 451 F.3d at 634-36.

[83] Notably, this argument was rejected in *Scarborough*.

[84] 18 U.S.C. §922(d)(1).

[85] United States v. Rose, 522 F.3d 710, 717 (6th Cir. 2008). *See also* United States v. Monteleone, 77 F.3d 1086, 1091- 92 (8th Cir. 1996); United States v. Peters, 403 F.3d 1263 (11th Cir. 2005); United States v. Haskins, 511 F.3d 688, 695 (7th Cir. 2007) (declining to directly address the Commerce Clause issue but citing *Peters* and *Monteleone* with approval).

[86] As described above, the Court in *Raich* upheld the application of the federal law to California users of homegrown marijuana because the Court determined that Congress had a rational basis to conclude that failure to regulate homegrown marijuana, a fungible product, would undercut the larger regulatory scheme of the interstate market in the commodity.

[87] *Id.* at 718.

[88] *Id.* at 719 (reviewing the legislative history of the 1968 firearms laws, which emphasized that the principal way to address the widespread prevalence of lawlessness and violent crime is to have "adequate Federal control over interstate and foreign commerce in these weapons,

and over all *persons engaging in the business of importing, manufacturing, or dealing in them* ... (emphasis added)").

[89] P.L. 103-159 (1994), *codified at* 18 U.S.C. §922(t).

[90] 18 U.S.C. §922(s).

[91] *Printz*, 521 U.S. at 926.

[92] 18 U.S.C. §922(t). FFLs may only transfer handguns to residents who reside within the state in which the FFL is located, and they may transfer long guns (i.e., rifles and shotguns) to both in-state and out-of-state residents.

[93] H.R. 137, the Fix Gun Checks Act of 2013 (113th Cong.); S. 374, the Fix Gun Checks Act of 2013 (113th Cong.).

[94] *See also* Morrison v. United States, 529 U.S. 598 (2000) (holding unconstitutional under the Commerce Clause a provision of the Violence Against Women Act that created a federal civil remedy for the victims of gender-motivated crimes of violence which was enforceable in both state and federal courts).

[95] S. Rept. No. 90-1097 (1968). The Gun Control Act, like the CSA in *Raich*, is a statute that "directly regulates economic, commercial activity." *Raich*, 545 U.S. at 26. Furthermore, similar to the Court in *Raich*, which found that failure to regulate intrastate manufacture and possession of marijuana would leave a "gaping hole" in the CSA, were such a measure to be enacted and subsequently challenged, it is conceivable for a reviewing court to conclude that not regulating background checks on intrastate firearms transactions between non-licensees also potentially leaves significant room for an unregulated secondary market in which firearms could be diverted into illicit channels, ultimately having a substantial effect on the national market for legal firearms.

In: Firearms in America
Editor: Alfonso D. Sutton

ISBN: 978-1-63117-823-8
© 2014 Nova Science Publishers, Inc.

Chapter 2

SECOND AMENDMENT CHALLENGES TO FIREARMS REGULATIONS POST-*HELLER*[*]

Vivian S. Chu

SUMMARY

The U.S. Supreme Court in *District of Columbia v. Heller* held that the Second Amendment to the U.S. Constitution protects an individual right to possess a firearm, unconnected with service in a militia, and the use of that firearm for traditionally lawful purposes, such as self-defense within the home. It also held that the Second Amendment applies to the states in *McDonald v. City of Chicago*. Since then, federal and state firearms laws have been challenged under the Second Amendment. Lower courts have been disputed in determining how to evaluate these provisions, given that the *Heller* decision was not an exhaustive analysis of the scope of the Second Amendment.

This report first discusses the two-step inquiry fashioned by the lower courts to analyze provisions under the Second Amendment. It proceeds to highlight how this test has been employed on a select number of firearms laws—namely, the federal age requirement and prohibition on possession by those convicted of a misdemeanor crime of domestic violence; and state requirements to obtain a concealed carry permit and a state assault weapons ban. How courts have applied the test to these categories may provide some indication as to how future firearms

---

[*] This is an edited, reformatted and augmented version of Congressional Research Service Publication, No. R43031, dated April 4, 2013.

regulations may be considered by the Supreme Court. The report concludes with a discussion on how varied interpretations by the lower courts of the *Heller* decision may affect the burden upon the federal government to defend firearms provisions, as well as new analytical frameworks that have been suggested.

INTRODUCTION

In 2008, the U.S. Supreme Court decided *District of Columbia v. Heller*, in which the Court held that the Second Amendment to the U.S. Constitution protects an individual right to possess a firearm, unconnected with service in a militia, and the use of that firearm for traditionally lawful purposes, such as self-defense within the home.[1] Shortly afterward in *McDonald v. City of Chicago*, the Supreme Court held that the Second Amendment also applies to the states, but it did not further explore the scope of the Second Amendment.[2] Although *Heller* did not constitute "an exhaustive historical analysis ... of the full scope of the Second Amendment,"[3] the Court noted that its decision "does not imperil every law regulating firearms," and "[does] not cast doubt [] on longstanding regulatory measures [such] as 'prohibitions on the possession of firearms by felons and the mentally ill,' 'laws forbidding the carrying of firearms in sensitive places such as schools and government buildings, or laws imposing conditions and qualifications on the commercial sale of arms.'"[4] Since *Heller* and *McDonald*, both federal and state firearms laws have been regularly challenged under the Second Amendment.

This report first discusses the standard of judicial review that the lower courts generally have fashioned to determine if a firearm law is in violation of the Second Amendment. Next, the report examines select categories of firearms laws that have been challenged under the Second Amendment. These include (1) prohibitions on certain persons based on age and on criminal history; (2) state concealed carry laws; and (3) state and local assault weapons bans. An examination of these categories could provide some insight as to how courts might assess future firearms legislation on Second Amendment grounds.

In the 113th Congress, several gun control proposals have been introduced. These include, among others, measures that would ban certain assault weapons and prohibit possession of large capacity magazines (e.g., S. 150/ H.R. 437/ S. 33); and measures that would require background checks on private transfers of firearms or ammunition (e.g., S. 22/ S. 174/ S. 374/ H.R. 141).[5]

WHAT STANDARD OF JUDICIAL SCRUTINY SHOULD BE APPLIED?

A significant question left open by the Court in *Heller* centers on the standard of scrutiny that should be applied to laws regulating the possession and use of firearms. Generally, there are three levels of judicial scrutiny. First, strict scrutiny, the most rigorous, requires a statute to be narrowly tailored to serve a compelling state interest.[6] Second, intermediate scrutiny, requires a statute to further a government interest in a way that is substantially related to that interest.[7] Third, the rational basis standard merely requires the statute to be rationally related to a legitimate government function.[8] The Court in *Heller* rejected the rational basis test[9] and also explicitly rejected Justice Breyer's "interest-balancing" inquiry, distinguishing this "judge-empowering" approach from the "traditionally expressed levels" of scrutiny.[10] However, the Court did not establish or clearly apply any judicial standard, declaring instead that the challenged firearms provisions were unconstitutional "[u]nder any of the standards of scrutiny that [the Court has] applied to enumerated constitutional rights."[11]

Lower Court Approaches to the Second Amendment after *Heller*

After *Heller*, some lower courts seemingly did not perform an extensive analysis or apply a particular standard of scrutiny in determining that a challenged federal firearms law was valid under the Second Amendment. Rather, they analogized the challenged firearms provisions to those listed as "presumptively lawful" in *Heller* and found them to be constitutional. Under this approach, courts have upheld bans on possession by felons,[12] by substance abusers,[13] by illegal aliens,[14] and by people convicted of domestic violence.[15] Interestingly, some of these categories, as well as those not listed in the Court's dicta as "presumptively lawful regulatory measures," are not necessarily "longstanding," as they were enacted in the 20th century.[16] As touched upon below, courts have wrestled with how to interpret and incorporate the "presumptively lawful" language from *Heller* with an analytical framework that involves application of means-end scrutiny.

However, the U.S. Court of Appeals for the Third Circuit (Third Circuit), in *United States v. Marzzarella*,[17] attempted to establish a framework for how to evaluate firearms laws that did not fall within those identified as "presumptively lawful." The statute at issue in *Marzzarella* was 18 U.S.C. §922(k), which is the federal ban on the possession of unmarked firearms.[18] In the Third Circuit's view, there are two possibilities of how the "presumptively lawful" categories are to be treated. The first possibility is that these types of firearms regulations could be those which regulate "conduct outside the scope of the Second Amendment," meaning that they would not be subject to any heightened judiciary scrutiny. Or, the language "may suggest the restrictions are presumptively lawful because they pass muster under any standard of scrutiny."[19] The Third Circuit favored its first interpretation, finding it more consistent based on the text and structure of the *Heller* decision.[20]

With this view, the Third Circuit noted that *Heller* suggested a two-step approach: "First, we ask whether the challenged law imposes a burden on conduct falling within the scope of the Second Amendment's guarantee (citations omitted). If it does not, our inquiry is complete. If it does, we evaluate the law under some form of means-end scrutiny. If the law passes muster under the standard, it is constitutional. If it fails, it is invalid."[21]

With respect to scope, the Court in *Heller* seemed to indicate that the "core" Second Amendment right protects "the right of law-abiding citizens to possess non-dangerous weapons for self-defense in the home."[22] It is less clear, however, the types of regulation that might burden conduct protected by the Second Amendment. The defendant, Marzzarella, argued that firearms without serial numbers must come within the scope of the Second Amendment because firearms in common use in 1791 did not have serial numbers. The Third Circuit rejected this because it found that "it would make little sense to categorically protect a class of weapons [under the Second Amendment] bearing a certain characteristic wholly unrelated to their utility."[23] The court was further skeptical of the defendant's argument that "possession in the home is conclusive proof that §922(k) regulates protected conduct [under the Second Amendment]."[24] Due to a lack of historical evidence, however, the court could not conclude with certainty that the Second Amendment did not protect possession of unmarked firearms in the home.[25]

The Third Circuit, therefore, proceeded to assume that the federal ban burdened the defendant's Second Amendment right and examined the law under "some form of means-end scrutiny." Looking to First Amendment jurisprudence for guidance,[26] the court noted that even an enumerated, fundamental right may be subjected to varying levels of scrutiny depending on the circumstances.[27] The court chose to apply an intermediate scrutiny standard to evaluate §922(k) finding that, similar to content-neutral time, place, and manner restrictions on speech, the firearms provision also regulated the manner in which persons could lawfully exercise their Second Amendment rights.[28] Although the intermediate scrutiny standard in the First Amendment context is articulated in different ways, "[t]hey all require the asserted governmental end to be more than just legitimate, either 'significant,' 'substantial,' or 'important,'" and require "the fit between the challenged regulation and the asserted objective be reasonable, not perfect."[29] With respect to §922(k), the Third Circuit held that the statute passes muster under intermediate scrutiny because it does not "severely limit the possession of firearms," and reasonably fits to achieve the government's substantial and important interest in preserving serial numbers for tracing purposes.[30]

As discussed below, many courts generally have employed the Third Circuit's two-part inquiry when determining if a challenged federal or state firearms provision violates the Second Amendment, including those the Court in *Heller* determined to be presumptively lawful.[31]

ARE CERTAIN INDIVIDUALS NOT PROTECTED BY THE SECOND AMENDMENT?

Both federal and state laws have long prohibited certain categories of individuals from possessing firearms.[32] Congress enacted the Gun Control Act of 1968[33] (GCA or Act) to "keep firearms out of the hands of those not legally entitled to possess them because of age, criminal background, or incompetency, and to assist law enforcement authorities in the states and their subdivisions in combating the increasing prevalence of crime in the United States."[34] The GCA establishes a comprehensive statutory scheme that regulates the manufacture, sale, transfer, and possession of firearms and ammunition.[35] For instance, the GCA prohibits federal firearms licensees (or licensed dealers) from selling handguns to any person under the age of 21 and long guns (i.e., rifles and shotguns) to any person under the age of 18.[36]

Licensed dealers are also subject to several requirements designed to ensure that a firearm is not transferred to an individual disqualified from possession under the act.[37] Under federal law there are nine categories of persons who prohibited from possessing, receiving, or transferring a firearm.[38] The individuals targeted by this provision include (1) persons convicted of a crime punishable by a term of imprisonment exceeding one year; (2) fugitives from justice; (3) individuals who are unlawful users or addicts of any controlled substance; (4) persons legally determined to be mentally defective, or who have been committed to a mental institution; (5) aliens illegally or unlawfully in the United States, as well as those who have been admitted pursuant to a nonimmigrant visa; (6) individuals who have been discharged dishonorably from the Armed Forces; (7) persons who have renounced United States citizenship; (8) individuals subject to a pertinent court order; and, finally, (9) persons who have been convicted of a misdemeanor domestic violence offense.

The following section reviews judicial decisions that have evaluated the constitutionality of the federal age requirement to purchase firearms, as well as the federal prohibition on misdemeanants of domestic violence from possessing firearms. While these and other categorical restrictions on certain individuals can be likened to the long-standing, presumptively lawful regulatory measures identified in *Heller*, reviewing courts have generally employed the two-step inquiry fashioned in *Marzzarella*.

Federal Age Requirement

Section 922(b)(1) of title 18 prevents licensed dealers from selling handguns to any individual under the age of 21 and long guns to any individual under the age of 18. The constitutionality of this law and its attendant regulations were challenged for violating "the right of 18-to-20-year-old adults to keep and bear arms under the Second Amendment" in *Nat'l Rifle Assoc. v. Bureau of Alcohol, Tobacco, Firearms, and Explosives*.[39] The U.S. Court of Appeals for the Fifth Circuit (Fifth Circuit) adopted the two-step approach from *Marzzarella*.[40] To determine if the law burdens protected conduct as historically understood, the Fifth Circuit relied on a "wide array of interpretive materials to conduct a historical analysis" to determine if the "law harmonizes with the historical traditions associated with the Second Amendment guarantee."[41] After reviewing both founding-era attitudes toward gun restrictions on certain groups,[42] as well as the laws and jurisprudence of the 19th century,[43] the Fifth Circuit concluded "the present ban is consistent with a longstanding tradition of targeting select groups' ability to access and to use arms for the sake of public safety." The court believed that the first step of the inquiry was satisfied, such that the regulation did not burden conduct protected by the Second Amendment, given the "considerable historical evidence of age- and safety- based restrictions on the ability to access arms."[44]

However, in "an abundance of caution," the Fifth Circuit proceeded to analyze the federal law under intermediate scrutiny (the second step) primarily due to two factors. First, the age restriction is similar to the other "longstanding, presumptively lawful bans on possession by felons and the mentally ill" identified in *Heller*[45]; second, the prohibition does not "disarm an entire community" like the D.C. ban in *Heller*.[46] In applying intermediate scrutiny, the court concluded that the government satisfied its burden of demonstrating that Congress "deliberately adopted a calibrated, compromise approach" to achieve an important government interest.[47]

Misdemeanants of Domestic Violence

The following two cases demonstrate the federal appellate courts' treatment of the GCA provision that prohibits misdemeanants of domestic violence from possessing or transporting firearms. Notably, this provision— codified at 18 U.S.C. §922(g)(9)—was enacted into law in 1996.[48]

The U.S. Court of Appeals for the Seventh Circuit (Seventh Circuit) in *United States v. Skoien* (*Skoien I*) vacated and remanded for further proceedings a defendant's conviction under 18 U.S.C. §922(g)(9).[49] The court noted the limiting language in *Heller* regarding presumptively lawful measures and declared it "would be a mistake to uphold this or other gun laws simply by invoking the Court's reference to these ... measures ... without more."[50] The court favored an analytical framework not unlike the two-step approach from *Marzzarella*.[51] It stated: "[C]onstitutional text and history come first, then (if necessary) an analysis of the public-benefits justification for the regulation follows.... If the first inquiry into the founding-era scope of the right doesn't resolve the case, then the second inquiry into the law's contemporary means-end justification is required."[52] The court moved to evaluate the prohibition under means-end scrutiny, given that the first inquiry did not resolve whether an individual who falls under §922(g)(9) is "categorically excluded from exercising the Second Amendment right as a matter of founding-era history and background legal assumptions."[53] Consequently, it applied intermediate scrutiny because the challenged provision "is several steps removed from the core constitutional right identified in *Heller*."[54] This is not to say that "domestic-violence misdemeanants have no Second Amendment rights, but it does support the application of a more lenient standard of review."[55] However, the Seventh Circuit in *Skoien I* vacated the charges against the defendant because the government "made little effort to discharge its burden of demonstrating the relationship between §922(g)(9)'s means and its end" and instead "rested nearly its entire case on *Heller*'s reference to felon-dispossession laws, asserting, without analysis, that 'Congress permissibly concluded that a narrow additional range of serious criminal offenses should likewise result in the forfeiture of the right to possess a firearm, even though the offenses are defined as misdemeanors under applicable law.'"[56] Because the government did not carry its burden of establishing a reasonable fit between the important objective of reducing domestic gun violence and §922(g)(9)'s permanent disarmament of all domestic-violence misdemeanants, the court vacated the defendant's charges but gave the government time to make its case.

Upon rehearing, the Seventh Circuit, sitting en banc, resisted delving "more deeply into the 'levels of scrutiny' quagmire."[57] It rejected the Second Amendment challenge to 18 U.S.C. §922(g)(9) on the basis that the government apparently met its burden by demonstrating that "logic and data establish a substantial relation between §922(g)(9) and [an important governmental] objective."[58]

In *United States v. Chester*, the U.S. Court of Appeals for the Fourth Circuit (Fourth Circuit) issued a decision to provide district courts in its circuit guidance on the framework for deciding Second Amendment challenges.[59] The Fourth Circuit followed the two-step approach delineated in *Marzzarella*: first, a historical inquiry "seek[ing] to determine whether the conduct at issue was understood to be within the scope of the right at the time of ratification;" and second, if the regulation burdens conduct within the scope of the Second Amendment as historically understood, "... mov[ing] up to the second step of applying the appropriate form of means-end scrutiny."[60]

The Fourth Circuit remanded the case to the district court but noted that, under the first prong, §922(g)(9)—like the GCA provision prohibiting convicted felons from possession—should be evaluated based on whether a person, rather than a person's conduct, is unprotected by the Second Amendment, and that "the historical data is not conclusive on the question of whether the Founding era understanding was that the Second Amendment did not apply to felons."[61] Thus, as in *Marzzarella*, the Fourth Circuit assumed, due to a lack of historical evidence, that the defendant was entitled to some Second Amendment protection to keep and possess firearms in his home for self-defense. For this defendant and other similarly situated persons, the court declared that the government, upon remand, must meet the intermediate scrutiny standard and not strict scrutiny, because the defendant's claim "was not within the 'core right' identified in *Heller*—the right of a *law-abiding*, responsible citizen to possess and carry a weapon for self-defense—by virtue of [the defendant's] criminal history as a domestic violence misdemeanant."[62]

Upon remand, the government presented empirical evidence to support its contention that the ban on misdemeanants of domestic violence is a reasonable fit in achieving the important government objective at stake, namely decreasing firearm use in domestic violence incidents.[63] The U.S. District Court for the Southern District of West Virginia upheld the statute, concluding the government demonstrated a reasonable fit between the statute and the substantial governmental objective at stake.[64]

These decisions indicate there may be variation with respect to how courts apply the two-step inquiry to assess whether a class of persons is entitled to protection under Second Amendment. As seen above, the Fifth Circuit did not find it necessary to its holding to analyze the federal age requirement under the second prong of the two-step analysis, because it concluded that historical evidence indicated individuals under a certain age are not entitled Second Amendment protection. The Fourth Circuit in *Chester*, on the other hand, could not determine if domestic violence misdemeanants are entitled to protection under the Second Amendment as historically understood, and therefore, it assumed they were protected, stating that application of intermediate scrutiny under the second prong would be appropriate upon remand. When faced with a Second Amendment challenge to prohibition on a category of persons that does not have a historical basis, it seems that a reviewing court will proceed with analysis of a regulation under a heightened means-end scrutiny and place even more emphasis on the responsibility of the government to meet its burden under intermediate scrutiny.[65]

DOES THE SECOND AMENDMENT EXTEND BEYOND THE HOME?

Traditionally, states have regulated concealed carrying of firearms and generally, they are categorized as either "shall-issue" or "may-issue" states. Among these states, some issue permits only to residents, while others issue permits to both residents and non-residents. In "shall-issue" jurisdictions, the issuing authority is required to grant the applicant a concealed carry permit (CCP) if he or she meets the statutory requirements. In "may-issue" jurisdictions, the issuing authority generally has the discretion to grant or deny a CCP based on a variety of statutory factors. Furthermore, each state decides which out-of-state permits to recognize.[66] Since *Heller*, several states' concealed carry laws have been challenged under the Second Amendment. For the most part, challenged concealed carry laws have been those in may-issue states that require an applicant to show good or proper cause in order to be eligible for a CCP.

Both *Heller* and *McDonald* emphasized that the right to keep and bear arms is not "a right to keep and carry any weapon whatsoever in any manner whatsoever and for whatever purpose."[67] *Heller* also indicated that mere regulation of a right would not sufficiently infringe upon, or burden, the Second Amendment right, when it pointed out that certain colonial-era ordinances did not "remotely burden the right of self-defense as much as an absolute ban on handguns."[68] In other words, it appears that to be burdensome, a regulation must also substantially infringe on the self-defensive right. Notably, *Heller* declared that the pre-ratified Second Amendment right was "understood to be an individual right protecting against both *public* and private violence," perhaps suggesting that the Second Amendment right extends beyond the home.[69] Yet the Court listed measures that forbid the carrying of firearms in sensitive places as presumptively lawful, perhaps suggesting that these are the types of regulatory measures excepted from the Second Amendment.

Therefore, with respect to concealed carry laws, courts have been confronted with determining whether the Second Amendment's protections extend beyond the home and, if so, whether concealed carry laws substantially burden the right of self-defense. Not surprisingly, courts have evaluated the challenged provisions differently, given the nuances of each state's concealed carry provisions. The following decisions indicate how reviewing courts have evaluated the constitutionality of concealed carry laws, and thus, how courts may assess future challenges to these laws.

For example, in *Peruta v. County of San Diego*, the U.S. District Court for the Southern District of California turned to the text and structure of *Heller* to determine whether California's concealed carry laws burden the Second Amendment. The court determined that the law, which requires an applicant for a CCP to be a resident and demonstrate "good cause," does not violate the Second Amendment.[70] Although the court raised the issue whether the Second Amendment right as delineated in *Heller* extends to the right to carry a loaded handgun in public, either openly or concealed, the court concluded it did not need to decide the issue.[71] It found California's CCP scheme similar to the 19th century cases cited in *Heller* that upheld state prohibitions on carrying concealed weapons because alternative forms of carrying arms were available.[72] To the extent that California's concealed carry scheme burdened the Second Amendment, the court declared this burden mitigated by

California's open carry provisions, which, although generally restrictive, permit the open carry of a loaded firearm under certain circumstances for immediate selfdefense.[73] The court also concluded that California's concealed carry measure passes muster under intermediate scrutiny.[74] Similarly, in *Williams v. Maryland*, the Maryland Court of Appeals upheld the state provision which prohibits the wearing, carrying, or transporting of a handgun openly or concealed without a permit.[75] The court reached this conclusion on the basis that the general ban on carrying a firearm includes an exception for home possession of a handgun without obtaining a permit. According to the court, the exception for the home "takes the statutory scheme outside the scope of the Second Amendment, as articulated in *Heller* and *McDonald*."[76] This reading is "wholly consistent with *Heller's* proviso that handguns are 'the most preferred firearm in the nation to keep and use for protection of one's home and family.'"[77]

On the other hand, the U.S. Court of Appeals for the Tenth Circuit (Tenth Circuit) used a two-step inquiry to analyze Colorado's concealed carry provision. The court, in *Peterson v. Martinez*, held that the carrying of concealed firearms is not protected by the Second Amendment.[78] The challenger, a resident from the State of Washington, sought review of Colorado's concealed carry law, which only issues CCPs for handguns to residents of the state.[79] After reviewing both early 19th century decisions and regulations on concealed carry cases, the court concluded that restrictions on concealed carry qualify as long-standing, and therefore fit within the Supreme Court's "presumptively lawful regulatory measures."[80] Moreover, because "the law harmonizes with the historical traditions associated with the Second Amendment guarantee," the challenger's claim "fail[ed] at step one" of the two-step analysis. As such, the Tenth Circuit did not engage in a means-end analysis of the provision.[81]

Other decisions have proceeded to the second prong of the two-step inquiry and have reached opposite conclusions after applying an intermediate scrutiny analysis on substantially similar concealed carry regulations that require an applicant to show proper cause. For instance, the U.S. District Court for the District of Maryland in *Woollard v. Sheridan* analyzed the requirement in the State of Maryland's statute that an applicant demonstrate "good and substantial reason" in order to obtain a CCP.[82] Although the U.S. Court of Appeals for the Fourth Circuit (Fourth Circuit) has since reversed the judgment of the court,[83] this report proceeds to review the district court's decision as it could be an approach that other courts may follow. In *Woollard*

I, the district court was mindful of an earlier Fourth Circuit decision that had refrained from concluding whether the scope of the Second Amendment as recognized in *Heller* applies outside the home.[84]

However, the district court in *Woollard I* found it necessary to conduct this analysis so as to determine if Maryland's restriction on handgun possession burdens any Second Amendment right. The district court concluded that *Heller* itself suggests the Second Amendment applies beyond the home, when it declared the right applicable to the home where the need "for defense of self, family, and property is most acute."[85] This particular language "suggests that the right also applies in some form 'where that need is not 'most acute.'"[86] The district court also reasoned that the Second Amendment must extend beyond the home because it protects lawful purposes such as hunting and militia training, neither of which are household activities.[87] Having determined that the regulation burdens conduct protected by the Second Amendment, the district court in *Woollard I* applied intermediate scrutiny and held that the "good and substantial reason" requirement infringes upon the Second Amendment because it is not reasonably adapted to a substantial government interest. Although public safety and crime prevention are considered substantial and compelling governmental interests, the district court found the state's good cause requirement overly broad and that it did nothing to advance the interests of public safety.[88]

In contrast, the U.S. Court of Appeals for the Second Circuit (Second Circuit) in *Kachalsky v. County of Westchester* upheld the State of New York's law which provides that a license to carry a concealed handgun shall only be issued when "proper cause exists."[89] The Second Circuit also determined that the Second Amendment "*must* have some application in the very different context of public possession of firearms."[90] Because the regulation places "substantial limits on the ability of law-abiding citizens to possess firearms for self-defense in public," some form of heightened scrutiny is appropriate. The court declared that it made "eminent sense" to apply intermediate scrutiny because the regulation does not touch upon the "core" protection of self-defense in the home.[91] Unlike the Maryland regulation in *Woollard I*, the Second Circuit decided that the New York proper cause requirement passes muster under intermediate scrutiny. Deferring to the state legislature's policy judgments, the court concluded that rather than forbidding anyone from carrying a handgun in public, New York took "a more moderate approach to fulfilling its important objective and reasonably concluded that only individuals having a bona fide reason to possess handguns should be allowed to introduce them into the public sphere."[92]

ARE CERTAIN TYPES OF WEAPONS NOT PROTECTED BY THE SECOND AMENDMENT?

Courts have employed a mixed approach when evaluating whether the Second Amendment protects certain types of weapons. Unlike other laws that have been scrutinized before the courts, the Supreme Court in *Heller* briefly addressed whether certain types of weapons would fall outside the protection of the Second Amendment. It declared that the Second Amendment "does not protect those weapons not typically possessed by law-abiding citizens for lawful purposes, such as short-barreled shotguns."[93] The Court found that its prior 1939 decision in *United States v. Miller*[94] supported this conclusion. Relying on *Miller*, the Court acknowledged that this limitation is supported by the "historical tradition of prohibiting the carrying of 'dangerous and unusual weapons'" and that the "sorts of weapons protected were those 'in common use at the time'" because those capable of service in the militia at the time of ratification would have brought "the sorts of lawful weapons that they possessed at home to militia duty."[95]

Since *Heller*, cases that have evaluated the constitutionality of state assault weapons bans have generally found them to be valid under the Second Amendment. These courts have relied on either, or both, the "common use" language found in *Heller* and the two-step inquiry set forth in *Marzzarella* to evaluate bans on assault weapons.

California

In 2009, the California Court of Appeals decided *People v. James*, which held that possession of an assault weapon in California remains unlawful and is not protected by the Second Amendment.[96] California's Roberti-Roos Assault Weapons Control Act of 1989, like the 1994 federal assault weapons ban, defines "assault weapons" by providing a list of proscribed weapons and through characteristics "which render these weapons more dangerous than ordinary weapons typically possessed by law-abiding citizens for lawful purposes."[97] Relying on *Heller*'s brief discussion that the Second Amendment does not protect a military weapon, such as an M16 rifle, the court in *James* declared that the prohibited weapons on the state's list "are not the types of weapons that are typically possessed by law-abiding citizens for lawful purposes such as sport hunting or self-defense; rather these are weapons of war."[98] It concluded that the relevant portion of the act did not prohibit conduct protected by the Second Amendment as defined in *Heller* and therefore the state was within its ability to prohibit the types of dangerous and unusual weapons an individual can use.[99]

District of Columbia

The District of Columbia amended its firearms regulations after the *Heller* decision and enacted new firearms regulations including an assault weapons ban that is similar to California's. In 2011, the D.C. Circuit issued its decision in *Heller v. District of Columbia* (*Heller II*) which upheld the District's ban on certain semiautomatic rifles and large capacity ammunition feeding devices (LCAFD).[100] Under the "common use" factor delineated in *Heller*, the D.C. Circuit acknowledged that "it was clear enough in the record that certain semi-automatic rifles and magazines holding more than 10 rounds are indeed in 'common use.'"[101] However, the court could not conclude definitely whether the weapons are "commonly used or are useful specifically for self-defense or hunting" such that they "meaningfully affect the right to keep and bear arms."[102] Therefore, the court went on to analyze the bans under the two-step approach to determine their validity under the Second Amendment.[103]

Assuming that the ban impinged on the right protected under *Heller* (i.e., to possess certain arms for lawful purposes such as individual self-defense or hunting), the court found that such regulations should be reviewed under intermediate scrutiny because the prohibition "does not effectively disarm individuals or substantially affect their ability to defend themselves."[104] Under intermediate scrutiny, the government has the burden of showing that there is a substantial relationship or reasonable "fit" between the regulation and the important governmental interest "in protecting police officers and controlling crime."[105] The D.C. Circuit held that the District carried this burden and that the evidence demonstrated that a ban on both semiautomatic assault rifles and LCAFDs "is likely to promote the Government's interest in crime control in the densely populated urban area that is the District of Columbia."[106]

Illinois—Cook County

In 2012, the Supreme Court of Illinois decided *Wilson v. Cook County*, a case that evaluated the constitutionality of the Blair Holt Assault Weapons

Ban of Cook County, a long-standing ordinance that was amended to similarly reflect provisions of the 1994 Assault Weapons Ban.[107] Among other claims, the plaintiffs argued that the ordinance violates the Second Amendment. With respect to the Second Amendment claim, the court indicated that it would follow the two-step approach similar to the *Heller II* court. While the court acknowledged that the ordinance banned only a subset of weapons with particular characteristics similar to other jurisdictions, it found that it could not "conclusively say ... that assault weapons as defined in the [o]rdinance categorically fall outside the scope of the rights protected by the [S]econd [A]mendment."[108] The court ultimately remanded the Second Amendment claim to the trial court for further proceedings, because unlike the *James* and *Heller II* decisions, the county did not have an opportunity to present evidence to justify the nexus between the ordinance and the governmental interest it seeks to protect.[109]

Summary

These cases demonstrate that courts evaluating various assault weapons bans, and to a limited extent LCAFD bans, have looked to the *Heller* decision and the general framework that has developed in the lower courts for analyzing claims under the Second Amendment. Based on the *Heller* decision where the Supreme Court indicated that certain weapons fall outside the protection of the Second Amendment, lower courts have examined whether the prohibited weapons are considered in "common use" or "commonly used" for lawful purposes or "dangerous and unusual." It is uncertain whether, to be protected under the Second Amendment, the weapon must be in "common use" by the people and if so, whether it must be in "common use" for self-defense or hunting; it is likewise uncertain what constitutes "dangerous and unusual." *Heller* could arguably be taken to indicate that if the prohibited weapons do not meet these criteria then they are not protected by the Second Amendment, in which case no heighted judicial scrutiny would be applied.

As seen above, a reviewing court could evaluate such measures under the two-step inquiry. If the restriction to certain types of firearms and firearms accessories imposes a burden on conduct protected by the Second Amendment, then a heightened level of judicial scrutiny will be applied to determine the ban's constitutionality. Yet how the "common use" and "dangerous and unusual" criteria should be read, if at all, in connection with the two-step approach remains unclear. Neither the *James*, *Heller II*, nor *Wilson* courts appear to have fully explained the connection between the two approaches.

IMPLICATIONS FOR FUTURE SECOND AMENDMENT CHALLENGES

Although many firearms laws have been upheld as constitutional, the differences in how courts interpret the text of *Heller*, insofar as providing some guidance on the scope of the Second Amendment, as well as how they apply the two-step inquiry may impact the burden upon the government to prove its case. For instance, courts have reached different conclusions on how to interpret the language on presumptively lawful restrictions. As noted above, it could be that these presumptively lawful measures are "so ingrained in our understanding of the Second Amendment that there is little doubt that they withstand the applicable level of scrutiny. Alternatively, the right itself can be seen as failing to extend into areas where, historically, limitations were commonplace and well accepted."[110]

While the court in *Woollard* believed the former reading was correct,[111] the Third Circuit in *Marzzarella* believed the latter was the correct interpretation for how to treat measures identified as presumptively lawful by the Court in *Heller*.[112] In each case, the court went on to apply intermediate scrutiny; however, the potential impact in selecting the latter interpretation—i.e., exceptions to the Second Amendment—may mean that as long as a challenged regulation was included among, or analogous to, the provisions noted in *Heller*,[113] there would be no burden imposed on the government to submit evidence demonstrating that the firearms regulation is a narrow fit to meet a substantial government interest. As such, this interpretation arguably would favor the government, and there could be a greater chance that a firearms regulation would be upheld. In contrast, the alternative interpretation is arguably not as favorable to the government, and a reviewing court could be less likely to uphold the constitutionality of a provision, unless the government is able to provide "meaningful evidence," as some courts have required. Moreover, the interpretation of the presumptively lawful language likely affects how lower courts define the nature of the right conferred by the Second Amendment and thus the level of scrutiny, if any, that should be applied.

Other Tests to Evaluate the Second Amendment

Although the prevailing test to evaluate challenges under the Second Amendment is the two-step inquiry, at least one judge, through dissent, has proposed a different approach. In *Heller II*, Judge Kavanaugh opined: "In my view, *Heller* and *McDonald* leave little doubts that courts are to assess gun bans and regulations based on the text, history, and tradition, not by a balancing test such as strict or intermediate scrutiny."[114] Under this test, he would have found that D.C.'s ban on semiautomatic rifles to be unconstitutional. However, the Second Circuit in *Kachalsky* seemed to implicitly reject this test. After reviewing the history of concealed carry laws and accompanying jurisprudence, the court stated: "History and tradition do not speak with one voice here. What history demonstrates is that states often disagreed as to the scope of the right to bear arms, whether the right was embodied in a state constitution or the Second Amendment."[115]

Moreover, some parties challenging firearms laws, such as the proper cause requirement for concealed carry, have also started to advocate that the court take a different approach to evaluate gun measures. They suggest applying First Amendment prior restraint doctrine instead of means-end scrutiny. In the First Amendment context, any law that makes "freedoms which the Constitution guarantees contingent upon the uncontrolled will of an official—as by requiring a permit or license which may be granted or withheld in the discretion of such official—is an unconstitutional censorship or prior restraint upon the enjoyment of those freedoms."[116] Thus far, this argument has been rejected and no court has taken this "quantum leap" of "import[ing] substantive First Amendment principles wholesale into Second Amendment jurisprudence."[117]

CONCLUSION

Firearms laws, both existing and new, will undoubtedly continue to be challenged under the Second Amendment. The Supreme Court's decision in *Heller* appears to have provided limited guidance on how to analyze firearms regulations under the Second Amendment. Yet lower courts have fashioned and primarily applied a two-step inquiry, which asks whether the regulated conduct burdens the Second Amendment right, and if so, whether it passes muster under means-end scrutiny. Although several firearms provisions have been upheld, it remains difficult to discern if there is a better understanding of the scope of the Second Amendment outside the "core" right identified in *Heller*, as courts have evaluated firearms provisions differently under the two-part test. As the post-*Heller* challenges to firearms provisions continue to percolate through the lower courts, it remains to be seen if any begin to use other analytical frameworks proposed, such as the "history, text, and tradition" test from the *Heller II* dissent or the prior restraints analysis suggested by parties challenging regulations under the Second Amendment.

End Notes

[1] 554 U.S. 570 (2008).

[2] 130 S. Ct. 3020 (2010).

[3] *Heller*, 554 U.S. at 626.

[4] *Heller*, 554 U.S. at 626-27. The Court reiterated this dicta in *McDonald*. *See McDonald*, 130 S. Ct. at 3047. However, the Court in *Heller* also noted that "since this case represents this Court's first in-depth examination of the Second Amendment, one should not expect it to clarify the entire field ... And there will be time enough to expound upon the historical justifications for the exceptions we have mentioned if and when those exceptions come before us." *Heller*, 554 U.S. at 635.

[5] For more on gun measures introduced in the 113th Congress, *see* CRS Report R42987, *Gun Control Proposals in the 113th Congress: Universal Background Checks, Gun Trafficking, and Military Style Firearms*, by William J. Krouse.

[6] F.E.C. v. Wis. Right to Life, Inc., 551 U.S. 449, 465 (2007).

[7] Bd. of Trs. of State Univ. of N.Y. v. Fox, 492 U.S. 469, 480 (1989).

[8] City of Cleburne v. Cleburne Living Ctr., 473 U.S. 432, 440 (1985). *See also* Erwin Chemerinsky, Constitutional Law: Principles and Policies §§6.5, 10.1.2 (3d ed. 2006).

[9] The Court stated "if all that was required to overcome the right to keep and bear arms was a rational basis, the Second Amendment would be redundant with the separate constitutional prohibitions on irrational laws, and would have no effect." *Heller*, 554 U.S. at 628 n.27.

[10] *Id*. at 634. In his dissent, Justice Breyer proposed an "interest-balancing" test, which "asks whether the statute burdens a protected interest in a way or to an extent that is out of proportion to the statute's salutary effects upon other important governmental interests." *Id*. at 634-35 (quoting Breyer, J. dissenting). The Court in *Heller* rejected it, stating: "We know of no other enumerated constitutional right whose core protection has been subjected to a freestanding "interest-balancing" approach. The very enumeration of the right takes out of the hands of government—even the Third Branch of Government—the power to decide on a case-by-case basis whether the right is *really worth* insisting upon. A constitutional guarantee subject to future judges' assessments of its usefulness is no constitutional guarantee at all." *Id*.

[11] *Id*. at 628. The challenged provisions were: D.C. Code §7-2501.01 (2001); §7-2502 (2001); §7-2507 (2001).

[12] *See, e.g.*, United States v. Barton, 633 F.3d 168, 171-72 (3d Cir. 2011) (finding the Supreme Court's discussion on categorical exceptions to the Second Amendment binding and not dicta and affirming a lower court's decision that the felon dispossession statute (§922(g)(1)) is presumptively lawful).

[13] *See, e.g.*, United States v. Richard, 350 F. App'x 252, 260 (10th Cir. 2009) (stating that the Second Amendment is subject to appropriate restrictions like those contained in 18 U.S.C. §923(g)(3)).

[14] *See, e.g.*, United States v. Yanez-Vasquez, No. 09-40056-01-SAC, 2010 U.S. Dist. LEXIS 8166, at *1 (D. Kan. Jan. 28, 2010) (upholding 18 U.S.C. §922(g)(5) that prohibits illegal aliens from possessing a firearm).

[15] *See, e.g.*, United States v. White, 593 F.3d 1199, 1205 (11th Cir. 2010) (holding that 18 U.S.C. §922(g)(9) is a presumptively lawful long-standing prohibition on the possession of firearms).

[16] *White*, 593 F.3d at 1206 ("We see no reason to exclude §922(g) from the list of long-standing prohibitions on which *Heller* does not cast doubt."). *See also* United States v. Booker, 570 F. Supp. 2d 161, 163 (D. Me. 2008) (stating, "persons who have been convicted of a misdemeanor crime of domestic violence must be added to the list of 'felons and the mentally ill' against whom the 'longstanding prohibitions on the possession of firearm' survive Second Amendment scrutiny"); United States v. Luedtke, 589 F. Supp. 2d 1018, 1021 (E.D. Wis. 2008) (noting that while 18 U.S.C. §§922(g)(8)-(9) do not represent "'longstanding prohibition on the possession of firearms,' nothing in *Heller* suggests the Court intended to permit only those *precise* regulations accepted at the founding").

[17] United States v. Marzzarella, 614 F.3d 85 (3d Cir. 2010), *cert. denied* Marzzarella v. United States, 131 S. Ct. 958 (2011).

[18] 18 U.S.C. §922(k) ("It shall be unlawful for any person, knowingly ... to possess or receive any firearm which has had the importer's or manufacturer's serial number removed, obliterated, or altered and has, at any time, been shipped or transported in interstate or foreign commerce.").

[19] *Id.* at 91.

[20] As discussed *infra*, other lower courts have had difficulty understanding what the Supreme Court meant by characterizing certain long-standing gun control measures as "presumptively lawful."

[21] *Marzzarella*, 614 F.3 at 89.

[22] *Id.* at 94.

[23] *Id.* ("The mere fact that some firearms possess a nonfunctional characteristic should not create a categorically protected class of firearms on the basis of that characteristic.").

[24] *Id.*

[25] *Id.* 94-5.

[26] For example, content-based restrictions on speech in a public forum trigger strict scrutiny, whereas content-neutral time, place, manner restrictions on speech in a public forum trigger intermediate scrutiny. *Id.* at 96.

[27] *Id.* at 97-100 ("In sum, the right to speech, an undeniably enumerated fundamental right, [citation omitted] is susceptible to several standards of scrutiny, depending upon the type of law challenged and the type of speech at issue. We see no reason why the Second Amendment would be any different." *Id.* at 96-7.).

[28] *Id.* at 96 ("Discrimination against particular messages in a public forum is subject to the exacting scrutiny. [citation omitted] Regulations of the manner in which that speech takes place, however, receive intermediate scrutiny, under the time, place, and manner doctrine. [citation omitted] Accordingly, we think §922(k) also should merit intermediate, rather than strict scrutiny." *Id.* at 97.).

[29] *Id.* at 98 (citing Turner Broad Sys., Inc. v. FCC, 512 U.S. 622, 662 (1994) and Ward v. Rock Against Racism, 491 U.S. 781, 791 (1989) and Lorillard Tobacco Co. v. Reilly, 533 U.S. 525, 526 (2001)).

[30] *Id.* at 97. The Third Circuit also held that the statute would still pass muster under strict scrutiny because it is "narrowly tailored to serve a compelling state interest." *Id.* at 99.

[31] *See, e.g.,* United States v. Greeno, 679 F.3d 510 (6th Cir. 2012) (applying two-step inquiry to determine if sentencing enhancement violates Second Amendment); Ezell v. City of Chicago, 651 F.3d 684 (7th Cir. 2011) (applying two-step inquiry to determine if class training requirement necessary to lawfully obtain firearm and firing range prohibition violates Second Amendment); United States v. Reese, 627 F.3d 792 (10th Cir. 2010) (applying two-step inquiry to review whether 18 U.S.C. §922(g)(8)—prohibiting those subject to a certain court order—is constitutional).

[32] The Federal Firearms Act of 1938, 52 Stat. 1250 (1938), was the first federal firearms law to regulate the possession, manufacture, and sale of firearms. It also made it unlawful at the federal level for certain individuals with criminal history to possess firearms.

[33] P.L. 90-618 (1968).

[34] S. Rept. No. 90-1097 (1968).

[35] 18 U.S.C. §§922 *et seq.*

[36] 18 U.S.C. §922(b)(1). Furthermore, the GCA places significant restrictions on the transfer to, and possession of, firearms by persons under the age of 18. 18 U.S.C. §922(x). *See also* United States v. Rene E., 583 F.3d 8 (1st Cir. 2009) (upholding federal ban on juvenile handgun possession).

[37] For example, federal firearms licensees (FFLs) must verify the identity of a transferee by examining a government-issued identification document bearing a photograph of the transferee, such as a driver's license; conducting a background check on the transferee using the National Instant Criminal Background Check System (NICS); maintaining records of the acquisition and disposition of firearms; reporting multiple sales of handguns to the Attorney General; responding to an official request for information contained in the licensee's records within 24 hours of receipt; and complying with all other relevant state and local regulations. *See* 18 U.S.C.§§922(t); 923.

[38] 18 U.S.C. §922(g). Individuals who are under indictment for a felony are also prohibited from receiving or transporting firearms or ammunition. 18 U.S.C. §922(n).

[39] 700 F.3d 185 (5th Cir. 2012). The other related regulations challenged were 18 U.S.C. §922(c)(1) and 27 C.F.R. §§478.99(b)(1), 478.124(a), and 478.96(b), all of which relate to firearm sales by a licensed dealer to persons of the requisite age. The appellants also asserted that the federal law denied them equal protection under the Due Process Clause of the Fifth Amendment of the U.S. Constitution. *NRA*, 700 F.3d at 188. The court rejected the equal protection claim, holding that age is not a suspect classification and that appellants failed to show the federal laws are not rationally related to a legitimate state interest. *Id.* at 212.

[40] *Id.* at 194-98 (reviewing the two-step test and discussing why the Fifth Circuit will adopt it).

[41] *Id.* at 194.

[42] *Id.* at 200-02 ("If a representative citizen of the founding era conceived of a 'minor' as an individual who was unworthy of the Second Amendment guarantee, and conceived of 18-to-20-year-olds as 'minors,' then it stands to reason that the citizen would have supported restricting an 18-to-20-year-old's right to keep and bear arms." *Id.* at 202.).

[43] *Id.* at 202-03 (reviewing state laws from the 19th century that prohibited selling deadly weapons to minors and state cases that upheld the validity of laws prohibiting weapons ownership by minors).

[44] *Id.* at 204.

[45] *Id.* at 205. Similar to the Third Circuit in *Marzzarella*, the Fifth Circuit opined that it is "difficult to map *Heller's* 'longstanding' ... 'presumptively lawful regulatory measures' ... onto [the] two-step framework," because it is unclear whether the long-standing regulations

"(i) presumptively fail to burden conduct protected by the Second Amendment, or (ii) presumptively trigger and pass constitutional muster under a lenient level of scrutiny." *Id*. at 196. Notwithstanding this confusion over how to approach evaluating long-standing prohibitions, the Fifth Circuit concluded that 18 U.S.C. §922(b)(1) would probably fall outside the protection of the Second Amendment or would probably only trigger and pass muster under intermediate scrutiny. *Id*.

[46] The Fifth Circuit also justified applying intermediate scrutiny because *Heller's* identification of certain longstanding, presumptively valid prohibitions indicates that the "Second Amendment permits 'categorical regulation of gun possession by classes of persons.'" *Id*. at 205 (citations omitted). Moreover, 18-to-20-year-old individuals will be temporarily be affected by the age qualification, and are not otherwise prohibited from possessing handguns for lawful purposes or acquiring them from parents or guardians. *Id*. at 206-07.

[47] *Id*. at 207-10. ("Overall, the government has marshaled evidence showing that Congress was focused on a particular problem: *young persons under 21*, who are immature and prone to violence, easily accessing *handguns*, which facilitate violent crime, primarily by way of *FFLs*. Accordingly, Congress restricted the ability of *young persons under 21* to purchase *handguns* from *FFLs*." *Id*. at 208 (emphasis in the original)).

[48] P.L. 104-208 (1996).

[49] United States v. Skoien (Skoien I), 587 F.3d 803 (7th Cir. 2009), *vacated by, rehearing granted, en banc*, by United States v. Skoien, No. 08-3770, 2010 U.S. App. LEXIS 6584, at *1 (7th Cir. Feb. 22, 2010).

[50] *Skoien I*, 587 F.3d at 808.

[51] *Id*. at 809.

[52] *Id*.

[53] *Id*. at 810 (noting that scholars disagree about whether and to what extent persons convicted of crimes—more specifically, felons—were considered excluded from the right to bear and keep arms during the founding era).

[54] *Id*. at 812 (stating that strict scrutiny cannot be applied to all gun restrictions as doing so would be incompatible with *Heller's* dicta about "presumptively lawful" firearms laws. *Id*. at 811.).

[55] *Id*.

[56] *Id*. at 814 ("In fairness, because *Heller* did not establish a standard of review, the government did not know what its burden would be. Like the district court, it proceeded on the assumption that the highest standard of scrutiny applied and then relied almost entirely on conclusory reasoning by analogy from *Heller's* reference to the 'presumptive' constitutionality of felon-dispossession laws.... In any event, our discussion here of the appropriate standard of review should provide guidance for the proceedings on remand." *Id*. at 815.).

[57] United States v. Skoien (Skoien II), 614 F.3d 638, 642 (7th Cir. 2010) (en banc).

[58] *Id*. at 641.

[59] United States v. Chester (Chester I), 628 F.3d 673 (4th Cir. 2010).

[60] *Id*. at 680.

[61] *Id*.

[62] *Id*. at 683 (emphasis in the original).

[63] United States v. Chester (Chester II), 847 F. Supp. 2d 902, 906-08 (S.D.W.Va. 2012).

[64] *Id*. at 906 (relying on *United States v. Carter*, 669 F.3d 411, 418 (4th Cir. 2012), in declaring that there is no precise formula the government must follow to make the required showing and that the government "may resort to a wide range of sources, such as legislative text and

history, empirical evidence, case law, common sense, as circumstances and context require").

[65] *Id.* at 906 (citing United States v. Carter, 669 F.3d 411 (4th Cir. 2012) (vacating and remanding the decision on basis that the government did not present sufficient evidence to demonstrate that 18 U.S.C. §922(g)(3)—prohibiting drug users from possessing firearms—was a substantial fit to achieve the important government interest)). *See also* District of Columbia v. Heller (Heller II), 670 F.3d 1224, 1254-59 (D.C. Cir. 2011) (holding that District's "novel registration" requirements were subject to intermediate scrutiny but remanding the case on this issue because the government did not meet its burden under the standard as it did not present any "meaningful evidence ... to justify its predictive judgments").

[66] For more on concealed carry and federal laws that regulate concealed carry for certain professions, *see* CRS Report R42099, *Federal Laws and Legislation on Carrying Concealed Firearms: An Overview*, by Vivian S. Chu.

[67] *McDonald*, 130 S. Ct. at 3047 (Alito, J., plurality) (citing Heller, 554 U.S. at 626).

[68] *Heller*, 554 U.S. at 632.

[69] *Id.* at 594 (emphasis added).

[70] Peruta v. County of San Diego, 758 F.Supp.2d 1106 (S.D. Cal. 2010).

[71] *Id.* at 1115.

[72] *Id.* at 1114 (citing State v. Chandler, 5 La. Ann. 489, 490 (1850) (holding that a ban on carrying concealed weapons "interfered with no man's right to carry arms ... in full open view."); Nunn v. State, 1 Ga. 243, 251 (1846) (holding a ban on carrying concealed weapons to be valid so long as it does not impair the right to bear arms altogether)). Notably, the court emphasized that concealed weapons bans "cannot be viewed in isolation; they must be viewed in the context of the government's overall scheme." *Id.*

[73] *Id.* at 1114-15 (citing Cal. Penal Code §12031 (2010)).

[74] The court found that the good cause requirement reasonably relates and is adapted to serving the government's "important and substantial interest in public safety and in reducing the rate of gun use in crime." *Id.* at 1117.

[75] Williams v. Maryland, 10 A.3d 1167, 1169 (Md. 2011) (referencing Md. Crim. Code §4-203(a)(1)(i) (2002)).

[76] *Id.* at 1178.

[77] *Id* (citing *Heller*, 554 U.S. at 628).

[78] Peterson v. Martinez, No. 11-1149, 2013 U.S. App. LEXIS 3776, at *1 (10th Cir. Feb. 22, 2013).

[79] Colo. Rev. Stat. §18-12-203. The State of Colorado recognizes out-of-state CCPs as long as the other state recognizes its CCP. The State of Washington does not recognize out-of-state CCPs and therefore a Washington CCP is not honored in Colorado. While the challenger also had other non-resident, out-of-state CCPs, Colorado only recognizes CCPs that are issued by an individual's state of residence. Colo. Rev. Stat. §18-12-213.

[80] *Peterson*, 2013 U.S. App. LEXIS 3776, at *33.

[81] *Id.* at *34.

[82] Woollard v. Sheridan (Woollard I), 863 F. Supp. 2d 462 (D. Md. 2012), *rev'd sub nom.* Woollard v. Gallagher (Woollard II), No. 12-1437, slip op. at 6 (4th Cir. Mar. 21, 2013). Similarly, the U.S. Court of Appeals for the Seventh Circuit (Seventh Circuit) also determined that the Second Amendment "implies a right to carry a loaded gun outside the home" as "[c]onfrontations are not limited to the home." Moore v. Madigan, 702 F.3d 933 (7th Cir. 2012), *rehearing denied*, Moore v. Madigan, No. 12-1269(L) (7th Cir. Feb. 22, 2013). The Seventh Circuit declared the Illinois carrying ban unconstitutional because it

simply goes too far in that it is "a blanket prohibition on carrying [a] gun in public [and] prevents a person from defending himself anywhere except inside his home." *Id.* at 940. However, the court did not apply a standard of scrutiny, but primarily found that Illinois "did not make strong showing" to justify the law and that the "empirical literature on the effects of allowing the carriage of guns in public fails to establish a pragmatic defense of the Illinois law." *Id.* at 939-40.

[83] *Woollard II*, No. 12-1437, slip op. at 20 ("We hew to a judicious course today, refraining from any assessment of whether Maryland's ... requirement for obtaining a handgun permit implicates Second Amendment protections. That is, we merely assume that the *Heller* right exists outside the home and that such right of Appellee Woollard has been infringed. We are free to make that assumption because the good-and-substantial reason requirement passes muster under what have deemed to be the applicable standard—intermediate scrutiny.").

[84] *Woollard I*, 863 F. Supp. 2d. at 469. In *United States v. Masciandaro*, 638 F.3d 458 (4th Cir. 2011), the Fourth Circuit upheld a conviction under a Department of Interior regulation that prohibited the possession or carrying of a loaded firearm in a motor vehicle within national park areas. Judge Niemeyer, writing for court, applied and upheld the regulation under intermediate scrutiny because the regulation did not burden the "'fundamental,' core right of self-defense in the home by a law-abiding citizen." *Id.* at 471. However, he was alone in his opinion regarding the scope of the Second Amendment. Judge Wilkinson, writing for the court only on this issue, stated that it was unnecessary to decide this issue and would await direction from the Supreme Court itself because "it is not clear what places public authorities may ban firearms altogether without shouldering the burdens of litigation." *Id.* at 475 (Wilkinson, J. majority). "The whole matter strikes us as a vast *terra incognita* that courts should enter only upon necessity and only then by small degree." *Id.*

[85] *Woollard I*, 863 F. Supp. 2d at 469 (citing *Heller*, 554 U.S. at 628).

[86] *Id.* at 469. The district court's analysis built upon Judge Niemeyer's reasoning in *Masciandaro* where he also opined that "if the Second Amendment right were confined to self-defense *in the home*, the Court not would not have needed to express reservation for 'sensitive places' outside of the home." *Masciandaro*, 638 F.3d at 468 (Niemeyer, J. Part III.B).

[87] *Woollard I*, 863 F. Supp. 2d at 469.

[88] *Id.* at 474-75 (The State "does not ban handguns from places where the possibility of mayhem is most acute, ... It does not attempt to reduce accidents, as would a requirement that all permit applicants complete a safety course. It does not even, as some other States' laws do, limit the carrying of handguns to persons deemed 'suitable' by denying a permit to anyone 'whose conduct indicates that he or she is potentially a danger to the public if entrusted with a handgun.'" *Id.*).

[89] *Kachalsky v. County of Westchester*, 701 F.3d 81 (2d Cir. 2012) (citing N.Y. Penal Law §400.00(2)(f)).

[90] *Id.* at 89 ("The plain text of the Second Amendment does not limit the right to bear arms to the home." *Id.* at n.10.).

[91] *Id.* at 93 (reviewing historical state regulation of firearms outside the home and declaring that "[S]tates have long recognized a countervailing and competing set of concerns with regard to handgun ownership and use in public. Understanding the scope of the constitutional right is the first step in determining the yard stick by which we measure the state regulation." *Id.* at 95-6.).

[92] *Id.* at 98.

[93] *Id.*

[94] United States v. Miller, 307 U.S. 174 (1939) (holding that the Second Amendment did not protect an individual's right to transport an unregistered short-barreled shotgun in interstate commerce).

[95] *Heller*, 540 U.S. at 627. The Court recognized that "it may be true that no amount of small arms could be useful against modern-day bombers and tanks." However, it noted that modern day developments "cannot change our interpretation of the right." *Id.*

[96] People v. James, 94 Cal. Rptr. 3d 576 (Cal. Ct. App. 2009), *rev. denied* by People v. James, 2009 Cal. LEXIS 9895 (Cal. Sept. 17, 2009), *cert. denied* James v. Cal. 2010 U.S. LEXIS 1284 (U.S., Feb. 22, 2010). Notably, a petitioner challenging an assault weapons ban could make an argument that civilian versions of military weapons, like the AR-15, should be differentiated from military weapons, like the M16, which the Supreme Court does not considered protected under the Second Amendment. However, the Supreme Court's denial of certiorari in the *James* case could indicate that the Court does not distinguish between military and civilian versions of military style weapons, considering both beyond the scope of the Second Amendment's guarantee.

[97] *James*, 94 Cal. Rptr. 3d at 579-580 (citing Cal. Penal Code §§12276, 12276.1).

[98] *Id.* at 585-86 (quoting Cal. Penal Code §122275.5(a) (West 2006)).

[99] *James*, 94 Cal. Rptr. 3d at 586 (citing the Cal. Penal Code §§12280(b)-(c) which imposes penalties for possession of assault weapon or .50 BMG rifle).

[100] Heller v. District of Columbia (Heller II), 670 F.3d 1244 (D.C. Cir. 2011) (affirming in part and vacating in part the lower court's decision, remanding to the lower court the petitioner's challenge to the District's "novel registration requirements").

[101] *Id.* at 1261.

[102] *Id.*

[103] The D.C. Circuit adopted from other circuits a two-step approach to determining the constitutionality of the gun laws at issue. *See, e.g.*, *Marzzarella*, 614 F.3d at 89. This D.C. Circuit indicated that this two-step approach is taken if the challenged regulation is not one that the *Heller* decision identified as a "longstanding" regulation that is "presumptively lawful." *Id.* (citing *Heller*, 554 U.S. at 626-27, n.26).

[104] *Heller II*, 670 F.3d 1261-62. The court did not resolve the question of whether the ban on certain long gun assault weapons or high capacity magazines impinged on the Second Amendment right as historically understood. *Id.* at 1261.

[105] *Id.* at 1262.

[106] *Id.* at 1263.

[107] Wilson v. Cook County, 968 N.E.2d 641 (Ill. 2012). The challengers in *Wilson* also argued that the ordinance violates the Due Process and Equal Protection Clauses of the U.S. Constitution. Regarding the due process claim, the court concluded that the ordinance is not unconstitutionally vague such that it "fails to provide people of ordinary intelligence a reasonable opportunity to understand what conduct it prohibits." *Id.* at 650-53. The court also dismissed the equal protection claim, finding that the "[o]rdinance does not arbitrarily differentiate between two owners with similar firearms because the banned firearms are either listed, a copy or duplicate, or fall under the characteristics-based test." *Id.* at 658.

[108] *Id.* at 655.

[109] *Id.* at 657. ("Without a national uniform definition of assault weapons from which to judge these weapons, it cannot be ascertained at this stage of the proceedings whether these arms with these particular attributes as defined in this [o]rdinance are all well suited for self-defense or support or would be outweighed completely by the collateral damage resulting from their use, making them 'dangerous and unusual' as articulated in *Heller*. This question

requires us to engage in an empirical inquiry beyond the scope of the record and beyond the scope of judicial notice about the nature of weapons that are banned under this [o]rdinance and the dangers of these particular weapons." *Id.* at 656.).

[110] *Woollard I*, 863 F. Supp. 2d at 470.

[111] *Id.* ("[I]t did seem to indicate that the former reading is more likely correct than the latter: 'The Court's use of the word 'presumptively' suggests that the articulation of sensitive places may not be a limitation on the scope of the Second Amendment, but rather on the analysis to be conducted with respect to the burden on that right.'" (citing *Masciandaro*, 638 F.3d at 472)).

[112] *Marzzarella*, 614 F.3d at 91 ("[W]e think the better reading based on the text and structure of *Heller*, is ... that these longstanding prohibitions are exceptions to the right to bear arms."). Notably, some courts do not resolve or address this text from *Heller*. For example, the Second Circuit in *Kachalsky* stated, "We do not view this language as a talismanic formula for determining whether a law regulating firearms is consistent with the Second Amendment. While we find it informative, it simply makes clear that the Second Amendment right is not unlimited." *Kachalsky*, 701 F.3d at 90 n.11.

[113] The measures identified by the *Heller* Court were "prohibitions on the possession of firearms by felons and the mentally ill, or laws for forbidding the carrying of firearms in sensitive places such as schools and government buildings, or laws imposing conditions and qualifications on the commercial sale of arms." *Heller*, 554 U.S. at 626-27.

[114] *Heller II*, 670 F.3d at 1271 (Kavanaugh, J. dissent).

[115] *Kachalsky*, 701 F.3d at 91.

[116] Staub v. City of Baxley, 335 U.S. 313, 322 (1958).

[117] *Kachalsky*, 701 F.3d at 91-93. *See also Woollard I*, 863 F. Supp. 2d at 472; Piszczatoski v. Filko, 840 F. Supp. 2d 813, 835-36 (D.N.J. 2012).

In: Firearms in America
Editor: Alfonso D. Sutton

ISBN: 978-1-63117-823-8
© 2014 Nova Science Publishers, Inc.

Chapter 3

FEDERAL ASSAULT WEAPONS BAN: LEGAL ISSUES[*]

Vivian S. Chu

SUMMARY

In the 113th Congress, there has been renewed congressional interest in gun control legislation. On January 16, 2013, President Obama announced his support for legislation on gun control, including a ban on certain semiautomatic assault firearms and large capacity ammunition feeding devices. Senator Dianne Feinstein introduced S. 150, the Assault Weapons Ban of 2013, which would prohibit, subject to certain exceptions, the sale, transfer, possession, manufacturing, and importation of specifically named firearms and other firearms that have certain features, as well as the transfer and possession of large capacity ammunition feeding devices. Representative Carolyn McCarthy introduced a companion measure, H.R. 437, in the House of Representatives. S. 150 is similar to the Assault Weapons Ban of 1994 (P.L. 103-322) that was in effect through September 13, 2004.

The Assault Weapons Ban of 1994 was challenged in the courts for violating, among other things, the Equal Protection Clause and the Commerce Clause. This report reviews the disposition of these challenges. It also discusses Second Amendment jurisprudence in light of the Supreme Court's

---

[*] This is an edited, reformatted and augmented version of a Congressional Research Service publication, CRS Report for Congress R42957, dated February 14, 2013.

decision in *District of Columbia v. Heller* and how lower courts have evaluated state and local assault weapons bans post-*Heller*.

INTRODUCTION

At the outset of the 113th Congress, there has been renewed congressional interest in gun control legislation. Senator Dianne Feinstein introduced S. 150, the Assault Weapons Ban of 2013, which would prohibit, subject to certain exceptions, the sale, transfer, possession, manufacturing, and importation of specifically named firearms and other firearms that have certain features, as well as the transfer and possession of large capacity ammunition feeding devices. Representative Carolyn McCarthy introduced a companion measure, H.R. 437, in the House of Representatives. S. 150 is similar to the Assault Weapons Ban of 1994 that was in effect through September 13, 2004.[1] As Congress considers S. 150 and other gun control measures, it may be useful to review the 1994 law and its relation to federal firearms law, as well as the disposition of the legal challenges to the ban.

GUN CONTROL ACT OF 1968

Congress enacted the Gun Control Act of 1968[2] (GCA or Act) to "keep firearms out of the hands of those not legally entitled to possess them because of age, criminal background, or incompetency, and to assist law enforcement authorities in the states and their subdivisions in combating the increasing prevalence of crime in the United States."[3] The GCA establishes a comprehensive statutory scheme that regulates the manufacture, sale, transfer, and possession of firearms and ammunition.[4]

In particular, the GCA establishes nine classes of individuals who are prohibited from shipping, transporting, possessing, or receiving firearms and ammunition.[5] The individuals targeted by this provision include (1) persons convicted of a crime punishable by a term of imprisonment exceeding one year; (2) fugitives from justice; (3) individuals who are unlawful users or addicts of any controlled substance; (4) persons legally determined to be mentally defective, or who have been committed to a mental institution; (5) aliens illegally or unlawfully in the United States, as well as those who have been admitted pursuant to a nonimmigrant visa; (6) individuals who have been discharged dishonorably from the Armed Forces; (7) persons who have renounced United States citizenship; (8) individuals subject to a pertinent court order; and, finally, (9) persons who have been convicted of a misdemeanor domestic violence offense.[6]

When the GCA was enacted, the transfer and sale of ammunition appear to have been regulated in the same manner as firearms. In 1986, Congress passed the Firearm Owners' Protection Act[7] (FOPA), which repealed many of the regulations regarding ammunition. Consequently, the transfer and sale of ammunition is not as strictly regulated as the transfer and sale of firearms.[8]

Restrictions on Sales

In order to effectuate the general prohibitions outlined above, the GCA imposes significant requirements on the transfer of firearms. Pursuant to the Act, any person who is "engaged in the business"[9] of importing, manufacturing, or dealing in firearms must apply and be approved as a Federal Firearms Licensee (FFL).[10] FFLs are subject to several requirements designed to ensure that a firearm is not transferred to an individual disqualified from possession under the Act. For example, FFLs must verify the identity of a transferee by examining a government-issued identification document bearing a photograph of the transferee, such as a driver's license;[11] conduct a background check on the transferee using the National Instant Criminal Background Check System (NICS);[12] maintain records of the acquisition and disposition of firearms;[13] report multiple sales of handguns to the Attorney General;[14] respond to an official request for information contained in the licensee's records within 24 hours of receipt;[15] and comply with all other relevant state and local regulations.[16]

Not all sellers of firearms are required to be approved FFLs, however. The GCA contains a specific exemption for any person who makes "occasional sales, exchanges, or purchases of firearms for the enhancement of a personal collection or for a hobby, or who sells all or part of his personal collection of firearms."[17] Although private sellers are not required to conduct a background check or maintain official records of transactions under federal law, they are prohibited from transferring a firearm if they know or have reasonable cause to believe that the transferee is a disqualified person.[18]

Restrictions on Interstate Transfers

In addition to the requirements imposed upon the sale of firearms by FFLs and non-FFLs (or private individuals) generally, federal law also places significant limitations on the actual interstate transfer of weapons. Although FFLs have the ability to sell and ship firearms in interstate or foreign commerce, the GCA places several restrictions on the manner in which a transfer may occur. Specifically, while FFLs may make an in-person, over-the-counter sale of a long gun (i.e., shotgun or rifle) to any qualified individual regardless of her state of residence,[19] they may only sell a handgun to a person who is a resident of the state in which the dealer's premises are located.[20] Relatedly, FFLs are prohibited from shipping firearms, both handguns and long guns, directly to consumers in other states.[21] Instead, FFLs making a firearm sale to a non-resident must transfer the weapon to another FFL that is licensed in the transferee's state of residence and from whom the transferee may obtain the firearm after passing the required NICS background check.[22]

Firearm transfers between non-FFL sellers are also strictly regulated. Specifically, whereas FFLs may transfer a long gun to any individual regardless of her state of residence in an over-the - counter sale, the GCA specifically bars a non-FFL from directly selling or transferring any firearm to any person who is not a resident of the state in which the non -FFL resides.[23] Instead, interstate transactions between non-FFLs result in the transferring party shipping the firearm to an FFL located in the transferee's state of residence.

THE 1994 ASSAULT WEAPONS BAN

Congress enacted, as part of the Violent Crime Control and Law Enforcement Act of 1994, the Public Safety and Recreational Firearms Act (referred to as the "Assault Weapons Ban"), which established a 10-year prohibition on the manufacture, transfer, or possession of "semiautomatic assault weapons," as defined by the act, as well as large capacity ammunition feeding devices.[24] The act contained several exceptions, including a "grandfather clause" allowing for the possession of such items that were otherwise lawfully possessed on the date of enactment. The Assault Weapons Ban expired on September 13, 2004.[25]

Generally speaking, an "assault weapon" is considered to be a military style weapon capable of providing by a selector switch either semiautomatic—

that is, the firearm discharges one round, then loads a new round, each time the trigger is pulled until the magazine is exhausted—or a fully automatic firearm—that is, continuous discharge of rounds while the trigger is depressed until all rounds are discharged. Under federal law, a fully automatic firearm falls under the definition "machinegun," which is defined as "any weapon that shoots ... automatically more than one shot, without manual reloading, by a single function of the trigger."[26] Semiautomatic firearms, including semiautomatic assault weapons, are "produced with semiautomatic fire capability only."[27]

Banned Weapons and Exemptions

The 1994 act made it "unlawful for a person to manufacture, transfer, or possess a semiautomatic assault weapon."[28] Weapons banned were identified either by specific make or model (including copies or duplicates thereof, in any caliber), or by specific characteristics that slightly varied according to whether the weapon was a pistol, rifle, or shotgun.[29]

> For example, a semiautomatic rifle fell under the term "semiautomatic assault weapon" if it had the ability to accept a detachable magazine and possessed two of the following five features: (1) a folding or telescopic stock; (2) a pistol grip that protrudes conspicuously beneath the action of the weapon; (3) a bayonet mount; (4) a flash suppressor or threaded barrel designed to accommodate a flash suppressor; or (5) a grenade launcher. See Former 18 U.S.C. §921(a)(30)(B).
>
> For the feature-based definition semiautomatic pistols and semiautomatic shotguns that would be included under the term "semiautomatic assault weapon." See Former 18 U.S.C. §§921(a)(30)(C), (D).

The act also made it unlawful to transfer and possess large capacity ammunition feeding devices (LCAFD).[30] An LCAFD was defined as "any magazine, belt, drum, feed strip, or similar device manufactured after the date [of the act] that has the capacity of, or that can be readily restored or converted to accept, more than 10 rounds of ammunition."[31] LCAFDs manufactured after the date of enactment were required to have a serial number that "clearly shows" that they were manufactured after such date, as well as other markings prescribed by regulation.[32]

The 1994 act included a grandfather clause and therefore allowed for the transfer of any "semiautomatic assault weapon" or LCAFD that was otherwise lawfully possessed on the date of enactment.[33] Additionally, Congress exempted roughly 650 types or models of firearms, such as various models of Browning, Remington, and Berettas, deemed mainly suitable for target practice, match competition, hunting, and similar sporting purposes.[34] This list was not exhaustive and the act provided that the absence of a firearm from the exempted list did not mean it was banned unless it met the definition of "semiautomatic assault weapon." The act also exempted any firearm that (1) is manually operated by bolt, pump, lever, or slide action; (2) has been rendered permanently inoperable; or (3) is an antique firearm. The act also did not apply to any semiautomatic rifle that cannot accept a detachable magazine that holds more than five rounds of ammunition nor any semiautomatic shotgun that cannot hold more than five rounds of ammunition in a fixed of detachable magazine.[35]

Furthermore, there were exemptions that permitted semiautomatic assault weapons and LCAFDs to be manufactured for, transferred to, and possessed by law enforcement and for authorized testing or experimentation purposes. The other exemptions included a transfer for purposes of federal security pursuant to the Atomic Energy Act, as well as possession by retired law enforcement officers who are not otherwise a prohibited possessor under law.[36]

Importation of Assault Weapons under 18 U.S.C. Section 925(d)(3)

The 1994 Assault Weapons Ban did not address the importation of semiautomatic assault weapons, rather Section 925(d)(3) of the GCA provides that the Attorney General[37] shall authorize a firearm or ammunition to be imported or brought into the United States if it does not meet the definition of a firearm under the National Firearms Act,[38] and is "generally recognized as particularly suitable for or readily adaptable to sporting purposes, excluding surplus military rifles." Notably, the statute does not specifically describe or list any criteria that the Attorney General is required to take into consideration when determining what constitutes "suitable for or readily adaptable to sporting purposes." This provision permitting the importation of firearms is generally known as "the sporting purposes test," and its implementation appears to be left to the Attorney General's discretion.

Prior to the implementation of the 1994 Assault Weapons Ban, the Bureau of Alcohol, Tobacco, Firearms and Explosives (ATF) identified several semiautomatic assault rifles that it determined did not meet the sporting suitability standard of Section 925(d)(3). On July 6, 1989, ATF prohibited importation of these rifles.[39] This decision was, in part, based on ATF's finding that "these rifles have certain characteristics that are common to modern military assault rifles and that distinguish them from traditional sporting rifles."[40] Subsequent to this decision, domestic manufacturing of semiautomatic assault weapons reportedly increased, and foreign manufacturers reportedly "circumvented the strictures of the [1989] ban [under President Bush] by reconfiguring their weapons and shipping them out under different models," as well as attempting to give the weapons a sporting appearance.[41]

The enactment of the 1994 Assault Weapons Ban addressed these developments to a certain degree; however, ATF subsequently determined in 1997 that certain semiautomatic assault rifles could no longer be imported even though they were permitted to be imported under the 1989 "sporting purposes test" because they had been modified to remove all of their military features other than the ability to accept a detachable magazine. Accordingly, on April 6, 1998, ATF prohibited the importation of 56 such rifles, determining that they did not meet the "sporting purposes test."

S. 150 and H.R. 437 Assault Weapons Ban of 2013

S. 150, the Assault Weapons Ban of 2013, was introduced by Senator Dianne Feinstein in the 113th Congress. A companion measure, H.R. 437, was introduced by Representative Carolyn McCarthy in the House of Representatives. S. 150 would establish a regulatory scheme for "semiautomatic assault weapons" similar to the 1994 law with a few differences.

First, it would ban approximately 157 specifically named firearms and any copies, duplicates, or variants thereof. It differs from the 1994 law because a semiautomatic firearm would be considered a "semiautomatic assault weapon" if it accepts a detachable magazine and has any one of five features (compared to two of five features in the 1994 law).

The features listed in S. 150 are slightly different than those listed in the 1994 law. The bill also further provides definitions for each of the features listed.

For example, under S. 150, a semiautomatic rifle would fall under the term "semiautomatic assault weapon" if it has the capacity to accept a detachable magazine and any one of the following: (1) a pistol grip; (2) a forward grip; (3) a folding, telescoping, or detachable scope; (4) a grenade launcher or rocket launcher; (5) a barrel shroud; or (6) a threaded barrel.

The bill further defines "semiautomatic assault weapon" as any semiautomatic rifle that has a fixed magazine with the capacity to accept more than 10 rounds, except for an attached tubular device designed to accept, and capable of operating only with, .22 caliber rimfire ammunition.

With respect to rifles, it also includes under the definition of "semiautomatic assault weapon" any part, combination of parts, component, device, attachment, or accessory that is designed or functions to accelerate the rate of fire of a semiautomatic rifle but not convert the semiautomatic rifle into a machinegun.

The bill also provides altered definitions for the semiautomatic pistols and shotguns that would fall under the term "semiautomatic assault weapon."

Second, the bill would prohibit the importation of—in addition to the sale, manufacture, transfer, and possession of—such weapons and LCAFDs. The bill's exemptions are similar to the 1994 law; however, it would exempt more hunting and sporting rifles and shotguns by make and model (approximately 2,258), and prohibit the transfer of grandfathered semiautomatic assault weapons to other private individuals unless a background check is conducted through an FFL. Other differences from the 1994 law include an absence of a sunset provision; requirements for safe storage of semiautomatic assault weapons by any private persons; and a requirement for the Attorney General to establish, maintain, and annually report to Congress the make, model, and if available, the date of manufacture of any semiautomatic assault weapon which the Attorney General is made aware has been used in relation to a crime under federal or state law.

LEGAL CHALLENGES TO THE 1994 ASSAULT WEAPONS BAN

The Assault Weapons Ban of 1994 was unsuccessfully challenged as violating several constitutional provisions. While arguments that the act constituted an impermissible Bill of Attainder,[42] is unconstitutionally vague,[43] and is contrary to the Ninth Amendment [44] were readily dismissed by the courts, challenges to the ban based on the Commerce Clause and the Equal Protection Clause received more measured consideration.

Commerce Clause

The 1994 Assault Weapons Ban was challenged on the basis that it violated the Commerce Clause.[45] The ban was evaluated under the factors delineated by the Supreme Court in *United States v. Lopez*,[46] which held that Congress had exceeded its constitutional authority under the Commerce Clause by passing the Gun Free School Zone Act of 1990[47] (School Zone Act) . The Court in *Lopez* clarified the judiciary's traditional approach to Commerce Clause analysis and identified three broad categories of activity that Congress may regulate under its commerce power. These are (1) the channels of commerce; (2) the instrumentalities of commerce in interstate commerce, or persons or things in interstate commerce; and (3) activities which "substantially affect" interstate commerce.[48]

In examining the School Zone Act, the Court concluded that possession of a gun in a school zone was neither a regulation of the channels nor the instrumentalities of interstate commerce.[49] Because the conduct regulated was considered to be a wholly intrastate activity, the Court concluded that Congress could only regulate if it fell within the third category and "substantially affect[ed]" interstate commerce. The Court indicated that intrastate activities have been, and could be, regulated by Congress where the activities "arise out of or are connected with a commercial transaction" and are "part of a larger regulation of economic activity, in which the regulatory scheme could be undercut unless the intrastate activity were regulated."[50] With respect to the School Zone Act, the Court declared that the intrastate activity was not a part of the larger firearms regulatory scheme.[51] Moreover, the Court found it significant that the act did not require that interstate commerce be affected, such as by requiring the gun to be transported in interstate commerce.[52]

Commerce Clause challenges to the 1994 Assault Weapons Ban were evaluated under the framework provided by the *Lopez* decision, and lower courts readily determined that the act met minimum constitutional requirements under the Commerce Clause. For example, in *Navegar, Inc. v. United States*, the U.S. Court of Appeals for the District of Columbia Circuit

(D.C. Circuit) addressed the question of whether the act fell within one of the three categories of activity identified in *Lopez*.[53] Like the Court in *Lopez*, the D.C. Circuit determined that it was not required to analyze the act under the first or second categories because the "[it] readily falls within category 3 as a regulation of activities having a substantial [e]ffect on interstate commerce."[54] The court analyzed individually the act's prohibitions on manufacture, transfer, and possession.

Regarding the manufacturing prohibition, the D.C. Circuit declared that "[t]he Supreme Court has repeatedly held that the manufacture of goods which may ultimately never leave the state can still be activity which substantially affects interstate commerce."[55] Regarding the prohibition on transfers, the court similarly remarked that "the Supreme Court precedent makes clear that the transfer of goods, even as part of an intrastate transaction, can be an activity which substantially affects interstate commerce."[56] Based on these maxims, the court held that "it is not even arguable that the manufacture and transfer of 'semiautomatic assault weapons' for a national market cannot be regulated as activity substantially affecting interstate commerce."[57]

However, with respect to the possession of a semiautomatic assault weapon, the court in *Navegar* noted that the *Lopez* decision raised a question of whether "mere possession" can substantially affect interstate commerce. The court proceeded to analyze the purposes behind the act to determine whether "it was aimed at regulating activities which substantially affect interstate commerce."[58] Analyzing the congressional hearings, the court determined that the ban on possession was "conceived to control and restrict the interstate commerce in 'semiautomatic assault weapons,'" and that the "ban on possession is a measure intended to reduce the demand for such weapons."[59] The D.C. Circuit stated that the ban on possession was "necessary to allow law enforcement to effectively regulate the manufacture and transfers where the product comes to rest, in the possession of the receiver."[60] Based on these factors, the court held that the "purpose of the ban on possession has an 'evident commercial nexus.'"[61]

Although the Supreme Court further clarified its Commerce Clause jurisprudence in later decisions, such as *Gonzales v. Raich*,[62] it appears that the Commerce Clause analysis applicable to the ability of Congress to regulate or ban certain semiautomatic assault weapons would not be fundamentally altered by these later developments.

Equal Protection Clause

The Assault Weapons Ban of 1994 was also challenged on Equal Protection Clause grounds, with opponents arguing that it prohibited weapons that were the functional equivalents of weapons exempted under the Act, and because the prohibition of other semiautomatic assault weapons based upon their characteristics served no legitimate governmental interest.

A court must employ one of the three levels of judicial scrutiny[63] in an Equal Protection Clause analysis to determine whether a law negatively impacts a suspect class or a fundamental right. If there is such an impact, the law is subjected to strict scrutiny, requiring the government to prove that the law is necessary to satisfy a compelling governmental interest.[64] If a law does not affect a suspect class or a fundamental right, the court engages in a "rational basis" review, requiring only that the law be rationally related to a legitimate governmental interest.[65]

Applying these standards, the U.S. Court of Appeals for the Sixth Circuit (Sixth Circuit) held that the provisions of the 1994 law did not violate the Equal Protection Clause. In *Olympic Arms v. Buckles*, the Sixth Circuit first noted that the lower court had held that the plaintiffs' claim was non-cognizable, given that the "Equal Protection Clause protects against inappropriate classifications of people, rather than things."[66] However, the court stated that other rulings have held that since persons may have an interest in things, their classification may be challenged on equal protection grounds.[67] Rather than resolve this disparity on the scope of the Equal Protection Clause, the Sixth Circuit went on to declare that "even if we were to assume that equal protection analysis is appropriate here, we would have to conclude that the semi-automatic assault weapons ban meets all equal protection requirements."[68]

The court first addressed the argument "that variations in the specificity of weapon descriptions and lack of common characteristics in the list of weapons outlawed destroy the constitutional legitimacy of the 1994 Act."[69] The Sixth Circuit found this argument to be without merit for several reasons. First, the court found it significant that the list of prohibited firearms was developed to target weapons commonly used in the commission of violent crimes. Additionally, the court found that the prohibition on copies or duplicates of listed firearms was incorporated to prevent manufacturers from circumventing the act's terms "by simply changing the name of the specified weapons."[70] Finally, the court noted that the list of exempted weapons was based on the determination that they were particularly suited to sporting purposes. Taking these factors together, the Sixth Circuit held that it was "entirely rational for Congress ... to choose to ban those weapons commonly used for criminal purposes and to exempt those weapons commonly used for recreational purposes."[71] The fact that many of the protected weapons were somewhat similar in function to those that were banned does not destroy the rationality of the congressional choice.[72]

The Sixth Circuit next addressed whether prohibiting weapons based upon having two or more qualifying features was irrational, given that the act allowed a weapon to possess one such feature and that the individual features did not operate in tandem with one another. The court also rejected this argument, explaining that each characteristic served to make the weapon "potentially more dangerous," and were not "commonly used on weapons designed solely for hunting."[73] The court also explained that "Congress could have easily determined that the greater the number of dangerous add-ons on a semi-automatic weapon, the greater the likelihood that the weapon may be used for dangerous purposes."[74] Accordingly, the Sixth Circuit concluded that the plaintiffs had "failed to meet the heavy burden required to show that the 1994 Act violates equal protection."[75]

Notably, the Sixth Circuit reviewed the equal protection claim under the rational basis test finding that "precedent does not recognize a fundamental right to individual weapon ownership or manufacture, and the plaintiffs, gun retailers and owners, are not a suspect class."[76] While the latter is still accurate, precedent regarding a fundamental right to individual weapon ownership has changed with the Supreme Court's decision in *District of Columbia v. Heller*.[77] As discussed below, the full nature of the right guaranteed by the Second Amendment has yet to be determined by the courts. Therefore, a court considering an equal protection claim in the context of a semiautomatic assault weapons ban could conceivably determine that it is necessary to first address the fundamental issue of whether assault weapons are protected by the Second Amendment.

SECOND AMENDMENT CONSIDERATION

If enacted, an assault weapons ban could also be challenged on Second Amendment grounds in light of the Supreme Court's decision in *District of Columbia v. Heller*. In *Heller*, the Court recognized that the Second Amendment protects an individual right to bear arms for lawful purposes such as self-defense within the home.[78] The decision was not an exhaustive analysis of the full scope of the right guaranteed by the Second Amendment,[79] but the Court stated that "[l]ike most rights, the right secured by the Second Amendment is not unlimited."[80] One limitation upon the Second Amendment the Court addressed is that it "does not protect those weapons not typically possessed by law-abiding citizens for lawful purposes, such as short-barreled shotguns."[81] The Court found that its prior 1939 decision in *United States v. Miller*[82] supported this conclusion. Relying on *Miller*, the Court acknowledged that this limitation is supported by the "historical tradition of prohibiting the carrying of 'dangerous and unusual weapons'" and that the "sorts of weapons protected were those 'in common use at the time'" because those capable of service in the militia at the time of ratification would have brought "the sorts of lawful weapons that they possessed at home to militia duty."[83]

Since *Heller*, cases that have evaluated the constitutionality of state assault weapons bans have generally found them to be valid under the Second Amendment. In 2009, the California Court of Appeals decided *People v. James*, which held that possession of an assault weapon in California remains unlawful and is not protected by the Second Amendment.[84] California's Roberti-Roos Assault Weapons Control Act of 1989, like the 1994 federal assault weapons ban, defines "assault weapons" by providing a list of proscribed weapons and through characteristics "which render these weapons more dangerous than ordinary weapons typically possessed by law-abiding citizens for lawful purposes."[85] Relying on *Heller*'s brief discussion that the Second Amendment does not protect a military weapon, such as an M16 rifle, the court in *James* declared that the prohibited weapons on the state's list "are not the types of weapons that are typically possessed by law-abiding citizens for lawful purposes such as sport hunting or self-defense; rather these are weapons of war."[86] It concluded that the relevant portion of the act did not prohibit conduct protected by the Second Amendment as defined in *Heller* and therefore the state was within its ability to prohibit the types of dangerous and unusual weapons an individual can use.[87]

The District of Columbia amended its firearms regulations after the *Heller* decision and enacted new firearms regulations including an assault weapons ban that is similar to California's. In 2011, the D.C. Circuit issued its decision in *Heller v. District of Columbia* (*Heller II*) which upheld the District's ban on certain semiautomatic rifles and LCAFDs.[88] Under the "common use" factor delineated in *Heller*, the D.C. Circuit acknowledged that "it was clear enough in the record that certain semi-automatic rifles and magazines holding more than 10 rounds are indeed in 'common use.'"[89] However, the court could not conclude definitely whether the weapons are "commonly used or are useful specifically for self-defense or hunting" such that they "meaningfully affect the right to keep and bear arms."[90] Therefore, the court went on to analyze the bans under a two-stepped approach to determine their validity under the Second Amendment.[91]

Under this approach, the court first asks whether a particular provision impinges upon a right protected by the Second Amendment as historically understood. If it does, then it goes on to determine whether the provision passes muster under the appropriate level of constitutional scrutiny.[92] Assuming that the ban impinged on the right protected under *Heller* (i.e., to possess certain arms for lawful purposes such as individual self-defense or hunting), the court found that such regulations should be reviewed under intermediate scrutiny because the prohibition "does not effectively disarm individuals or substantially affect their ability to defend themselves."[93] Under intermediate scrutiny, the government has the burden of showing that there is a substantial relationship or reasonable "fit" between the regulation and the important governmental interest "in protecting police officers and controlling crime."[94] The D.C. Circuit held that the District carried this burden and that the evidence demonstrated that a ban on both semiautomatic assault rifles and LCAFDs "is likely to promote the Government's interest in crime control in the densely populated urban area that is the District of Columbia."[95]

In 2012, the Supreme Court of Illinois decided *Wilson v. Cook County*, a case that evaluated the constitutionality of the Blair Holt Assault Weapons Ban of Cook County, a long-standing ordinance that was amended to similarly reflect provisions of the 1994 Assault Weapons Ban.[96] The plaintiffs argued that the ordinance violates the Due Process and Equal Protection Clauses of the U.S. Constitution as well as the Second Amendment. Regarding the due process claim, the court concluded that the ordinance is not unconstitutionally vague such that it "fails to provide people of ordinary intelligence a reasonable opportunity to understand what conduct it prohibits."[97] The court also dismissed the plaintiff's equal protection claim, finding that the "[o]rdinance does not arbitrarily differentiate between two owners with similar firearms because the banned firearms are either listed, a copy or duplicate, or fall under the characteristics-based test."[98] With respect to the Second Amendment claim, the court indicated that it would follow the two-step approach similar to the *Heller II* court. While the court acknowledged that the ordinance banned only a subset of weapons with particular characteristics similar to other jurisdictions, it found that it could not "conclusively say ... that assault weapons as defined in the [o]rdinance categorically fall outside the scope of the rights protected by the [S]econd [A]mendment."[99] The court ultimately remanded the Second Amendment claim to the trial court for further proceedings, because unlike the *James* and *Heller II* decisions, the county did not have an opportunity to present evidence to justify the nexus between the ordinance and the governmental interest it seeks to protect.[100]

These cases demonstrate that courts evaluating various assault weapons bans, and to a limited extent LCAFD bans, have looked to the *Heller* decision and the general framework that has developed in the lower courts for analyzing claims under the Second Amendment. Based on the *Heller* decision where the Supreme Court indicated that certain weapons fall outside the protection of the Second Amendment, lower courts have examined whether the prohibited weapons are considered in "common use" or "commonly used" for lawful purposes or "dangerous and unusual." It is uncertain whether, to be protected under the Second Amendment, the weapon must be in "common use" by the people and if so, must it be in "common use" for self-defense or hunting, or what constitutes "dangerous and unusual." *Heller* could arguably be taken to indicate that if the prohibited weapons do not meet these criteria then they are not protected by the Second Amendment, in which case no heighted judicial scrutiny would be applied.

Courts also could evaluate such measures under the two -step approach laid out by the lower courts. This asks whether a ban on certain weapons and firearm accessories imposes a burden on conduct falling within the scope of the Second Amendment. If so, then a heightened level of judicial scrutiny will be applied to determine the ban's constitutionality. How the "common use" and "dangerous and unusual" criteria should be read, if at all, in connection with the two-step approach remains unclear. Neither the *James*, *Heller II*, nor *Wilson* courts appear to have fully explained the connection between the two approaches.

Lastly, while it appeared that constitutional claims under the Due Process and Equal Protection Clauses were largely dismissed when the 1994 Assault Weapons Ban was in effect, the *Wilson* case demonstrates that they are claims challengers may still consider raising.

End Notes

[1] P.L. 103-322 (1994).
[2] P.L. 90-618 (1968).
[3] S. Rept. No. 90-1097 (1968).
[4] 18 U.S.C. §§922 *et seq*.
[5] 18 U.S.C. §922(g).

[6] The GCA also prohibits the receipt, transport, or shipment of firearms or ammunition by individuals under felony indictment. 18 U.S.C. §922(n). Furthermore, the GCA places significant restrictions on the transfer to, and possession of, firearms by persons under the age of 18. *See* 18 U.S.C. §922(x).

[7] P.L. 99-308 (1986).

[8] *See* CRS Report R42687, *Internet Firearm and Ammunition Sales*, by Vivian S. Chu.

[9] "Engaged in the business" means one who "devotes time, attention, and labor" to manufacturing, importing, or dealing firearms "as a regular course of trade or business with the principal objective of livelihood and profit." 18 U.S.C. §§921(a)(21)-(22).

[10] 18 U.S.C. §922(a); §923.

[11] 18 U.S.C. §922(t)(1)(c).

[12] 18 U.S.C. §922(t).

[13] 18 U.S.C. §923(g)(1)(A).

[14] 18 U.S.C. §923(g)(3)(A).

[15] 18 U.S.C. §923(g)(7).

[16] 18 U.S.C. §§922(b)(2), 923(d).

[17] 18 U.S.C. §921(a)(21)(C).

[18] 18 U.S.C. §§922(d), (t).

[19] 18 U.S.C. §922(b)(3)(A).

[20] 18 U.S.C. §922(b)(3).

[21] 18 U.S.C. §922(a)(2). Regarding the mailing of firearms, federal law prohibits the shipment of any firearm other than a shotgun or rifle via the United States Postal Service, except for firearms shipped for official law enforcement purposes. 18 U.S.C. §1715. Firearms, including handguns, may be shipped by common carrier (*e.g.*, FedEx or UPS) upon disclosure and subject to the restrictions discussed above. *See* 18 U.S.C. §922(a)(2)(A); §922(3); 27 C.F.R. §178.31.

[22] 18 U.S.C. §922(b)(3); §922(t).

[23] 18 U.S.C. §922(a)(3); §922(a)(5); §922(b)(3).

[24] P.L. 103-322, Title XI (1994). The 1994 ban marked only the second time that Congress has prohibited the manufacture of specific firearms. The Undetectable Firearms Act of 1988 (P.L. 100-649 (1988)) bans the manufacture, importation, possession, transfer, or receipt of firearms that are undetectable by metal detectors at security checkpoints at certain locations. 18 U.S.C. §922(p).

[25] Prior to its expiration in 2004, several bills were introduced that would strike the expiration date and impose a ban in the importation on large capacity ammunition feeding devices, subject to the same exceptions, or make other amendments to the 1994 law that was in effect. *See* S. 1034, Assault Weapons Reauthorization Act of 2003 (108th Cong. 1st sess.); H.R. 2038, Assault Weapons Ban and Law Enforcement Protection Act of 2003 (108th Cong., 1st sess.), and S. 1431, the Assault Weapons Ban and Law Enforcement Protection Act, (108th Cong., 1st sess.).

[26] *See* 26 U.S.C. §5845. Since 1934, the National Firearms Act has regulated the traffic in, and possession of, machineguns, other weapons and destructive devices. 26 U.S.C. §§5801 *et seq.*

[27] Public Safety and Recreational Firearms Use Protection Act, Hearing Before the H. Comm. on the Judiciary, 103d Cong. at 18 (H. Rept. 103-489).

[28] Former 18 U.S.C. §922(v).

[29] Former 18 U.S.C. §921(a)(30). Specific models included: the Norinco, Mitchell, and Poly Technologies Avtomat Kalashnikovs (all models); Action Arms Israel Military Industries UZI and Galil; Beretta Ar70 (SC-70); Colt AR-15; Fabrique National FN/FAL, FN/LAR, and FNC; Steyr AUG; INTRATEC TEC-9 TEC-DC9 and TEC-22; and revolving cylinder shotguns, such as (or similar to) the Street Sweeper and Striker 12. Former 18 U.S.C. §921(a)(30)(A).

[30] Former 18 U.S.C. §922(w).

[31] Former 18 U.S.C. §921(31). The term did not include an attached tubular device designed to accept and capable of operating only with .22 caliber rimfire ammunition.

[32] 18 U.S.C. §923(i) (as amended by P.L. 103-322). The Bureau of Alcohol, Tobacco, Firearms and Explosives issued regulations requiring that LCAFDs manufactured or imported under the act be identified with a serial number, and domestically manufactured devices bear the name, city, and state of the manufacturer. Imported devices were required to bear the manufacturer and country of origin as well as the name of the importer. Finally, LCAFDs manufactured after September 13, 1994 to be exempted by the ban were required to be marked "RESTRICTED LAW ENFORCEMENT/GOVERNMENT USE ONLY," or, in the case of devices manufactured for export (since July 5, 1995) "FOR EXPORT ONLY." 27 C.F.R. §478.92(c).

[33] Former 18 U.S.C. §§922(v)(2); (w)(2).

[34] Former 18 U.S.C. §922(v)(3).

[35] Former 18 U.S.C. §922(v)(3)(B)-(D).

[36] Former 18 U.S.C. §922(4).

[37] It should be noted that the Homeland Security Act of 2002 transferred the Bureau of Alcohol, Tobacco, Firearms and Explosives to the Department of Justice from the Department of Treasury. P.L. 107-296, Title XI, Subtitle B, §1111 (2002).

[38] 26 U.S.C. §5845(a).

[39] See 1989 Study on ATF's website; see also Bureau of Alcohol, Tobacco, Firearms and Explosives, "Federal Firearms Reference Guide," General Information Question 20 at 167-68 (2005).

[40] See Federal Firearms Reference Guide, supra note 39.

[41] See Scott Dailard, "The Role of Ammunition in a Balanced Program of Gun Control: A Critique of the Moynihan Bullet Bills," 20 J. Legis. 19, 33 (1994).

[42] See Navegar, Inc. v. United States, 192 F.3d 1050, 1066-68 (D.C. Cir. 1999), rehearing en banc denied, 200 F.3d, 868 (D.C. Cir. 2000), cert. denied 531 U.S. 816 (2000) (the assault weapons ban does not constitute a Bill of Attainder as it does not impose a legislative punishment, does not exhibit a purely punitive purpose, and does not manifest a congressional intent to punish specific individuals, but rather specifies conduct from which individuals must refrain in order to avoid punishment).

[43] See United States v. Starr, 945 F.Supp. 257, 259 (M.D. Ga. 1996), aff'd 144 F.3d 56 (11th Cir. 1998) (assault weapons ban was not unconstitutionally vague because it defines "a criminal offense with sufficient definiteness that ordinary people can understand what conduct is prohibited and in a manner that does not encourage arbitrary and discriminatory enforcement" and court had "no difficulty finding that an ordinary person" would conclude that the provisions of the federal law applied to the firearms possessed by the defendant). The district court also cited Boyce Motor Lines v. United States, 342 U.S. 337 (1952), which stated: "Nor is it unfair to require that one who deliberately goes perilously close to an area of proscribed conduct shall take the risk that he may cross the line."

[44] See San Diego Gun Rights Committee v. Reno, 98 F.3d 1121, 1125 (9th Cir.1996) (The Ninth Amendment states: "The enumeration in the Constitution, of certain rights, shall not be construed to deny or disparage others retained by the people." Joining other circuit court decisions, the Ninth Circuit concluded that the Ninth Amendment "has not been interpreted as independently securing any constitutional rights for purposes of making out a constitutional violation" and thus does not encompass an unenumerated, fundamental individual right to bear firearms.).

[45] U.S. Const., art. I, §8, cl. 3.

[46] 514 U.S. 549 (1995).

[47] P.L. 101-647 (1990). The act had made it a federal offense for "any individual to knowingly possess a firearm at a place the individual knows, or has reasonable cause to believe, is a school zone." 18 U.S.C. §922(q) (1988 ed. Supp. V).

[48] Lopez, 514 U.S. at 558-59.

[49] *Id*. at 559-60.

[50] *Id*. at 561 (referencing *Wickard v. Filburn*, 317 U.S. 111 (1942)).

[51] *Id*.

[52] *Id*. at 561-62. The Court found it significant that that the act "contains no jurisdictional element which would ensure, through a case-by-case inquiry, that the firearm possession in question affects interstate commerce." A jurisdictional element would also "limit [the statute's] reach to a discrete set of firearms possessions that additionally have an explicit connection with or effect on interstate commerce." *Id*. at 562. In 1996, Congress passed a new version of the Gun Free School Zone Act (P.L. 104-208) that added a jurisdictional hook. The provision reads: "It shall be unlawful for any individual to knowingly possess a firearm that has moved in or otherwise affects interstate or foreign commerce at ... a school zone."

[53] 192 F.3d 1050, 1066-68 (D.C. Cir. 1999), rehearing *en banc* denied, 200 F.3d, 868 (D.C. Cir. 2000), *cert. denied* 531 U.S. 816 (2000).

[54] *Id*. at 1055.

[55] *Id*. at 1057 (citing *United States v. Darby*, 312 U.S. 100, 118-19 (1941); *NLRB v. Jones & Laughlin Steel*, 301 U.S. 1, 37 (1937)).

[56] *Id*. at 1058 (citing *Lopez*, 514 U.S. at 560-61 (citing *Wickard v. Filburn*, 317 U.S. 11, 127-28 (1942)(noting that farmer's home consumption of wheat substantially affected interstate commerce and that farmer's selling of homegrown wheat and local marketing substantially affects interstate commerce)).

[57] *Id*.

[58] To determine whether an activity that does not have an clear connection with interstate commerce, the Court in *Lopez* stated that it would consider legislative findings and even congressional committee findings to determine if there was a rational basis for congressional action. *Lopez*, 514 U.S. at 562.

[59] *Navegar*, 192 F.3d at 1058-59 (citing other cases such as *United States v. Rybar*, 103 F.3d 273 (3d. Cir 1996) (holding that the Firearm Owners Protection Act of 1986 targets the mere intrastate possession of machine guns as a "demand-side measure to lessen the stimulus that prospective acquisition would have on the commerce of machine guns"); *United States v. Rambo*, 74 F.3d 948 (9th Cir. 1995) (holding that the ban on possession is in effect "an attempt to control the interstate market ... by creating criminal liability for the demand-side of the market, i.e., those who would facilitate illegal transfer out of the desire to acquire mere possession" [citation omitted])).

[60] *Id*. at 1059.

[61] *Id*. (citing *Lopez*, 514 U.S. at 580 (Kennedy, J., concurring)).

[62] 545 U.S. 1 (2005) (holding that Congress' Commerce Clause authority includes the power to prohibit the local cultivation and use of marijuana in compliance with California law).

[63] Generally there are three levels of judicial scrutiny. First, strict scrutiny, the most rigorous, requires a statute to be narrowly tailored to serve a compelling state interest. Second, intermediate scrutiny, requires a statute to further a government interest in a way that is substantially related to that interest. Third, the rational basis standard merely requires the statute to be rationally related to a legitimate government function. *See* Erwin Chemerinsky, Constitutional Law: Principles and Policies §§ 6.5, 10.1.2 (3d ed. 2006).

[64] *See, e.g.*, City of Cleburne v. Cleburne Living Center, 473 U.S. 432, 439-40 (1985).

[65] *See, e.g.*, Heller v. Doe, 509 U.S. 312, 319 (1993). Intermediate scrutiny has also been applied in equal protection analysis. *See, e.g.*, Craig v. Boren, 429 U.S. 190 (1976) (applying intermediate scrutiny when declaring unconstitutional an Oklahoma law that allowed women to buy low alcohol, 3.2 percent beer, at age 18, but men could not buy such beer until age 21).

[66] Olympic Arms v. Buckles, 301 F.3d 384, 388 (6th Cir. 2002) (referring to *Olympic Arms v. Magaw*, 91 F.Supp.2d 1061 (E.D. Mich. 2000)).

[67] *Id*. at 388.

[68] *Id*.

[69] *Id*. at 389.

[70] *Id*.

[71] *Id*. at 390.

[72] *Id*. The court in *Olympic Arms* further stated: "A classification does not fail because it 'is not made with mathematical nicety or because in practice it results in some inequality.'" (citing *Dandridge v. Williams*, 397 U.S. 471, 488 (1970)).

[73] *Id*.

[74] *Id*.

[75] *Id*.

[76] *Id*. at 389.

[77] 554 U.S. 570 (2008).

[78] *Id*.

[79] *Id*. at 626.

[80] *Id*.

[81] *Id*.

[82] *United States v. Miller*, 307 U.S. 174 (1939) (holding that the Second Amendment did not protect an individual's right to transport an unregistered short-barreled shotgun in interstate commerce).

[83] *Heller*, 540 U.S. at 627. The Court recognized that "it may be true that no amount of small arms could be useful against modern-day bombers and tanks." However, it noted that modern day developments "cannot change our interpretation of the right." *Id*.

[84] People v. James, 94 Cal. Rptr. 3d 576 (Cal. Ct. App.2009), *rev. denied* by People v. James, 2009 Cal. LEXIS 9895 (Cal. Sept. 17, 2009), *cert. denied* James v. Cal. 2010 U.S. LEXIS 1284 (U.S., Feb. 22, 2010). Notably, a petitioner challenging an assault weapons ban could make an argument that civilian versions of military weapons, like the AR-15, should be differentiated from military weapons, like the M16, which the Supreme Court does not considered protected under the Second Amendment. However, the Supreme Court's denial of certiorari in the *James* case could indicate that the Court does not distinguish between military and civilian versions of military style weapons, considering both beyond the scope of the Second Amendment's guarantee.

[85] *James*, 94 Cal. Rptr. 3d at 579-580 (citing Cal. Penal Code §§12276, 12276.1).

[86] *Id*. at 585-86 (quoting Cal. Penal Code § 122275.5(a) (West 2006)).

[87] *James*, 94 Cal. Rptr. 3d at 586 (citing the Cal. Penal Code §§ 12280(b)-(c) which imposes penalties for possession of assault weapon or .50 BMG rifle).

[88] Heller v. District of Columbia (Heller II), 670 F.3d 1244 (D.C. Cir. 2011) (affirming in part and vacating in part the lower court's decision, remanding to the lower court the petitioner's challenge to the District's "novel registration requirements").

[89] *Id*. at 1261.

[90] *Id*.

[91] The D.C. Circuit adopted from other circuits a two-step approach to determining the constitutionality of the gun laws at issue. *See, e.g.*, United States v. Marzzarella, 614 F.3d 85, 89 (3d Cir. 2010). This D.C. Circuit indicated that this two-step approach is taken if the challenged regulation is not one that the *Heller* decision identified as a "longstanding" regulation that is "presumptively lawful." *Id*. (citing *Heller*, 554 U.S. at 626-27, n.26).

[92] *Heller II*, 670 F.3d at 1252.

[93] *Id*. at 1261-62.

[94] *Id*. at 1262.

[95] *Id*. at 1263.

[96] Wilson v. Cook County, 968 N.E.2d 641 (Ill. 2012).

[97] *Id*. at 650-53.

[98] *Id*. at 658.

[99] *Id*. at 655.

[100] *Id.* at 657. ("Without a national uniform definition of assault weapons from which to judge these weapons, it cannot be ascertained at this stage of the proceedings whether these arms with these particular attributes as defined in this [o]rdinance are all well suited for self-defense or support or would be outweighed completely by the collateral damage resulting from their use, making them 'dangerous and unusual' as articulated in *Heller*. This question requires us to engage in an empirical inquiry beyond the scope of the record and beyond the scope of judicial notice about the nature of weapons that are banned under this [o]rdinance and the dangers of these particular weapons." *Id.* at 656.).

In: Firearms in America ISBN: 978-1-63117-823-8
Editor: Alfonso D. Sutton © 2014 Nova Science Publishers, Inc.

Chapter 4

SUBMISSION OF MENTAL HEALTH RECORDS TO NICS AND THE HIPAA PRIVACY RULE[*]

Edward C. Liu, Erin Bagalman, Vivian S. Chu and C. Stephen Redhead

SUMMARY

Questions about the scope and efficacy of the background checks required during certain firearm purchases have gained prominence following recent mass shootings. These background checks are intended to identify whether potential purchasers are prohibited from purchasing or possessing firearms due to one or more "prohibiting factors," such as a prior felony conviction or a prior involuntary commitment for mental health reasons. Operationally, such background checks primarily use information contained within the National Instant Criminal Background Check System (NICS) and a particular focus of the debate in Congress has been whether federal privacy standards promulgated under the Health Insurance Portability and Accountability Act (i.e., the HIPAA privacy rule) or state privacy laws are an obstacle to the submission of mental health records to NICS.

Under the Gun Control Act of 1968 (GCA), as amended, persons adjudicated to be mentally defective or who have been committed to a mental institution are prohibited from possessing, shipping, transporting,

---

[*] This is an edited, reformatted and augmented version of Congressional Research Service Publication, No. R43040, dated April 15, 2013.

and receiving firearms and ammunition. Neither a diagnosis of a mental illness nor treatment for a mental illness is sufficient to qualify a person as "adjudicated as a mental defective." Rather, an individual's "adjudication as a mental defective" relies upon a determination or decision by a court, board, commission, or other lawful authority. The definition of "committed to a mental institution" may apply only to inpatient settings. At least one federal court has held that the Supreme Court's recent recognition of an individual right to possess a firearm suggests that some emergency hospitalization or commitment procedures, that may not have as many procedural safeguards as formal commitment, should not be included within the meaning of "involuntary commitment" for purposes of the GCA. In 2007, Congress passed the NICS Improvement Amendments Act (NIAA), which authorizes the Attorney General to make additional grants to states to improve electronic access to records as well as to incentivize states to turn over records of persons who would be prohibited from possessing or receiving firearms.

In 2012, the Government Accountability Office (GAO) reported that a variety of technological, coordination, and legal (i.e., privacy) challenges limit the states' ability to report mental health records to NICS. The HIPAA privacy rule, which applies to most health care providers, regulates the use or disclosure of protected health information. On February 14, 2013, HHS announced that it will seek to amend the HIPAA privacy rule to remove any potential impediments to state reporting of mental health records to NICS. The privacy rule is most relevant as a potential obstacle where information used to generate mental health records on individuals prohibited from gun possession under the GCA is held by health care providers in states that do not expressly require disclosure of such records to NICS. Courts and health care providers that generate such prohibiting mental health records may also be subject to state health privacy laws that may be more restrictive than the HIPAA privacy rule.

INTRODUCTION

Questions about the scope and efficacy of the background checks required during certain firearm purchases have gained prominence following recent mass shootings.[1] These background checks are intended to identify whether potential purchasers are prohibited from purchasing or possessing firearms due to one or more "prohibiting factors," such as a prior felony conviction or a prior involuntary commitment for mental health reasons. If disqualifying information surfaces during the background check, the transfer is not completed. Operationally, such background checks primarily use information contained within the National Instant Criminal Background Check System (NICS), maintained by the Federal Bureau of Investigation (FBI), and a particular focus of the debate in Congress has been whether the HIPAA privacy rule or state privacy laws are an obstacle to the population of NICS with prohibiting mental health records.

This report provides an overview of prohibiting mental health records under current federal law, and distinguishes those records from other types of mental health information that would not disqualify an individual from purchasing a firearm. This report also provides an overview of NICS and discusses potential issues arising from state and federal medical privacy laws that may impede states' efforts to submit prohibiting mental health records to NICS.[2]

PROHIBITING MENTAL HEALTH FACTORS UNDER THE GUN CONTROL ACT OF 1968

Under the Gun Control Act of 1968 (GCA)[3], as amended, certain categories of persons are prohibited from possessing, shipping, transporting, and receiving firearms and ammunition.[4] These nine categories of persons who are prohibited include:

1) Persons convicted of a crime punishable by a term of imprisonment exceeding one year;
2) Fugitives from justice;
3) Individuals who are unlawful users or addicts of any controlled substance;
4) Persons adjudicated to be mentally defective, or who have been committed to a mental institution;
5) Aliens illegally or unlawfully in the United States, as well as those who have been admitted pursuant to a nonimmigrant visa;
6) Individuals who have been discharged dishonorably from the Armed Forces;
7) Persons who have renounced United States citizenship;
8) Individuals subject to a pertinent court order; and
9) Persons who have been convicted of a misdemeanor domestic violence offense.[5]

Of these categories, only the fourth is primarily concerned with mental health issues.[6] The sections below provide a more detailed discussion of the scope of this category's two subcomponents: adjudication as a mental defective and commitment to a mental institution.

Adjudication As a Mental Defective

As noted above, the GCA prohibits individuals "adjudicated as a mental defective" from possessing, receiving, transferring, or transporting a firearm. The term has been further defined by federal regulation as:

> (a) A determination by a court, board, commission, or other lawful authority that a person, as a result of marked subnormal intelligence, or mental illness, incompetency, condition, or disease:
> (1) Is a danger to himself or to others; or
> (2) Lacks the capacity to manage his own affairs.
> (b) The term shall include—(1) a finding of insanity by a court in a criminal case, and (2) those persons found incompetent to stand trial or found not guilty by lack of mental responsibility [under the Uniform Code of Military Justice].[7]

It is important to note that despite references to "mental illness" in the definition, neither a diagnosis of a mental illness nor treatment for a mental illness appears, by itself, to qualify a person as "adjudicated as a mental defective."[8] Thus, while a health care provider may provide to a third party (i.e., a court, board, commission, or other lawful authority) an assessment of an individual's mental health for purposes of adjudication, the provision of mental health treatment alone is not considered a determination for purposes of being considered "adjudicated as a mental defective," nor is treatment necessary for the determination. Rather, an individual's "adjudication as a mental defective" relies upon a determination or decision by "a court, board, commission, or other lawful authority."

Physicians and other health care providers generally do not fall within this list of authorized decision-makers, with the exception of certain instances under state law where a health care provider may be authorized by statute to admit a patient to involuntary psychiatric treatment. A health care provider, under these circumstances, could potentially be considered an "other lawful authority," who makes a determination which falls within the federal statute criminalizing firearms possession by an individual who is "adjudicated as a mental defective" or "committed to a mental institution." See discussion below at "Emergency Admission or Hospitalization."

Whether the definition of "adjudicated as a mental defective" includes individuals who have been assigned fiduciaries to manage monetary benefits received from a federal agency is subject to interpretation, as illustrated by the different policies of the Department of Veterans Affairs (VA) and the Social Security Administration (SSA). In particular, the definition includes those who are determined "as a result of ... condition ...[to] lack[] the capacity to manage his own affairs." Accordingly, VA policy requires that an individual who receives VA monetary benefits and who "lacks the mental capacity to manage his or her own financial affairs regarding disbursement of funds without limitation, and is either rated incompetent by VA or adjudged to be under legal disability by a court of competent jurisdiction" be assigned a fiduciary (who manages the money disbursed by VA) and be reported to NICS.[9] SSA does not appear to have a comparable policy for representative payees (i.e., individuals who have been assigned a fiduciary to manage their SSA monetary benefits). In a letter to the Vice President, the National Council on Disability (NCD) urges him to

> avoid any proposal to link the Social Security Administration's database of representative payees with the FBI's National Instant Criminal Background Check System (NICS). Whatever merits such a proposal might seem to present, such benefits are outweighed by the inaccurate and discriminatory inference that would result: equating the need for assistance in managing one's finances with a presumption of incapacity in other areas of life.... NCD recommends you ensure that the selection of a representative payee continues to have no implication on other areas of rights beyond financial decision-making.[10]

Commitment to a Mental Institution

The term "committed to a mental institution" is defined through regulation as

> A formal commitment of a person to a mental institution by a court, board, commission, or other lawful authority. The term includes a commitment to a mental institution involuntarily. The term includes commitment for mental defectiveness or mental illness. It also includes commitments for other reasons, such as for drug use.

> The term does not include a person in a mental institution for observation or a voluntary admission to a mental institution.[11]

The use of the term "institution" suggests that the definition of "committed to a mental institution" may apply only to inpatient settings. The question of whether the definition applies to outpatient commitment was raised following the Virginia Tech shooting in 2007 (see textbox). In either case, the definition explicitly excludes "voluntary admission," and so would not apply to individuals voluntarily seeking treatment for mental illness in any setting.[12]

Emergency Admission or Hospitalization

As noted above, state law may authorize a health care provider to admit a patient to involuntary psychiatric treatment, particularly in emergency situations for a brief duration. In these limited instances, it is possible that a health care provider would be considered an "other lawful authority," and the patient receiving involuntary psychiatric treatment would fall within the definition of "committed to a mental institution" for purposes of the GCA. For example, in *United States v. Waters*, the U.S. Court of Appeals for the Second Circuit held that the involuntary hospitalization of an alleged mentally ill individual pursuant to New York state law[14] met the definition of an "involuntary commitment" for purposes of the GCA, even though the hospitalization was ordered by the director of a hospital upon the certification of two physicians.[15]

Example: Virginia Tech Shooting of April 16, 2007

On April 16, 2007, a student at Virginia Tech, Seung Hui Cho, shot and killed 32 students and faculty and wounded 17 more before killing himself. More than a year prior to the shootings, a series of events led to a commitment hearing for involuntary admission on December 14, 2005. At the hearing the special justice ruled that Cho "presents an imminent danger to himself as a result of mental illness" and ordered outpatient treatment. Following the shooting, a review determined that Cho had been ineligible to purchase a gun under federal law because he "had been judged to be a danger to himself and ordered to outpatient treatment." The review further determined that "Virginia law did not clearly require that persons such as Cho—who had been ordered into out-patient treatment but not committed to an institution—be reported to the [NICS] database."

On April 30, 2007, the Governor of Virginia issued Executive Order 50, requiring that any involuntary treatment order, whether inpatient or outpatient, be reported to the NICS. In 2008, the state legislature codified this requirement.[13]

Sources: Virginia Tech Review Panel, *Mass Shootings at Virginia Tech: April 16, 2007*, August 2007, http://www.governor. techPanelReport-docs/Full Report.pdf and Virginia Executive Order No. 50, (April 30, 2007), http://www.lva.virginia.gov/public/EO/ eo50%282007 %29.pdf.

However, at least one federal court has held that the Supreme Court's recent recognition of an individual right to possess a firearm in *District of Columbia v. Heller*,[16] suggests that some emergency hospitalization or commitment procedures should not be included within the meaning of "involuntary commitment" for purposes of the GCA. In *United States v. Rehlander*, the U.S. Court of Appeals for the First Circuit (First Circuit) considered a Maine law which provides authority for the brief, but involuntary, detention of individuals in mental institutions on the basis of a medical provider's examination and certification that the individual is mentally ill and poses a likelihood of serious harm.[17] In pre-*Heller* cases, the First Circuit had held that this emergency hospitalization under Maine law qualified as "involuntary commitment" under the GCA.[18] However, because the procedures under state law were *ex parte*[19] and did not have additional procedural safeguards, the court held that construing the emergency hospitalization procedures to qualify as "involuntary commitment" under the GCA post-*Heller* would risk depriving individuals of their right to bear arms without sufficient due process. Therefore, the appellate court overturned its earlier decisions and held that such emergency hospitalizations were not "involuntary commitments."

THE NATIONAL INSTANT CRIMINAL BACKGROUND CHECK SYSTEM (NICS)

Under the Brady Handgun Violence Prevention Act of 1993 (Brady Act), the Attorney General was required to establish a computerized system to facilitate background checks on individuals seeking to acquire firearms from federally licensed firearms dealers.[20] The National Instant Criminal Background Check System (NICS) was activated in 1998 and is administered by the Federal Bureau of Investigation (FBI). Through NICS, federal firearms licensees submit background checks on prospective transferees to the FBI, which queries other databases – including the National Crime Information Center (NCIC), the Interstate Identification Index (III), and the NICS index – to determine if the transferees are disqualified from receiving firearms.[21] According to the FBI, records in the NICS Index are voluntarily provided by local, state, tribal, and federal agencies, and it "contains [disqualifying records] that may not be available in the NCIC or the III of persons prohibited from receiving firearms under federal or state law."[22]

The Brady Act authorized the Attorney General to "secure directly from any [federal] department or agency of the United States" information on persons for whom receipt of a firearm would violate federal or state law. The act does not mandate that federal agencies disclose these records, rather it mandates that "upon request of the Attorney General, the head of such department or agency shall furnish such information to the system."[23] With respect to states, which are not required to submit records to NICS, the Brady Act provided grants to "improv[e] State record systems and the sharing ... of the records ... required by the Attorney General under [the Brady Act]."[24] However, it did not mandate that states turn over any specific records, even upon request.

NICS Improvement Amendments Act of 2007

In 2007, Congress passed the NICS Improvement Amendments Act (NIAA), which authorizes the Attorney General to make additional grants to states to improve electronic access to records as well as to incentivize states to turn over records of persons who would be prohibited from possessing or receiving firearms under 18 U.S.C. §922(g) or (n), *with an emphasis on providing accurate records relating to those who are prohibited under (g)(4) ("adjudicated as a mental defective") or (g)(9) ("convicted in any court of a misdemeanor crime of domestic violence").*[25] Moreover, it mandates that the Department of Homeland Security make available to the Attorney General any records that are related to being a prohibited possessor under federal law.[26]

For federal agencies, NIAA clarifies the standard for adjudication and commitments related to mental health. It provides that no department may provide any such record if the record has been set aside or the individual has been released from treatment; the person has been found by the court or board to no longer suffer from the condition that was the basis of the adjudication or commitment; or the adjudication or commitment is based solely on a medical finding of disability, without opportunity to be heard by a court or board.[27] It also requires agencies that do make such determinations to establish a program that permits a person to apply for relief from the disabilities imposed under §922(g)(4).[28]

With respect to states, NIAA allows a state to be eligible for a two year waiver of the matching requirement in the National Criminal History Improvements Grant program, established under the Brady Act, if the state provides at least 90% of the records relevant to determining whether a person is disqualified from possessing a firearm under federal or applicable state law.[29] To be eligible for such a waiver, other requirements include providing updates to NICS regarding any record that should be modified or removed from the system, and more detailed information regarding those who are convicted of a misdemeanor crime of domestic violence or adjudicated as a mental defective under federal law. NIAA also provides the Attorney General discretion to award additional grants for purposes of assisting states with upgrading information identification technologies for firearms disability determinations as long as they have implemented a relief from disabilities program that meets certain requirements.[30] This grant program is known as the NICS Act Record Improvement Program (NARIP).[31] If a state has received a waiver or an additional grant under NIAA, the act imposes penalties for non-compliance.[32] The act mandates reductions in Department of Justice Byrne Justice Assistance Grant funds and permits the Attorney General to make discretionary reduction of these funds if a state does not comply with eligibility requirements of NIAA.[33]

State Reporting of Prohibiting Mental Health Records to NICS

In 2012, five years after the NIAA was enacted, the Government Accountability Office (GAO) released a report that examined states' progress in reporting mental health records to the NICS databases.[34] It is important to keep in mind that the "mental health records" reported to NICS include only individual identifiers and no actual medical information. However, as discussed in more detail below, the preparation and submission of such records by health departments and health care facilities involves the use of patient information and thus is subject to federal and, in many instances, state health privacy laws.

GAO found that the total number of mental health records that states made available to NICS databases increased approximately nine-fold from about 126,000 to 1.2 million between 2004 and 2011. However, this increase largely reflected the efforts of 12 states. According to GAO, almost half of all states increased the number of mental health records they reported by fewer than 100 over the same time period.

Both DOJ and state officials told GAO that a variety of technological, coordination, and legal (i.e., privacy) challenges limit the states' ability to report mental health records. Technological challenges include updating aging computer systems and integrating existing record systems. Several states reported using their NARIP grant funding to automate the collection and transmission of records. DOJ officials further emphasized that the technological challenges

> are particularly salient for mental health records because these records originate from numerous sources within the state—such as courts, private hospitals, and state offices of mental health—and are not typically captured by any single state agency. For example, records that involve involuntary commitments to a mental institution typically originate in entities located throughout a state and outside the scope of law enforcement, and therefore a state may lack processes to automatically make these records available to the FBI.[35]

The fact that mental health records often originate in hospitals and health departments, which are typically not connected to law enforcement agencies that make the majority of records available to NICS, presents challenges in getting all the relevant entities to collaborate. As an example, GAO cited an April 2012 report by the state of Illinois, Office of the Auditor General, which found that for 2010, approximately 114,000 mental health records were maintained in nursing homes, private hospitals, state mental health facilities, and circuit courts. However, only about 5,000 records were reported to NICS because of a lack of coordination and other challenges. Citing privacy concerns, officials in three of the six states reviewed by GAO reported that the absence of explicit statutory authority to share mental health records was an impediment to NICS reporting.[36]

In a November 2011 report on NICS reporting, Mayors Against Illegal Guns (MAIG) drew conclusions that are broadly similar to those of GAO.[37] MAIG interviewed officials in all 50 states and the District of Columbia and found that state reporting of mental health records to NICS is impeded by a complex set of obstacles including technological and logistical problems, privacy concerns, insufficient funding, and a lack of leadership. The MAIG report noted that even among states with strong reporting programs, there is considerable variation in the number and type of mental health records submitted to NICS. It found that states that have significantly improved their reporting in the past few years share a number of common attributes including the ability to commit funding to their efforts and effective political leadership. MAIG also found a strong association between reporting levels and enactment of state laws that require or authorize agencies to report their records. According to MAIG, nine of the 10 states that had the greatest increase in records submitted to NICS between September 2010 and October 2011 have laws or policies requiring or permitting sharing mental health records with NICS.

Impact of the HIPAA Privacy Rule on NICS Reporting

Officials in approximately half of the states told MAIG that state health privacy laws as well as the privacy rule promulgated by the Department of Health and Human Services (HHS) under the Health Insurance Portability and Accountability Act (HIPAA) were potential obstacles to NICS reporting. In some states, officials cited privacy concerns as the primary impediment to reporting.

HIPAA Privacy Rule Overview
The HIPAA privacy rule established a set of federal standards to help safeguard the privacy of personal health information.[38] Those standards include certain individual privacy rights, such as the right of access to one's health information and the right to request corrections, as well as limitations on the use or disclosure of personal health information. The rule applies to (1) health plans;[39] (2) health care clearinghouses;[40] and (3) health care providers who transmit health information electronically in connection with one of the HIPAA-covered financial or administrative transactions.[41] These persons and organizations are collectively referred to as covered entities.

The privacy rule covers protected health information (PHI) in any form that is created or received by a covered entity. PHI is defined as individually identifiable information that relates to the past, present, or future physical or mental health of an individual; the provision of health care to an individual; or the past, present, or future payment for the provision of health care to an individual.[42]

In the broadest sense, *the privacy rule prohibits a covered entity from using or disclosing PHI except as expressly permitted or required by the rule.*[43] As briefly outlined below, the rule describes a range of circumstances under which it is permissible to use or disclose PHI. In all such instances covered entities can choose whether to use or disclose PHI based on their professional ethics and best judgment. The rule specifies only two circumstances when a covered entity is required to disclose PHI. A covered entity must disclose PHI to: (1) the individual who is the subject of the information, (i.e., patient right of access), and (2) HHS officials investigating potential violations of the rule.[44]

Generally, covered entities may use or disclose PHI for the purposes of treatment, payment, and other routine health care operations with few restrictions.[45] Under other specific circumstances (e.g., disclosures to family members and friends), the rule requires covered entities to give the individual the opportunity to object to the disclosure (i.e., opt out).[46] Importantly, the rule also permits the use or disclosure of PHI for several specified "national priority purposes" that are not directly connected to the treatment of the individual.[47] These uses and disclosures are permitted by the rule in recognition of the important uses made of health information outside of the health care context. They include the following uses and disclosures:

- **Required by law.** Covered entities may use or disclose PHI to the extent that such use or disclosure is required by (federal or state) law and the disclosure complies with and is limited to the relevant requirements of such law.[48]
- **Law enforcement purposes.** Covered entities may disclose PHI to law enforcement officials for certain specified law enforcement purposes.[49]
- **Averting a serious threat to health or safety.** Consistent with applicable law and standards of ethical conduct, a health care provider may use or disclose PHI if the provider in good faith believes the use or disclosure is necessary to prevent or lessen a serious and imminent threat to the health or safety of a person or the public.[50]
- **Specialized government functions.** Covered entities may use or disclose PHI for several specified essential government functions.[51]

For all uses or disclosures of PHI that are not otherwise permitted or required by the rule, covered entities must obtain a patient's written authorization.

As discussed above, prohibiting mental health records under the GCA are typically generated by the courts that adjudicate persons as mentally defective, and by the courts and health care providers that involuntarily commit individuals to mental health facilities. While courts are not covered entities and are not subject to the HIPAA privacy rule, health care providers such as hospitals and state health departments are covered by the privacy rule and, therefore, may not use or disclose PHI for the purpose of NICS reporting without express permission under the rule. As described below, it is necessary to look to the states to determine whether such permission exists.

Interaction of HIPAA Privacy Rule and State Privacy Laws

Although the HIPAA privacy rule provides a federal floor with respect to the uses and disclosures of PHI, the overall scope of the privacy rule may be modulated by state law. If a state requires covered entities to disclose prohibiting mental health records to NICS, the HIPAA privacy rule does not prohibit that disclosure.[52] Therefore, the privacy rule is most relevant as a potential obstacle where prohibiting mental health records are held by covered entities in a state that does not require disclosure of such records to NICS. This would be the case even if the state expressly allowed, but did not explicitly require, disclosure of prohibiting mental health records to NICS because merely permissive state laws are insufficient to exempt disclosure from the HIPAA privacy rule.

It should also be noted that both types of entities—courts and health care providers—may also be subject to state health privacy laws that may be more protective of individually identifiable health information than the HIPAA privacy rule and other state-level requirements and policies. State laws that are more protective of privacy include those that prohibit or restrict a use or disclosure that would otherwise be permitted under the privacy rule, and those that provide individuals with greater access to their own health information. This final section of the report provides a basic overview of the different types of state privacy laws that may impact the sharing of prohibiting mental health records with NICS.

Figure 1 summarizes state laws that address the reporting of mental health records for use in firearm purchaser background checks. Twenty-three states have NICS reporting mandates.[53] These laws require courts and, in some instances, mental health facilities to report (1) to NICS directly, or (2) to a state agency that in turn reports to NICS. As noted above, the HIPAA privacy rule would not bar the mandated disclosures in these states. Note that in one of the states— Delaware—reporting by mental health facilities takes the place of court reporting (see Figure 1).

Seven states have laws that authorize, but do not require, reporting to NICS.[54] In these states that do not mandate reporting, HIPAA-covered entities do not appear to have permission under the privacy rule to use or disclose PHI for the purpose of preparing and reporting mental health records to NICS. Absent a state reporting mandate, it is not clear that there are any other provisions in the privacy rule that provide such permission.

None of the three other national priority purposes in the privacy rule discussed earlier (under "HIPAA Privacy Rule Overview") address reporting to federal databases for the purposes of future background checks. The disclosure of PHI for law enforcement purposes has to be (1) as required by law; (2) pursuant to various specified judicial and administrative processes and procedures such as court orders, subpoenas, and summonses; or (3) in response to one of several other specified law enforcement activities.[55] The privacy rule's provisions authorizing the use or disclosure of PHI for various specialized government functions list a number of specific activities, none of which includes reporting information to the NICS databases.[56] Finally, the rule's provisions that permit the use and disclosure of PHI to avert a serious threat to health or safety focus on two types of situations, neither of which appears to include NICS reporting. The first permits the disclosure of PHI to a person or persons reasonably able to prevent or lessen a serious and imminent threat to the health or safety of a person or the public. The second concerns alerting law enforcement authorities about an individual involved in a violent crime or who has escaped from prison or lawful custody.[57]

An additional eight states collect mental health records pursuant to state law, but these laws do not address NICS reporting.[58] Again, without a NICS reporting mandate, HIPAA-covered entities do not appear to have permission under the privacy rule to use PHI for the purpose of reporting mental health records to the federal databases. These states include California, which despite the absence of a NICS reporting mandate, has one of the best NICS reporting rates for mental health records. In part this is because of a state law that requires mental health facilities to report mental health records to the California Department of Justice (DOJ). That requirement effectively removes HIPAA as an impediment to such reporting by HIPAA-covered entities. While state law is silent on DOJ reporting to NICS, California has developed a reporting infrastructure and entered into an agreement with the federal government to report mental health records to NICS.

Finally, 13 states are without laws requiring or authorizing the collection or reporting of mental health records for use in firearm purchaser background checks, either at the state or federal level. Once again, HIPAA-covered entities in these states that are in possession of disqualifying mental health records appear to lack the authority under the privacy rule to report such information to NICS.

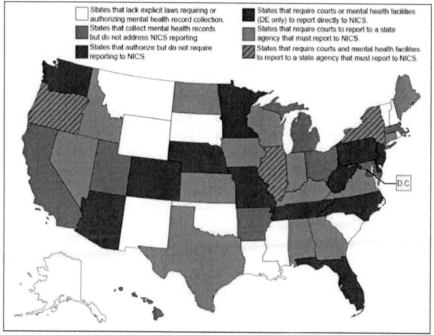

Source: Prepared by CRS based on a review and analysis of laws in all 50 states and the District of Columbia that address the reporting of mental health records for use in firearm purchaser background checks.

Note: CRS's characterization of state laws is in broad agreement with a similar analysis by the Law Center to Prevent Gun Violence—a nonprofit organization that advocates for gun-control legislation and provides legal expertise and information on U.S. gun laws—but with one key difference. Whereas the Law Center characterized Virginia as a state that authorizes but does not require reporting to NICS, CRS concluded that Virginia's law requires NICS reporting. The Law Center's analysis is available at http://smartgunlaws.org/mental-health

Figure 1. State Laws That Require or Authorize the Reporting of Mental Health Records to NICS, As of January 1, 2013.

On February 14, 2013, in response to the President's instruction to address any potential legal barriers to NICS reporting, HHS announced that it will seek to amend the HIPAA privacy rule to remove any potential impediments to state reporting of mental health records to NICS.[59] The HHS Office for Civil Rights (OCR), which administers and enforces the privacy rule, plans to issue an advance notice of proposed rulemaking (ANPRM) to solicit public comment on this issue prior to proposing any changes to the privacy rule.[60]

While a detailed examination of state-level activities is beyond the scope of this report, it should be emphasized that many states collect and use mental health records (and other relevant information) pursuant to state law or policies for their own background checks of firearm purchases. Some states are "Point-Of-Contact" (POC) states, meaning that the state agency is responsible for electronically accessing NICS and for implementing and maintaining their own Brady NICS program.[61] Often times a POC state will run the background check against the state's own records, some of which may not be in NICS. In some instances, background checks conducted by POCs may be more stringent than non-POC states because they have access to more access to disqualifying records. In addition, these states could be more thorough in their background checks because statutory prohibitions on firearm possession in these states sometimes exceed the federal prohibitions under the Brady Act. However, unlike the nationwide NICS background checks, state-level checks do not capture prohibited individuals who cross state lines to purchase long guns.

End Notes

[1] See CRS Report R43004, Public Mass Shootings in the United States: Selected Implications for Federal Public Health and Safety Policy, coordinated by Jerome P. Bjelopera.

[2] This report is limited to a discussion of currently applicable law, and does not discuss proposals to revise the types of mental health records that would disqualify an individual from purchasing or possessing a firearm.

[3] P.L. 90-618 (1968).

[4] 18 U.S.C. §922(g). Individuals who are under indictment for a felony are also prohibited from receiving or transporting firearms or ammunition. 18 U.S.C. §922(n).

[5] 18 U.S.C. §922(g).

[6] In the 113th Congress, Senator Lindsey Graham introduced S. 480, the NICS Reporting Improvement Act of 2013, that would revise 18 U.S.C. 922(g)(4) to replace references to "mental defective" with "mentally incompetent" and "mental institution" with "psychiatric hospital." The bill would also expressly define the type of hearings that qualify for purposes of being "adjudicated mentally incompetent or ... committed to a psychiatric hospital." A full discussion of the effects of these amendments is beyond the scope of this report.

[7] 27 C.F.R. §478.11. It is likely that any record that fits the definition under (b) would be related to criminal record histories that are more easily accessible by the states. However, it has been reported that a majority of states have low submission rates for the types of records that fall under subsection (a). MAIG Report.

[8] See, e.g., U.S. v. Vertz, 102 F. Supp.2d 787, 788 (W.D. Mich. 2000), aff'd on other grounds, 40 Fed. Appx. 69 (6th Cir. 2002) ("Despite the extensive evidence of medical illness, for purposes of criminal liability under the federal firearms statute, it is not sufficient that the defendant has been diagnosed as mentally ill by his treating physicians. The statute specifically requires that the individual have been adjudicated as a mental defective or committed to a mental institution.").

[9] DEPARTMENT OF VETERANS AFFAIRS, "Privacy Act of 1974; System of Records," 76 Fed. Reg. 14119, 14122 (Mar. 15, 2011). Pursuant to NIAA, the VA provides notice to veterans who may fall under the firearms disqualification, and the agency has established an administrative procedure that provides veterans with the ability to request relief from their firearms disability. See MR21-1MR VA Manual, Part III, Subpart v, Chapter 9 Section B, available at, http://www.benefits DEPARTMENT OF VETERANS AFFAIRS, Fast Letter to Regional Offices Re: Processing Requests for Relief from the Reporting Requirements of the National Instant Criminal Background Check System (NICS), available at https://docs.google 11ETxpq4dJiiJYcSD8 KYXtVTIOhKSqg5hAilxjNQ43OY/edit?pli=1.

[10] Letter from Jonathan M. Young, Chairman, National Council on Disability, to Joseph Robinette Biden, Jr., Vice President, United States of America, January 11, 2013, http://www.ncd.gov/publications/2013/Jan142013. Legislation to prevent these types of VA records from being transferred to NICS has been introduced in the 113th Congress. See, e.g., H.R. 577 and S. 572, Veterans Second Amendment Protection Act (113th Cong., 1st sess.). In other words, these bills would allow veterans who have been appointed a fiduciary to keep their firearms.

[11] 27 C.F.R. §478.11.

[12] The Judge David L. Bazelon Center for Mental Health Law, an advocacy organization that opposes involuntary outpatient commitment, has compiled a summary of state statutes allowing involuntary outpatient commitments; the summary includes a comparison with inpatient commitment statutes. See http://www.bazelon.org/LinkClick.aspx? fileticket= CBmfGyA4i-w%3D&tabid=324. For more about involuntary commitment, see National Conference of State Legislatures, Screening and Entry into Mental Health Treatment: Balancing Help for the Individual and the Community, http://www.ncsl.org/issues or National Conference of State Legislatures, Mental Health: What are the issues surrounding involuntary treatment?, http://www.ncsl.org/issues-research/health/mental-health-faq.aspx #issues.

[13] VA. CODE ANN. §37.2-819.

[14] N.Y. MENTAL HYG. LAW §9.27.

[15] U.S. v. Waters, 23 F.3d 29 (2d Cir. 1994). See also U.S. v. Vertz, 102 F. Supp. 2d at 787 ("prior hospitalization, which was supported by a second psychiatrist's certification, qualified as a commitment to a mental institution"). But see U.S. v. Giardina, 861 F.2d 1334 (5th Cir. 1988) (temporary, emergency detentions for treatment of mental disorders or difficulties, which did not lead to formal commitments under state law, did not constitute the commitment envisioned by the GCA).

[16] 554 U.S. 570 (2008).

[17] U.S. v. Rehlander, 666 F.3d 45 (1st Cir. 2012).

---

[18] U.S. v. Chamberlain, 159 F.3d 656 (1st Cir. 1998) and U.S. v. Holt, 464 F.3d 101 (1st Cir. 2006).

[19] The term ex parte refers to a legal proceeding brought by one person in the absence of and without representation or notification of other parties.

[20] P.L. 103-159, §103 (1994) [hereinafter Brady Act].

[21] The NCIC is a database of documented criminal justice information that is made available to law enforcement and authorized agencies, with the goal of assisting law enforcement in apprehending fugitives, finding missing persons, locating stolen property, and further protecting law enforcement personnel and the public. The III, or "Triple I," is a computerized criminal history index pointer system that the FBI maintains so that records on persons arrested and convicted of felonies and serious misdemeanors at either the federal or state level can be shared nationally. See Federal Bureau of Investigation, National Instant Criminal Background Check System 2011 Operations Report, available at http://www.fbi.gov/about-us/cjis/nics/reports/2011-operations

[22] See Federal Bureau of Investigation, Criminal Justice Information Services, National Instant Criminal Background Check System Index Brochure, available at http://www.fbi.go v/about-us/cjis/nics/general-information/nics-index.

[23] Brady Act, §103(e).

[24] Brady Act, §106. This program is known as the National Criminal History Improvement Program (NCHIP). This program is administered by the Department of Justice Bureau of Justice Statistics (BJS). See http://bjs.gov/index.cfm? ty=tp&tid=47.

[25] P.L. 110-180, §§102-104, 301 (2007) [hereinafter NIAA].

[26] NIAA, §101(b).

[27] NIAA, §101(c)(1).

[28] NIAA, §101(c)(2).

[29] NIAA, §102.

[30] NIAA, §§103, 105.

[31] This program is also administered by the Department of Justice's BJS. See http://bjs.gov/index.cfm?ty=tp&tid=49.

[32] NIAA, §104.

[33] For more information on the Byrne Justice Assistance Grant program, see CRS Report RS22416, Edward Byrne Memorial Justice Assistance Grant (JAG) Program, by Nathan James.

[34] U.S. Government Accountability Office, Gun Control: Sharing Promising Practices and Assessing Incentives Could Better Position Justice to Assist States in Providing Records for Background Checks, GAO-12-684, July 16, 2012, http://www.gao.gov/assets

[35] Id. at 11-12.

[36] Id. at 12.

[37] Mayors Against Illegal Guns, Fatal Gaps: How Missing Records in the Federal Background Check System Put Guns in the Hand of Killers, November 2011, http://www.mayorsagainstillegalguns.org/downloads/pdf/ maig_mimeo_revb.pdf. MAIG is a coalition of mayors from more than 900 cities and towns across the United States, co-chaired by New York City's Mayor Michael Bloomberg and Boston's Mayor Thomas Marino. The coalition shares best practices, develops policies, and supports legislation at all levels of government to reduce the distribution of, and access to, illegal and military-style firearms in U.S. cities and towns.

[38] The HIPAA privacy rule, and accompanying general administrative and enforcement requirements, are codified at 45 C.F.R. Part 160 and Part 164, Subparts A and E.

[39] Health plans include any individual or group plan that provides or pays for medical care. The term encompasses both private and government plans. Health maintenance organizations (HMOs) and high-risk pools are specifically covered. Most employee health benefit plans are covered. See 45 C.F.R. §160.103.

[40] Health care clearinghouse is a term of art under the privacy rule. It refers to an entity (e.g., claims processor) that translates health information received from other entities either to or from the standard format that is required for electronic transactions. See 45 C.F.R. §160.103.

[41] Health care providers include any person (e.g., physician, nurse, pharmacist) or entity (e.g., hospital, clinic) that furnishes, bills, or is paid for health care in the normal course of business. To be a covered entity, a provider must conduct one or more of the HIPAA-specified transactions, such as verifying insurance coverage or filing a health claim, by transmitting health information electronically in a standard format (i.e., the provider must include certain information and use specified codes for diagnosis and treatment) required by HIPAA. Providers that rely on third-party billing services to conduct such electronic transactions on their behalf are also covered under the privacy rule. Providers that operate solely on a paper basis and do not submit insurance claims electronically are not subject to the rule. See 45 C.F.R. §160.103.

[42] 45 C.F.R. §160.103.

[43] 45 C.F.R. §164.502(a)

[44] Id.

[45] 45 C.F.R. §164.506.

[46] 45 C.F.R. §164.510.

[47] 45 C.F.R. §164.512.

[48] 45 C.F.R. §164.512(a)

[49] 45 C.F.R. §164.512(f)

[50] 45 C.F.R. §164.512(j). On January 15, 2013, the HHS Office for Civil Rights issued a letter to health care providers in which he reminded them of the privacy rule's "duty to warn" provision, which permits the disclosure of patient information to avert threats to health or safety. See http://www.hhs.gov/ocr/office/lettertonationhcp.pdf.

[51] 45 C.F.R. §164.512(k)

[52] Id.

[53] AL, CO, CT, DE, GA, ID, IL, IN, IA, KS, KY, ME, MN, NV, NC, ND, NY, OR, TN, TX, WA, WI, and VA; see Figure 1.

[54] AZ, FL, MO, NE, NJ, PA, and WV; see Figure 1. In some cases, whether state law requires disclosure to NICS may be ambiguous. For example, New Jersey state law currently prohibits disclosure of commitment records disclosure except as needed to comply with the data reporting provisions of the NIAA or the Brady Act, but it is not clear that either of those laws impose any such requirements. The state is currently considering Assembly Bill No. 3717, which would amend state law to explicitly require reporting of institutionalized persons to NICS. http://www.njleg.state.nj.us/ 2012/Bills/A4000/3717_I1.HTM

[55] 45 C.F.R. §164.512(k)

[56] 45 C.F.R. §164.512(k)

[57] 45 C.F.R. §164.512(j)

[58] AR, CA, HI, MA, MD, MI, OH and UT; see Figure 1.

[59] HIPAA provides the HHS Secretary with authority to modify the privacy standards, as determined appropriate, but not more frequently than once every 12 months. Any addition

or modification to a standard must "be completed in a manner that minimizes the disruption and cost of compliance." 42 U.S.C. §1320d–3(b)(1).

[60] Kendra Casey Plank, "HIPAA Privacy Rule Changes Could Ease Sharing of Mental Health Records by States," Bloomberg BNA, Health Care Daily Report, February 15, 2013.

[61] See Federal Bureau of Investigation, National Instant Criminal Background Check System-Participation Map, available at, http://www.fbi.gov/about-us/cjis/nics/general-information /participation-map.

In: Firearms in America
Editor: Alfonso D. Sutton

ISBN: 978-1-63117-823-8
© 2014 Nova Science Publishers, Inc.

Chapter 5

INTERNET FIREARM AND AMMUNITION SALES[*]

Vivian S. Chu

SUMMARY

As the Internet has become a significant venue for facilitating commercial transactions, concerns have arisen regarding the use of this medium to transfer firearms. This report discusses the sale of firearms and ammunition over the Internet, with a focus on the extent to which federal law regulates such activity. A review of the relevant factors indicates Internet-based firearm transactions are subject to the same regulatory scheme governing traditional firearm transactions. Over the years, this has raised concern about the possibility of increased violation of federal firearm laws, as well as challenges that law enforcement may face when attempting to investigate violations of these laws. A review of the relevant factors also indicates that the sale and transfer of ammunition are not as strictly regulated as firearms, and that these changes came into effect in 1986. Lastly, this report highlights recent legislative proposals, S. 3458 and H.R. 6241, companion measures introduced by Senator Frank Lautenberg and Representative Carolyn McCarthy in the 112th Congress that would affect online ammunition transactions.

---

[*] This is an edited, reformatted and augmented version of Congressional Research Service Publication, No. R42687, dated August 28, 2012.

INTRODUCTION

As the Internet has become a significant venue for facilitating commercial transactions, it may be more common in this day and age for a consumer to first turn to the Internet to purchase goods than to go to a store. This could be said for almost all types of goods, including firearms and ammunition. A simple search for the terms "sale" and "firearm" results in a multitude of websites devoted to the sale of firearms or ammunition. Accordingly, questions and concerns have arisen regarding the extent to which federal law regulates the sale of such goods. A review of applicable federal laws, discussed below, establishes that Internet-based firearm sales are not imbued with a special character by virtue of their medium of transfer, and are in fact subject to the same degree of regulation as any other type of firearm transaction. The unique qualities of Internet transactions, however, may pose significant obstacles to enforcing these firearm regulations.[1] The sale of ammunition, however, is subject to less federal regulation than firearms. It is this latter fact that has become the subject of heightened scrutiny in the aftermath of the tragic mass shooting that occurred in a Colorado movie theater in July 2012. The suspected shooter, who killed 12 persons and injured at least 58, reportedly purchased at least 6,000 rounds of ammunition online.[2] Following this incident, Senator Frank Lautenberg and Representative Carolyn McCarthy have introduced new legislation, the Stop Online Ammunition Sales Act (S. 3458/H.R. 6241), that would more strictly regulate the online sale of ammunition.

THE GUN CONTROL ACT OF 1968

Congress enacted the Gun Control Act of 1968[3] (GCA or Act) to "keep firearms out of the hands of those not legally entitled to possess them because of age, criminal background or incompetency, and to assist law enforcement authorities in the states and their subdivisions in combating the increasing prevalence of crime in the United States."[4] To this end, the GCA prohibits certain classes of individuals from possessing firearms, and establishes a comprehensive regulatory scheme designed to prevent the transfer of firearms to such individuals.[5]

In particular, the GCA establishes nine classes of individuals who are prohibited from shipping, transporting, possessing, or receiving firearms in interstate commerce.[6] The individuals targeted by this provision include (1) persons convicted of a crime punishable by a term of imprisonment exceeding one year; (2) fugitives from justice; (3) individuals who are unlawful users or addicts of any controlled substance; (4) persons legally determined to be mentally defective, or who have been committed to a mental institution; (5) aliens illegally or unlawfully in the United States, as well as those who have been admitted pursuant to a nonimmigrant visa; (6) individuals who have been discharged dishonorably from the Armed Forces; (7) persons who have renounced United States citizenship; (8) individuals subject to a pertinent court order; and, finally, (9) persons who have been convicted of a misdemeanor domestic violence offense.[7]

These nine categories of persons are also prohibited from shipping, possessing, or receiving ammunition in interstate commerce. When the GCA was enacted, the transfer and sale of ammunition appear to have been regulated in the same manner as firearms. In 1986, Congress passed the Firearm Owners' Protection Act (FOPA),[8] which repealed many of the regulations regarding ammunition. Consequently, as discussed below, the transfer and sale of ammunition are not as strictly regulated as the transfer and sale of firearms.

Restrictions on Sales

In order to effectuate the general prohibitions outlined above, the GCA imposes significant requirements on the transfer of firearms. Pursuant to the Act, any person who is "engaged in the business"[9] of importing, manufacturing, or dealing in firearms must apply and be approved as a Federal Firearms Licensee (FFL or licensee).[10] FFLs are subject to several requirements designed to ensure that a firearm is not transferred to an individual disqualified from possession under the Act. For example, a licensee must verify the identity of a transferee by examining a government-issued identification document bearing a photograph of the transferee, such as a driver's license;[11] conduct a background check on the transferee using the National Instant Criminal Background Check System (NICS);[12] maintain records of the acquisition and disposition of firearms;[13] report multiple sales of handguns to the Attorney General;[14] respond to an official request for information contained in the licensee's records within 24 hours of receipt;[15] and comply with all other relevant state and local regulations.[16]

Not all sellers of firearms are required to be approved FFLs, however. The GCA contains a specific exemption for any person who makes "occasional sales, exchanges, or purchases of firearms for the enhancement of a personal collection or for a hobby, or who sells all or part of his personal collection of firearms."[17] Although private sellers are not required to conduct a background check or maintain official records of transactions under federal law, they are prohibited from transferring a firearm if they know or have reasonable cause to believe that the transferee is a disqualified person.[18]

When the GCA was originally enacted in 1968, the sale and transfer of ammunition were regulated in nearly the same manner as firearms. This meant that an individual "engaged in the business"[19] of dealing ammunition, among other things, had to be licensed under the GCA,[20] and was required to maintain records of the ammunition sale.[21] In 1986, however, Congress enacted the Firearm Owners' Protection Act (FOPA), which repealed these types of regulations for sales and transfer of ammunition.[22] Consequently, one does not need to be an FFL to deal in ammunition, nor are such sellers (including FFLs) required to keep a record of ammunition sales.[23] Notably, while FFLs have never been required under federal law to conduct a background check for purchasers of ammunition, they still may choose to do so because it remains unlawful for any seller of ammunition to transfer ammunition knowing or having reasonable cause to believe that such person is a prohibited possessor.[24]

Restrictions on Interstate Transfers

In addition to the aforementioned requirements imposed upon the sale of firearms by licensed and unlicensed individuals generally, federal law also places significant limitations on the actual interstate transfer of weapons. These provisions are of particular interest in analyzing Internet-based firearm sales, given the inherently interstate quality of such activity and the perceived potential for abuse in the Internet sale context.

Although FFLs have the ability to sell and ship firearms in interstate or foreign commerce, the GCA places several restrictions on the manner in which a transfer may occur. Specifically, while a licensee may make an in-person, over-the-counter sale of a long gun (i.e., shotgun or rifle) to any qualified individual regardless of her state of residence,[25] a licensee may only sell a handgun to a person who is a resident of the state in which the dealer's premises is located.[26] Relatedly, a licensee is prohibited from shipping firearms, both handguns and long guns, directly to consumers in other states.[27]

Instead, FFLs making a firearm sale to a non-resident must transfer the weapon to another FFL that is licensed in the transferee's state of residence and from whom the transferee may obtain the firearm after passing the required NICS background check.[28]

Firearm transfers between non-FFL sellers are also strictly regulated. Specifically, whereas FFLs may transfer a long gun to a non-resident non-licensee in an over-the-counter sale, the GCA specifically bars a non-FFL from directly selling or transferring any firearm to any person who is not a resident of the state in which the non-FFL resides.[29] Instead, interstate transactions between non-FFLs result in the transferring party shipping the firearm to an FFL located in the transferee's state of residence.

On the other hand, ammunition sales are currently less extensively regulated than firearm sales. Prior to 1986, however, not only were sales of ammunition conducted through FFLs who were required to be licensed to engage in the business of dealing ammunition, but FFLs were prohibited from shipping ammunition to a private person (non-FFL).[30] The transfer of ammunition to an out-of-state purchaser, therefore, had to be conducted much like a handgun sale to an out-of-state purchaser, with the FFL transferring the ammunition to another FFL located in the state of the purchaser. After FOPA repealed these provisions in 1986,[31] sellers no are no longer required to have a license to deal in ammunition and they are not prohibited from shipping ammunition directly to a private person regardless of the purchaser's state of residence. While there is less regulation of ammunition at the federal level, a few states have enacted legislation that requires either, or both, a seller and purchaser of ammunition to be licensed by the state.[32]

THE GCA AND THE INTERNET

It is these aforementioned provisions on interstate transfers that arguably control the present inquiry regarding the extent to which Internet-based firearm and ammunition transactions are regulated under federal laws.[33] The panoply of provisions discussed above establish a federal scheme that regulates every firearm sale, irrespective of the medium of transaction. Even though these laws do not specifically address online or Internet sales, they broadly address the transfer of any firearm in interstate or foreign commerce. The mere fact that a firearm transaction is negotiated over the Internet does not exempt it from the requirements that apply to traditional sales conducted in person or those facilitated through classified advertisements in newspapers.[34]

In other words, FFLs who advertise firearms over the Internet are still prohibited from directly shipping a firearm to a non-FFL purchaser. If an out-of-state non-FFL purchaser desired to buy a firearm (i.e., a handgun or long gun) from the FFL, then the FFL would have to arrange for the firearm to be transferred to another FFL located in the purchaser's state and from whom the nonFFL purchaser could obtain the firearm after passing a background check.[35] Similarly, private sellers of firearms who advertise the sale of firearms over the Internet could only make a direct transfer to a purchaser who is a resident of the seller's own state. The private seller would still be prohibited from directly transferring his firearms to an out-of-state non-FFL purchaser, and would be required to arrange for the firearm to be transferred to an FFL located in the purchaser's state.[36] Internet-based sales and transfers of ammunition, on the other hand, may be conducted freely by FFL and non-FFL sellers to in- or out-of-state purchasers, given the GCA's lack of proscription against such conduct.[37]

Concerns and Proposed Legislation

Although existing GCA provisions encompass Internet-based firearm transactions and freely permit the direct transfer of ammunition between seller and purchaser, concerns have arisen since the beginning of the Internet revolution that there is ample opportunity for abuse of the existing firearm regulations or an increased potential for violations of federal law.

Almost 12 years ago, the Department of Justice (DOJ) identified several factors it found unsettling regarding firearm sales over the Internet.[38] In addition to the possibility that prohibited persons may be successful in acquiring firearms over the Internet, DOJ stated that the Internet "provides convenient fora" for the advertisement and sale of firearms by non-licensed individuals who are not required to conduct background checks or retain records of sales. Because non-FFL transactions are regulated less strictly, DOJ observed that non-licensed individuals might be encouraged to illegally engage in the business of dealing in firearms. Furthermore, there could be an increase in violations of federal law, as the prospect of quick profits from Internet sales may "create a temptation on the part of FFLs to circumvent" existing federal laws.[39] During this time, the Working Group on Unlawful Conduct on the Internet (Working Group), established by President Clinton in 2000,[40] stated that the sale of firearms over the Internet poses "unique problems" for law enforcement.[41] The Working Group first maintained that illegal online sales would be more difficult to detect than sales facilitated through traditional venues such as print advertisements, since "the [I]nternet provides people with the means to advertise guns for sale on message boards, through e-mail, in chat rooms, or other websites that will be difficult to find and may even be inaccessible to law enforcement."[42] Another hindrance to law enforcement efforts suggested by the Working Group is the lack of a fixed physical location for the execution of Internet-based sales. Whereas the Bureau of Alcohol, Tobacco, Firearms and Explosives may conduct inspections and review records of transactions with traditional sales made at gun stores or gun shows, Internet-based transactions would be much more difficult to monitor.[43] It is unclear the extent to which law enforcement has experienced problems in detecting illegal firearm transactions, or whether it has the investigatory resources or capabilities to devote to enforcing firearm laws over the Internet.

It should also be noted that when these reports were issued, there was little substantive evidence to support the assumption that individuals advertising firearms over the Internet were more likely to ignore firearm laws than those employing traditional methods of sale. Even though the observations from DOJ and the Working Group have an intuitive appeal and appear logically sound, an investigation by the General Accounting Office[44] (GAO) from 2001 on Internet-based firearm sales detected no illegal activity with respect to FFLs. The GAO investigation was limited in scope, but none of the FFLs solicited by the undercover investigator agreed to engage in any illegal activity.[45] More recently, however, the City of New York issued a report in December 2011 on its undercover investigation, which specifically examined online gun sales from private sellers.[46] The results from this investigation present a marked contrast from the earlier GAO investigation. The city of New York's investigation examined 125 private sellers from 14 states who advertised on 10 different websites.[47] Investigators indicated to these private sellers that they "probably couldn't pass a background check."[48] Of the 125 private sellers, 77 agreed to sell a gun to someone who said he could not pass a background check.[49] While these investigations were conducted several years apart and were both limited in scope, results from the GAO investigation could be interpreted as undermining the contention that the use of the Internet to facilitate firearm transactions will result in increased illegal activity with respect to FFLs. In contrast, the city of New York's investigation could give credence to the observation that the Internet increases the potential for abuse by private sellers to make unlawful sales of firearms to prohibited purchasers.

In addition to these long-existing concerns regarding the sale of firearms over the Internet, concerns have also been raised with respect to online ammunition sales, especially in light of reports that the suspected gunman in the Colorado movie theater shootings purchased at least 6,000 rounds of ammunition online. In response to this, Senator Frank Lautenberg[50] and Representative Carolyn McCarthy introduced S. 3458 and H.R. 6241, the Stop Online Sales Ammunition Act of 2012.[51] Primarily, this legislation would reinstitute the ammunition regulation that had been repealed when FOPA was passed in 1986. It would require an individual who wishes to sell ammunition to be a licensed dealer, irrespective of whether such business is conducted with the principal objective of livelihood and profit, because the amendment does not include the phrase "engaged in the business."[52] Accordingly, the bill would arguably prevent any secondary sales of ammunition, that is, sales between non-FFLs, an action that is currently permitted with respect to secondary sales of firearms.[53] Although a licensee selling ammunition would not be required to conduct a NICS background check under the bill, the licensee would be required to examine a valid photo identification of the transferee before completing the transfer. It would also make it unlawful for a licensee to directly transfer or deliver ammunition to any non-licensee and would require licensees to keep track of ammunition transfers to the same extent that they keep track of firearm transfers. These requirements would have the likely effect of requiring the seller and buyer to meet in person to complete the transaction. Furthermore, one component of the bill that was not a part of the original ammunition regulations from 1968 is the requirement that licensees prepare a report of multiple sales for federal and local authorities whenever the licensee disposes of more than 1,000 rounds of ammunition to a non-licensee during any five consecutive business days.[54]

In contrast to the proposed ammunition bill discussed above, proposed gun control measures have primarily focused on extending the background check requirements to private sellers rather than targeting the interstate scheme under the GCA. Such measures, like Fixed Gun Checks Act of 2011 (H.R. 1781/S. 436), would effectively require some in-person contact to be made through an FFL or a law enforcement agency because they would require a background check be conducted for every firearm sale.[55] These measures perhaps focus on extending background check requirements because, as discussed above, the existing scheme on the interstate transfer of firearms arguably encompasses Internet-based firearms transactions, such that most firearm transactions are transferred through FFLs, unless it is an intrastate sale between two non-FFLs.

End Notes

[1] This report addresses the specific issue of whether the current federal firearm laws apply to Internet-based firearm sales and whether such laws are effective in the Internet context. The report does not purport to broach the related policy issue of whether additional firearm laws, either generally or specifically applicable to internet transactions, are warranted. For more on gun control policy, see CRS Report RL32842, *Gun Control Legislation*, by William J. Krouse.

[2] Thom Patterson, "Police Chief: Suspect bought over 6,000 rounds of ammunition through Internet," CNN, July 20, 2012, *available at*, http://articles.cnn.com/2012-07-20/justice/justice_colorado-shooting-weapons_

[3] P.L. 90-618 (1968), as amended *codified at* 18 U.S.C. §§921 *et seq.*

[4] S.Rept. 90-1097 (1968).

[5] 18 U.S.C. §921 *et seq.* (2006).

[6] 18 U.S.C. §922(g).

[7] The GCA also prohibits the receipt, transport, or shipment of firearms or ammunition by individuals under felony indictment. 18 U.S.C. §922(n). Furthermore, the GCA places significant restrictions on the transfer to, and possession of, firearms by persons under the age of 18. *See* 18 U.S.C. §922(x).

[8] P.L. 99-308 (1986).

[9] "Engaged in the business" means one who "devotes time, attention, and labor" to manufacturing, importing, or dealing firearms "as a regular course of trade or business with the principal objective of livelihood and profit." 18 U.S.C. §§921(a)(21)-(22).

[10] 18 U.S.C. §922(a); §923.

[11] 18 U.S.C. §922(t)(1)(c).

[12] 18 U.S.C. §922(t).

[13] 18 U.S.C. §923(g)(1)(A).

[14] 18 U.S.C. §923(g)(D)(3)(A).

[15] 18 U.S.C. §923(g)(D)(7).

[16] 18 U.S.C. §§922(b)(2), 923(d).

[17] 18 U.S.C. §921(a)(21)(C).

[18] 18 U.S.C. §§922(d), (t).

[19] *See supra* note 9 for definition of "engaged in the business." Notably, the definition of "engaged in the business" was added in 1986 when Congress enacted the Firearm Owners' Protection Act (P.L. 99-308).

[20] 18 U.S.C. §922(a)(1) (1970) ("It shall be unlawful for any person, except a licensed ... dealer, to engage in the *business of importing, manufacturing, or dealing in firearms or ammunition*, or in the course of such business to ship, transport, or receive any firearm or ammunition in interstate or foreign commerce.")(emphasis added) *cf.* 18 U.S.C. §922(a)(1)(B) (2006) ("It shall be unlawful for any person, except a licensed importer or licensed manufacturer, to engage in the *business of importing or manufacturing ammunition*, or in the course of such business to ship, transport, or receive any ammunition in interstate or foreign commerce.")(emphasis added).

[21] 18 U.S.C §923(g) (1970) (Each licensee "shall maintain such records of importation, production, shipment, receipt, sale or other disposition of *firearms and ammunition at such place* ...")(emphasis added) *cf.* 18 U.S.C. §923(g)(1)(A) (2006) (Each licensee "shall maintain such records of importation, production, shipment, receipt, sale or other disposition of *firearms at his place of business* ...")(emphasis added).

[22] P.L. 99-308 (1968).

[23] Armor piercing ammunition, however, is more strictly regulated than ammunition. Under federal law, FFLs are required to record sales and transfers of armor piercing ammunition, and it is generally unlawful for FFLs to transfer armor piercing ammunition unless it is for government use or for the purpose of exportation. 18 U.S.C. §922(a)(8) (2006).

[24] 18 U.S.C. §922(d) (2006).

[25] 18 U.S.C. §922(b)(3)(A).

[26] 18 U.S.C. §922(b)(3).

[27] 18 U.S.C. §922(a)(2). Regarding the mailing of firearms, federal law prohibits the shipment of any firearm other than a shotgun or rifle via the United States Postal Service, except for firearms shipped for official law enforcement purposes. 18 U.S.C. §1715. Firearms, including handguns, may be shipped by common carrier (*e.g.*, FedEx or UPS) upon disclosure and subject to the restrictions discussed above. *See* 18 U.S.C. §922(a)(2)(A); §922(3); 27 C.F.R. §178.31.

[28] 18 U.S.C. §922(b)(3); §922(t).

[29] 18 U.S.C. §922(a)(3); §922(a)(5); §922(b)(3).

[30] 18 U.S.C. §922(a)(2) (1970) ("It shall be unlawful for any [licensed] importer, manufacturer, dealer or collector ... to ship or transport ... any *firearm or ammunition to any person* other than a licensed" importer, manufacturer, dealer or collector.")(emphasis added) *cf.* 18 U.S.C. §922(a)(2) (2006) ("It shall be unlawful for any [licensed] importer, manufacturer, dealer, or collector ... to ship or transport ... *any firearm to any person* other than a licensed" importer, manufacturer, dealer, or collector.)(emphasis added).

[31] P.L. 99-308 (1986).

[32] *See, e.g.*, D.C. Code §§7-2504.01, 7-2504.04 (requires seller and purchaser to both be licensed or registered to sell, purchase, or possess ammunition); Md. Code Pub. Safety §11-105(a) (requires anyone engaged in the business of dealing or explosives (ammunition) for the use in firearms to be licensed); Wash. Rev. Code §9.41.110(3) (requires anyone who deals, sells, or transfers ammunition to be licensed).

[33] Some have posited that the "secondary gun market—i.e., the selling of guns at a gun show or over the internet—is in reality totally unregulated." *See* Violence Policy Center, "Unsafe in Any Hands: Why America Needs to Ban Handguns," *available at*, http://www.vpc.org/studies/unsafe.htm.

[34] 18 U.S.C. §922.

[35] 18 U.S.C. §922(a)(2).

[36] 18 U.S.C. §§922(a)(3), (5).

[37] While some states noted above (*supra* note 32) have enacted regulations that require sellers and/or purchasers to be licensed, at least one state has attempted to enact laws that proscribe mail order sales of ammunition. In 2009, the state of California passed a law that required the delivery or transfer of "handgun ammunition" to be conducted in person with the receiver presenting "bona fide evidence of identity." Cal. Penal Code §12318 (repealed 2010) and re-codified Cal. Penal Code §30312 (2010, effective February 1, 2011). A violation of this is a misdemeanor. However, this law was challenged based on the claim that the statutory definition of "handgun ammunition," that is, the type of ammunition that is required to be transferred in person, is unconstitutionally vague on its face. *See* Parker v. California, No.10CECG01226, January 31, 2011 (Super. Ct. Fresno)(Order Denying Pls' Mot. for Summ. J. and Grant. In Part and Den. In Part Pls' Mot. For Summ. Adjudication), *available at*, http://michellawyers.com/wp-content/uploads/2011/02/ Parker-Final-Order_R.pdf. The lower court ruled in favor of the challengers and held that the challenged

provisions failed to meet the requirements for a constitutionally valid criminal statute because (1) the statutory definition was not definite enough so that ordinary people can understand what conduct is prohibited, and (2) the statutory definition of the criminal offense was not definite enough to not encourage arbitrary and discriminatory enforcement. *Id*. The court issued an order of permanent injunction against enforcement or implementation of the challenged provisions. *See* Parker v. California, No.10CECG01226, January 21, 2011 (Super. Ct. Fresno)(Order for Permanent Inj), *available at*, http://www.calgunlaws.com/images

[38] *See* U.S. Department of Justice, "Gun Violence Reduction: National Integrated Firearms Violence Reduction Strategy," at 28, *available at*, http://www.justice.gov/archive/opd /gunviolence.htm.

[39] *Id*.

[40] President Clinton established the Working Group on Unlawful Conduct on the Internet in Executive Order 13133.

[41] *See* President's Working Group on Unlawful Conduct on the Internet, "The Electronic Frontier: The Challenge of Unlawful Conduct Involving the Use of the Internet," Appendix E, at 3.

[42] *Id*.

[43] *Id*.

[44] The General Accounting Office is now called the Government Accountability Office. P.L. 108-271 (2004).

[45] United States General Accounting Office, "Firearms Purchased From Federal Licensees Using Bogus Identification," GAO-01-427, March 2001. An undercover agent responded to 10 of 21 advertisements offering firearms for sale on an unidentified website. Eight of the 10 advertisers were federally licensed dealers, all of whom refused to ship the firearms offered for sale to anyone except another federally licensed dealer in compliance with the GCA. Of the two advertisers selling firearms in an individual capacity, the GAO report stated that one private seller refused to ship the firearm to anyone other than a licensee and that the other private seller "refused to send the firearm through the mail." The two individual sellers reportedly agreed to sell the firearms to the undercover agent in person, though the transaction was not pursued. The report did not provide sufficient evidence to determine whether such a transaction would have violated the GCA. *Id*. at 13.

[46] City of New York, Michael R. Bloomberg, "Point, Click, Fire: An Investigation of Illegal Online Gun Sales," December 14, 2011, *available at*, http://www.nyc.gov/html/cjc /downloads/pdf/nyc_pointclickfire.pdf.

[47] The city chose sites that had relatively few rules requiring buyers and sellers to identify themselves, and could therefore be more attractive to prohibited or unscrupulous purchasers. The sites visited by the investigators typically permit potential buyers to view firearm ads that include the cell phone number and e-mail address of the seller without registering with the site or otherwise revealing their identity. *Id*. at 9.

[48] *Id*. at 10.

[49] *Id*. Investigators met five of the sellers to exchange the gun for cash.

[50] After the events in Colorado, Senator Lautenberg also reintroduced S. 32 as an amendment to the cybersecurity bill (S. 3414). This proposed measure would prohibit the transfer or possession of "large capacity magazines" of more than 10 rounds.

[51] Following the Colorado shootings, it was reported that gun rights proponents were "holding off any effort to force action on a House-passed bill that would allow gun owners to carry concealed weapons across state lines," primarily because of "tight control" of the Senate floor rather than the "unfavorable climate for the legislation." *See* Alan K. Ota, "Gun Rights

Supporters Blame Reid for Inaction on Concealed-Weapons Bill," *CQ Today*, July 23, 2012, *available at*, http://cq.com/doc/news-4128218. The House-passed bill referred to is H.R. 822, the National Right-to-Carry Concealed Act of 2011. Senator Mark Begich has introduced S. 2188, the companion bill to H.R. 822, and Senator John Thune has introduced a very similar concealed carry bill, S. 2213, the Respecting States' Rights and Concealed Carry Reciprocity Act of 2012. For more on concealed carry, *see* CRS Report R42099, *Federal Laws and Legislation on Carrying Concealed Firearms: An Overview*, by Vivian S. Chu.

[52] 18 U.S.C. §§921(a)(21)-(22).

[53] 18 U.S.C. §§922(b)(3), (5).

[54] This proposed requirement mirrors the existing requirement under federal law that FFLs prepare a multiple sales report for federal and state authorities whenever they sell or dispose of two or more handguns during any five consecutive business days. 18 U.S.C. §923(g)(3).

[55] For a review of other gun control measures, *see* CRS Report RL32842, *Gun Control Legislation*, by William J. Krouse.

In: Firearms in America
Editor: Alfonso D. Sutton

ISBN: 978-1-63117-823-8
© 2014 Nova Science Publishers, Inc.

Chapter 6

THE PROTECTION OF LAWFUL COMMERCE IN ARMS ACT: AN OVERVIEW OF LIMITING TORT LIABILITY OF GUN MANUFACTURERS[*]

Vivian S. Chu

SUMMARY

The Protection of Lawful Commerce in Arms Act (PLCAA, P.L. 109-92) was passed in 2005. The PLCAA generally shields licensed manufacturers, dealers, and sellers of firearms or ammunition, as well as trade associations, from any civil action "resulting from the criminal or unlawful misuse" of a firearm or ammunition, but lists six exceptions where civil suits may be maintained. This act was introduced in response to litigation brought by municipalities and victims of shooting incidents against federally licensed firearms manufacturers and dealers, some of whom were located outside the state where the injuries occurred. Consequently, most lawsuits brought after the enactment of this law have been dismissed notwithstanding the exceptions that would permit a civil suit to proceed against a federal firearms licensee. This report provides an overview of the PLCAA and its exceptions, and discusses recent judicial developments.

---

[*] This is an edited, reformatted and augmented version of Congressional Research Service Publication, No. R42871, dated December 20, 2012.

OVERVIEW OF THE PROTECTION OF LAWFUL COMMERCE IN ARMS ACT

The Protection of Lawful Commerce in Arms Act (PLCAA) was passed in 2005.[1] The act generally shields federally licensed manufacturers, dealers, and sellers of firearms or ammunition, as well as trade associations, from any civil action "resulting from the criminal or unlawful misuse" of a firearms or ammunition. The act lists six exceptions where civil suits may be maintained but otherwise requires that lawsuits, pending at the time of enactment, brought by shooting victims and municipalities "be immediately dismissed by the court in which the action was brought or is currently pending."[2]

The PLCAA was considered and passed at a time when victims of shooting incidents, as well as municipalities with high incidences of firearms-related crimes, brought civil suits seeking damages and injunctive relief against out-of-state manufacturers and sellers of firearms as one tactic to inhibit the flow of firearms into illegal markets.[3] The statute's findings state that the lawsuits seeking to hold "an entire industry for harm that is solely caused by others is an abuse of the legal system," and that the businesses targeted should not be liable for the harm caused by third parties who criminally or unlawfully misuse firearms products that function as designed and intended.[4] Senator Larry E. Craig, sponsor of the legislation, said that the bill "will put an end to politically-motivated lawsuits against the firearms industry," and added, "[t]hese outrageous lawsuits attempting to hold law-abiding industry responsible for the acts of criminals are a threat to jobs and the economy, jeopardize the exercise of constitutionally-protected freedoms, undermine national security, and circumvent Congress and state legislatures."[5] In contrast, opponents of the legislation, like Dennis Henigan of the Brady Legal Action Project, countered, "The gun lobby is trying to radically change the rules, to make irresponsible gun dealers and the makers of defective guns the only business[es] in America exempt from longstanding principles of negligence, nuisance and product liability."[6]

PROVISIONS OF THE PLCAA

The main provision of the PLCAA provides: "A qualified civil liability action may not be brought in any Federal or State court."[7] Whether the

PLCAA bars a civil suit depends on if the action brought is a "qualified civil liability action," which is defined as:

> a civil action or proceeding or an administrative proceeding brought by any person against a manufacturer or seller of a qualified product, or a trade association, for damages, punitive damages, injunctive or declaratory relief, abatement, restitution, fines, or penalties, or other relief, resulting from the criminal or unlawful misuse of a qualified product by the person or a third party.... [8]

Although a qualified civil liability action, by its own definition, appears to bar administrative proceedings, it is unclear whether the statute actually does so because the main provision of the PLCAA prohibits civil suits from being brought in courts. Notably, administrative proceedings are not brought in courts although appeals of them may be. If the statute is meant to cover administrative proceedings, then the effect of its doing so is not clear.

Exceptions to the Prohibition on Civil Liability Action

The PLCAA lists six types of lawsuits that do not qualify as a "qualified civil liability action," and that therefore are not barred by the statute. [9] Each of these exceptions is discussed below.

> **First Exception:** An action brought against a transferor convicted under 18 U.S.C. § 924(h), or a comparable or identical state felony law, by a party directly harmed by the conduct of which the transferee is so convicted.

Under the first exception, a civil suit would not be prohibited against a transferor (*i.e.*, a federal firearms licensee) if the transferor was convicted under 18 U.S.C. § 924(h), which makes it unlawful for anyone to "knowingly transfer[] a firearm, knowing that such firearm will be used to commit a crime of violence ... or a drug trafficking crime." Additionally, the transferee, or receiver, of the firearm needs to have been convicted for the civil action to be permitted, but the type of conviction necessary is unclear. The transferee's conviction cannot refer to § 924(h) because this provision only applies to a transferor of a firearm. It may be the case that the conviction must be of a "crime of violence" or a "drug trafficking crime," as defined by federal statute, as those are the crimes that the transferor must have had knowledge of in order to be convicted under § 924(h).[10]

> **Second Exception:** An action brought against a seller for negligent entrustment or negligence per se.

The second exception specifically refers to actions against "a seller," and the PLCAA's definition of "seller" may exclude some manufacturers from being included under this second exception, in which case they would continue to be immune from suits for negligent entrustment or negligence per se.

Under the PLCAA, a "seller" includes a "dealer (as defined in section 921(a)(11) of title 18) ... who is engaged in the business as such a dealer *and* who is licensed to engage in the business" under title 18. A "dealer," under § 921(a)(11), includes a person who is "engaged in the business of selling firearms at wholesale or retail,"[11] and thus could include a manufacturer because it likely sells its products at wholesale. However, under limited circumstances,[12] federal regulation provides that a firearms manufacturer is *not* required "to obtain a dealer's license in order to engage in the business on the licensed premises as a dealer of the same type of firearms authorized by the license to be imported or manufactured." [13] If a manufacturer meets this condition, then it is not required to obtain a "dealer's license," in which case it would likely be excluded from the definition of "seller" under the PLCAA.

Although the PLCAA defines "negligent entrustment" as "the supplying of a qualified product by a seller for use by another person when the seller knows, or reasonably should know, the person to whom the product is supplied is likely to, and does, use the product in a manner involving unreasonable risk of physical injury to the person or others,"[14] a plaintiff's claim of negligent entrustment will be asserted under state law. For example, Washington state courts have held that a common law tort claim of negligent entrustment can be brought against both retail firearms dealers and manufacturers.[15] However, even if a state has its own interpretation and permits a suit for negligent entrustment to proceed against a manufacturer, the federal definition of "seller" might preclude such a suit.[16] This means that a manufacturer excepted from the federal requirement to obtain a "dealer's license," as described above, *would not* qualify as a "seller" under PLCAA and therefore would continue to be immune from suits for negligent entrustment. Alternatively, a manufacturer who is licensed as a dealer under federal law *would* qualify as a "seller" and would be subject to suits for negligent entrustment.

Under the second exception, a "seller" may also be subject to an action for "negligence per se," a term that the PLCAA does not define. This term generally means "[n]egligence established as a matter of law, so that breach of the duty is not a jury question."[17] In other words, a court could adopt the requirements of a legislative enactment or regulation as the standard of conduct for a reasonable person.[18] If it does so, then the individual who violates the legislation or regulation is automatically deemed negligent and the jury is not asked to determine if such individual acted in a reasonable manner.[19] Thus, whether a violation of a statute constitutes negligence per se is a question of state law.[20] Accordingly, a plaintiff may proceed under the second exception of the PLCAA if he alleges that the seller violated a statute and that relevant statute provides that one may be held strictly liable for violating the particular statute or regulation. Conversely, if applicable state law allows the question of negligence to go to the jury even when the defendant has violated a statute or regulation—in other words, there is no negligence per se rule—then the second exception would not apply and such a suit would be barred by the PLCAA unless it qualified as an another listed exception.

Third Exception: An action in which a manufacturer or seller of a qualified product violated a state or federal law applicable to the sale or marketing of the product, and the violation was a proximate cause of the harm for which relief is sought including:

(i) any case in which the manufacturer or seller knowingly made any false entry in, or failed to make appropriate entry in, any record required to be kept under Federal or State law with respect to the qualified product, or aided, abetted, or conspired with any person in making any false or fictitious oral or written statement with respect to any fact material to the lawfulness of the sale or other disposition of a qualified product; or

(ii) any case in which the manufacturer or seller aided, abetted, or conspired with any other person to sell or otherwise dispose of a qualified product, knowing, or having reasonable cause to believe, that the actual buyer of the qualified product was prohibited from possessing or receiving a firearm or ammunition under 18 U.S.C. § 922 (g) or (n).

This third exception to the PLCAA is known as the "predicate exception," because it essentially requires the plaintiff to assert, as part of her claim, that the manufacturer or seller knowingly committed a violation of an underlying statute, *i.e.*, a "predicate statute." A case that proceeds under the third exception has often turned on whether the predicate statute is "applicable to the sale or marketing of the product."

The U.S. Court of Appeals for the Second Circuit (Second Circuit) in *City of New York v. Beretta U.S.A. Corp.* held that the PLCAA barred the action because the criminal nuisance law upon which the City relied "does not fall within the contours of the Act's predicate exception."[21] The City had alleged that the firearms suppliers violated the State of New York's criminal nuisance provision, which provides that one is guilty of such an offense if, by conduct that is "either unlawful in itself or unreasonable under all circumstances, knowingly or recklessly creates or maintains a condition which endangers the safety or health of a considerable number of persons ... "[22] While the City acknowledged that the criminal nuisance statute was one of general applicability, it argued that the provisions could be applied to the sale or marketing and thus fell within the predicate exception. The firearms suppliers, on the other hand, argued that the predicate exception "was intended to include statutes that specifically and expressly regulate the firearms industry."[23] The Second Circuit, in determining the meaning of a law "applicable to the sale or marketing of [firearms]," agreed with neither the City nor the firearms suppliers.[24] Rather, the court concluded that the predicate exception: (1) does not include the New York criminal nuisance law asserted by the plaintiffs; (2) does encompass statutes that expressly regulate firearms, or that have been declared by courts to apply to the sale and marketing of firearms; and (3) does cover statutes that do not expressly regulate firearms, but that clearly implicate the purchase and sale of firearms.[25]

Similarly, the U.S. Court of Appeals for the Ninth Circuit (Ninth Circuit) in *Ileto v. Glock* rejected the plaintiffs' claim that California's public nuisance statutes can be predicate statutes that are encompassed under the PLCAA's third exception. The parties disputed whether the California tort statutes are "applicable to the sale or marketing of [firearms],"[26] and each side advanced an interpretation of "applicable" similar to their counterparts in *City of New York*. The Ninth Circuit also found that the term "'applicable' has a spectrum of meanings, including the two poles identified by the parties."[27] The court in *Ileto* declared that the PLCAA preempted common law claims, like general tort theories of liability, even if such claims are codified by state law, as is the case in California.[28] However, the Ninth Circuit did not go as far as the Second Circuit to outline the contours of the types of laws that might be acceptable as predicate statutes under the exception. Rather, it declined to "express any view on the scope of the predicate exception with respect to any other statute."[29]

Although the federal courts have rejected both criminal and public nuisance laws as statutes that would be encompassed by the predicate exception, it appears that only one state court reached the opposite conclusion. The State of Indiana court of appeals in *Smith & Wesson Corp. v. City of Gary, Indiana* rejected the manufacturers' argument that the term "applicable" is limited to those statutes that regulate the manner in which a firearm is sold or marketed, *i.e.*, "statutes specifying when, where, how, and to whom a firearm may be sold or marketed."[30] Rather, the court found that "on the face of the [predicate exception's language], Indiana's public nuisance statute appears applicable to the sale or marketing of firearms."[31] Furthermore, the court did not believe that the PLCAA requires an underlying violation of a statute applicable to the sale or marketing of firearms because "unlawful conduct was not a requirement of a public nuisance claim."[32] However, the appeals court recognized that even if the PLCAA were to require an underlying violation of a statute *directly* applicable to the sale of a firearm, the City already had alleged such violations in its complaint.[33] Despite reaching the opposite conclusion, the Ninth Circuit in *Ileto*, remarked that that this case was of "limited persuasive value," because the court's decision was based, in part, on the fact that the plaintiffs in *City of Gary* had alleged violations of the state's statutory firearms regulations, which did not occur in the Ninth Circuit case.[34]

As indicated by these cases, plaintiffs who have brought challenges under the predicate exception generally have not been successful.[35] Yet, the New York State appellate division in *Williams v. Beemiller, Inc.*, allowed a civil suit against a manufacturer, distributor, and dealer to proceed under the predicate exception.[36] The complaint listed several causes of action, including that the defendants had intentionally violated federal, state, and local legislative enactments by permitting straw purchases to occur, *i.e.*, the sale of firearms to an individual who purchased firearms on behalf of another whom the dealer knew or had reasonable cause to believe was ineligible to purchase weapons.[37] The court held that the claims were not barred by the PLCAA because the plaintiffs had sufficiently alleged facts to support a finding that the defendants knowingly violated the Gun Control Act, which makes it unlawful for any licensee to knowingly make any false entry in, or fail to properly maintain, any record that he is legally required to keep.[38] Unlike the rejected nuisance laws, the court, by allowing the suit to proceed, acknowledged that provisions of the Gun Control Act are "applicable to firearms" sales and therefore could be used as predicate statutes for the predicate exception.[39] Although the plaintiffs overcame this procedural hurdle, they must still demonstrate that the defendant knowingly violated the federal statute and that violation of the statute was the "proximate cause" of their injuries.[40] If the plaintiffs prevail in the *Williams* case, the door to civil litigation against licensed firearms suppliers might be once again slightly opened, as others could take similar action based on the same grounds.

Fourth Exception: An action for breach of contract or warranty in connection with the purchase of the product.

Fifth Exception: An action for death, physical injuries or property damage resulting directly from a defect in design or manufacture of the product, when used as intended or in a reasonably foreseeable manner, except that where the discharge of the product was caused by a volitional act that constituted a criminal offense, then such act shall be considered the sole proximate cause of any resulting death, personal injuries or property damage.

The fourth and fifth exceptions appear to be straightforward in that they permit breach of contract or warranty actions against a seller as well as tort actions for injuries incurred as a result of a design defect or manufacturing defect. Notably, there is an exception to the fifth exception. The exception appears to preclude a suit "where the discharge of the product was caused by a volitional act that constituted a criminal offense" because that act would be considered "the sole proximate cause of any resulting death, personal injuries, or property damage." For example, if a criminal fired a gun without aiming at his victim, but the bullet hit the victim as a result of a manufacturing or design defect, then the injured person would be statutorily barred from a suit against the manufacturer. However, if a criminal used a gun while committing an offense and the gun fired spontaneously without his pulling the trigger, different questions may be raised. Would committing the offense constitute a "volitional act" that would immunize the manufacturer from suit? Additionally, does the phrase "constituted a criminal offense" mean that the criminal had to have been convicted by proof beyond a reasonable doubt as required in criminal prosecution, or merely that the plaintiff would have to prove, by a preponderance of the evidence (the standard for civil suits), that the defendant's volitional act constituted a criminal offense? If the latter, would the plaintiff be permitted to prove in a civil suit that the criminal's volitional act constituted a criminal offense even if the criminal had been previously acquitted for that offense?

> **Sixth Exception**: An action or proceeding commenced by the Attorney General to enforce the provisions of chapter 44 of title 18 or chapter 53 of title 26.

The last exception to the PLCAA is also straightforward. The act does not prevent the Attorney General from enforcing the relevant Gun Control Act[41] or National Firearms Act[42] against federal firearms licensees through the administrative or civil proceedings provided for in those statutes.

CONCLUSION

Many civil lawsuits against federal firearms licensees have been dismissed since the enactment of the PLCAA. It may be the case that entities or individuals have been deterred from bringing suit due to the federal provision or from other plaintiffs' lack of success under the statutory exceptions. In the past year, however, at least one court has permitted a lawsuit to proceed under the predicate exception, finding that provisions of the Gun Control Act are "applicable to the sale or marketing of guns," and therefore may be used as the underlying predicate statute to assert a state tort law claim against a federal firearms licensee. Yet, whether the plaintiffs are able to prove their claims will likely depend on their success in the discovery process, in which case they may face other procedural obstacles to obtaining information.

End Notes

[1] P.L. 109-92 (2005), *codified at* 15 U.S.C. § 7901 *et seq.*

[2] 15 U.S.C. § 7902(b).

[3] *See, e.g.*, City of Cincinnati v. Beretta U.S.A. Corp., 768 N.E.2d 1136 (Ohio 2002) (appellate court reversing lower court dismissal and holding that distributors could be held liable for creating alleged nuisance); NAACP v. AcuSport, Inc., 271 F.Supp. 2d 435 (E.D.N.Y. 2003) (gun industry held to have created public nuisance after trial; case dismissed due to lack of organizational standing); Jefferson v. Rossi, No. 01-CV-2536, 2002 WL 32154285, (E.D. Pa. Jan. 22, 2002).

[4] 15 U.S.C. § 7901(a)(5).

[5] "Lawsuit Reform Legislation Introduced," *U.S. Fed News* (Feb. 16, 2005). In contrast to the legislation that was ultimately enacted, other Members in prior years had introduced legislation that would expressly permit a state, or an individual injured from the discharge of a firearm, to bring a lawsuit against a manufacturer, distributor of firearms if they were negligent in a firearm's manufacture, distribution or sale. *See, e.g.*, the Firearms Industry

Responsibility Enforcement Act, H.R. 1049, 106th Cong., 1st sess. (1999); the Gun Industry Responsibility Act, H.R. 1086, 106th Cong., 1st sess. (1999); the Firearm Rights, Responsibilities, and Remedies Act, H.R. 1233 (106th Cong., 1st sess. (1999).

[6] "Brady Campaign to Prevent Gun Violence: Extreme Gun Lobby Trying Again to Protect Reckless Gun Dealers," *U.S. Newswire* (Feb. 16, 2005).

[7] 15 U.S.C. § 7902(a).

[8] *Id.* at § 7903(5)(A). A "qualified product" means a firearm, including any antique firearm, or ammunition as defined in title 18 of the U.S. Code, or a component part of a firearm or ammunition, that has been shipped or transported in interstate or foreign commerce. *Id.* at § 7903(4). The term "unlawful misuse" is defined as "conduct that violates a statute, ordinance, or regulation as it relates to the use of a qualified product." *Id.* at § 7903(9).

[9] *Id.* at § 7903(5)(a)(i)-(vi).

[10] A "crime of violence" is defined as an offense that is a felony and "(A) has an element of use, attempted use, or threatened use of physical force against the person or property of another; or (B) that by its nature, involves a substantial risk that physical force against the person or property of another may be used in the course of committing the offense." 18 U.S.C. § 924(c)(3). A "drug trafficking crime" is defined as "any felony punishable under the Controlled Substances Act (21 U.S.C. § 801 *et seq*), the Controlled Substances Import and Export Act (21 U.S.C. § 951 *et seq*), or the Maritime Drug Law Enforcement Act (46 U.S.C. App. 1901 *et seq*)." 18 U.S.C. § 924(c)(2).

[11] 18 U.S.C. § 921(a)(11).

[12] 27 C.F.R. § 478.41(b). ("Payment of the license fee as an importer or manufacturer of destructive devices, ammunition for destructive devices or armor piercing ammunition or as a dealer in destructive devices *includes the privilege of importing or manufacturing firearms* other than destructive devices and ammunition ..., *or dealing in firearms* other than destructive devices, as the case may be, by such a licensee *at the licensed premises*.") (emphasis added).

[13] *Id.*

[14] 15 U.S.C. § 7903(5)(B).

[15] *See* Berthony v. Walt Failor's, Inc., 653 P.2d 280 (Wash. 1980) (holding that firearms dealers (1) owe a common law duty not to provide weapons to unfit persons and (2) owe a common law duty to third parties injured by weapons made available to an unfit person by a firearms dealer). *See also* Johnson v. Bulls Eye Shooter Supply, No. 03-2-093932-8, 2003 WL 21629244, at *4 (Wash. Jun. 27, 2003) (citing *Knott v. Liberty Jewelry and Loan, Inc.*, 748 P.2d 661 (Wash. Ct. App. 1988), as not precluding civil actions against retail dealers or manufacturers of firearms).

[16] U.S. Const., art. VI, cl. 2. ("This Constitution, and the Laws of the United States which shall be made in Pursuance thereof; and all Treaties made, or which shall be made, under the Authority of the United States, shall be the supreme Law of the Land; and the Judges in every State shall be bound thereby, any Thing in the Constitution or Laws of any State to the Contrary notwithstanding.").

[17] Black's Law Dictionary (7th ed. 1999) at 1057 ("Negligence per se usually arises from a statutory violation." *Id.*).

[18] Restatement (Second) of Torts § 286 (1965). A court may choose to adopt a law or regulation for the standard of a reasonable person if the law's purpose is found to be, exclusively or in part, "(a) to protect a class of persons which includes the one whose interest is invaded, (b) to protect the particular interest which is invaded, (c) to protect that interest against the kind

of arm harm which has resulted, and (d) to protect that interest against the particular hazard from which the harm results." *Id*.

[19] *Id*. at § 288B(1). This is the rule in followed in a majority of courts. *See* Stuart M. Speiser, Charles F. Krause and Alfred W. Gans, 2 The American Law of Torts (1985 cum. supp. 1998) at 1029. However, some courts appear to have limited the "per se" rule to situations where there has been a violation of a *specific* requirement of a law, *i.e.*, legislation that expresses rules of conduct in specific and concrete terms as opposed to general or abstract principles. *Id*. at 1034- 35.

[20] The statute in question in a negligence per se claim is most frequently statutes adopted by state legislatures, "but equally applies to regulations adopted by state administrative bodies, ordinances adopted by local councils, and federal statutes as well as regulations promulgated by federal agencies." Restatement (Third) of Torts: Liability for Physical and Emotional Harm § 14 cmt. a (2010).

[21] City of New York v. Beretta U.S.A. Corp., 524 F.3d 384, 390 (2d. Cir. 2008) (also holding that the PLCAA is a valid exercise of the powers granted to Congress pursuant to the Commerce Clause and that the act does not violate the doctrine of separation of powers or otherwise offend the Constitution), *cert. denied* New York v. Beretta U.S.A. Corp., 2009 U.S. LEXIS 1833 (U.S. Mar. 9, 2009).

[22] *Id*. at 399. (*citing* New York Penal Code § 240.45(1)).

[23] *Id*.

[24] The court found the firearms suppliers' reading of the PLCAA's third exception—i.e., that the predicate statute must expressly refer to the firearms industry—too narrow. Similarly, it found that the City's reading of the PLCAA exception—i.e., that the statute need only be "capable of being applied"—too broad. *Id*. at 400.

[25] *Id*. at 404.

[26] Ileto v. Glock, 565 F.3d 1126, 1133 (9th Cir. 2009), *cert. denied* Ileto v. Glock, 2010 U.S. LEXIS 4308 (U.S., May 24, 2010).

[27] *Id*. at 1134.

[28] *Id*. at 1135-36. The Ninth Circuit noted that the PLCAA's second exception further bolstered its conclusion that Congress intended to preempt common law claims, because the second exception, which only allows the common law claims of negligent entrustment and negligence per se, "demonstrates that Congress consciously considered how to treat tort claims." *Id*. at 1136 n.6. Furthermore, the court stated that accepting the plaintiffs' argument of recognizing codified common law claims but not non-codified common law claims under the predicate exception would lead to "a result that is difficult to square with Congress' intention to create national uniformity." *Id*. at 1136.

[29] *Id*. at 1138 n.9.

[30] Smith & Wesson Corp. v. City of Gary, Indiana, 875 N.E.2d 422 (Ind. Ct. App. 2007).

[31] *Id*. at 432.

[32] *Id*. (quoting the Indiana Supreme Court who declared "generally, gun regulatory laws leave room for the defendants to be in compliance with those regulations while still acting unreasonably and creating a public nuisance." City of Gary ex rel. King v. Smith & Wesson Corp., 801 N.E.2d 1222, 1232-33, 1235 (Ind. 2003)).

[33] *Id*. at 433.

[34] *Ileto*, 565 F.3d at 1135 n.5 ("Indeed, the *City of Gary* court distinguished the facts of this case on that basis [citation omitted] ("Here, unlike in *Ileto*, the City alleged activity on the part of the Manufacturers that facilitates unlawful sales and violates regulatory statutes.")).

[35] *See, e.g.,* District of Columbia v. Beretta U.S.A. Corp., 940 A.2d 163, 170-71 (D.C. 2008) (holding that the District of Columbia's Assault Weapons Manufacturing Strict Liability Act of 1990 does not qualify as a predicate statute because it does not impose any duty on firearms manufacturers or sellers to operate in any particular manner or according to any standards of reasonableness and that Congress could not have intended "to exempt an action founded on so attenuated a connection between statutory 'violation' and an injury from the reach of those civil actions the PLCAA proscribes.").

[36] 2012 N.Y. App. Div. LEXIS 6683; 952 N.Y.S.2d 333 (Oct. 5, 2012). The plaintiffs, an injured student and his father, alleged that the licensed dealer sold 87 handguns, including the weapon used to shoot the student in 2003, to a gun trafficker in one transaction in Ohio, as well as more than 50 additional sales within a period of months.

[37] *Id.* at *3-4.

[38] *Id.* at *10. *See* 18 U.S.C. § 922(m) (unlawful for any federal firearms licensee knowingly to make any false entry in, or fail to appropriately maintain, any record which he is required to keep by law). *See also* 18 U.S.C. § 923(g) (requires a federal firearms licensee to maintain records on the identity of an individual to whom he transfers firearms).

[39] *Id.* at *7-8.("[W]e agree with plaintiffs that the court erred in dismissing the complaint in asmuch as [the plaintiffs] sufficiently alleged that defendants knowingly violated various federal and state statutes applicable to the sale or marketing of firearms within the meaning of the PLCAA's predicate exception.").

[40] Any plaintiff could encounter difficulty proving his case because there are federal restrictions on the admissibility of certain firearms data in state or federal court proceedings. Firearms trace data is generally accumulated when investigators recover guns at a crime scene and trace the commercial trail of the gun to its first retail purchaser from a licensed dealer. This information is gathered and maintained by the Bureau of Alcohol, Tobacco, Firearms and Explosives (ATF). The restriction on the accessibility and use of this data is part of an appropriations restriction known as the Tiahrt amendment that was first passed in 2003. Currently, the appropriations restriction provides, in relevant part:

[N]o funds appropriated under this or any other Act may be used to disclose part or all of the contents of the Firearms Trace System ... and all such data shall be immune from legal process, shall not be subject to subpoena or other discovery, shall be inadmissible in evidence, and shall not be used, relied on, or disclosed in any manner, nor shall testimony or other evidence be permitted based on the data, in a civil action in any State (including the District of Columbia) or Federal court or an administrative proceeding other than a proceeding commenced by the [ATF]...

Continuing Appropriations Resolutions, 2013, P.L. 112-175 (2012) (*referring to* P.L. 112-55; 125 Stat. 609-610 (2012)).

[41] Gun Control Act, *codified at* 18 U.S.C. § 921 *et seq.*

[42] National Firearms Act, *codified at* 26 U.S.C. § 5801 *et seq.*

In: Firearms in America   ISBN: 978-1-63117-823-8
Editor: Alfonso D. Sutton   © 2014 Nova Science Publishers, Inc.

Chapter 7

FIREARM VIOLENCE, 1993-2011[*]

Michael Planty and Jennifer L. Truman

In 2011, a total of 478,400 fatal and nonfatal violent crimes were committed with a firearm (table 1). Homicides made up about 2% of all firearm-related crimes. There were 11,101 firearm homicides in 2011, down by 39% from a high of 18,253 in 1993 (figure 1). The majority of the decline in firearm-related homicides occurred between 1993 and 1998. Since 1999, the number of firearm homicides increased from 10,828 to 12,791 in 2006 before declining to 11,101 in 2011.

Nonfatal firearm-related violent victimizations against persons age 12 or older declined 70%, from 1.5 million in 1993 to 456,500 in 2004 (figure 2). The number then fluctuated between about 400,000 to 600,000 through 2011.[1] While the number of firearm crimes declined over time, the percentage of all violence that involved a firearm did not change substantively, fluctuating between 6% and 9% over the same period. In 1993, 9% of all violence was committed with a firearm, compared to 8% in 2011.

The primary source of information on firearm-related homicides was obtained from mortality data based on death certificates in the National Vital Statistics System of the National Center for Health Statistics (NCHS), Centers for Disease Control and Prevention's (CDC) Web-based Injury Statistics Query and Reporting System (WISQARS). These mortality data include

---

[*] This is an edited, reformatted and augmented version of special report NCJ 241730, released by the U.S. Department of Justice, Office of Justice Programs, Bureau of Justice Statistics, May 2013.

causes of death reported by attending physicians, medical examiners, and coroners, and demographic information about decedents reported by funeral directors who obtain that information from family members and other informants. The NCHS collects, compiles, verifies, and prepares these data for release to the public.

HIGHLIGHTS

- Firearm-related homicides declined 39%, from 18,253 in 1993 to 11,101 in 2011.
- Nonfatal firearm crimes declined 69%, from 1.5 million victimizations in 1993 to 467,300 victimizations in 2011.
- For both fatal and nonfatal firearm victimizations, the majority of the decline occurred during the 10-year period from 1993 to 2002.
- Firearm violence accounted for about 70% of all homicides and less than 10% of all nonfatal violent crime from 1993 to 2011.
- About 70% to 80% of firearm homicides and 90% of nonfatal firearm victimizations were committed with a handgun from 1993 to 2011.
- From 1993 to 2010, males, blacks, and persons ages 18 to 24 had the highest rates of firearm homicide.
- In 2007-11, about 23% of victims of nonfatal firearm crime were injured.
- About 61% of nonfatal firearm violence was reported to the police in 2007-11.
- In 2007-11, less than 1% of victims in all nonfatal violent crimes reported using a firearm to defend themselves during the incident.
- In 2004, among state prison inmates who possessed a gun at the time of offense, less than 2% bought their firearm at a flea market or gun show and 40% obtained their firearm from an illegal source.

The estimates of nonfatal violent victimization are based on data from the Bureau of Justice Statistics' (BJS) National Crime Victimization Survey (NCVS), which collects information on nonfatal crimes against persons age 12 or older reported and not reported to the police from a nationally representative sample of U.S. households. Homicide rates are presented per 100,000 persons and the nonfatal victimization rates are presented per 1,000 persons age 12 or older.

Additional information on firearm violence in this report comes from the School-Associated Violent Deaths Surveillance Study (SAVD), the FBI's Supplemental Homicide Reports (SHR), the Survey of Inmates in State Correctional Facilities (SISCF), and the Survey of Inmates in Federal Correctional Facilities (SIFCF).

Each source provides different information about victims and incident characteristics. Estimates are shown for different years based on data availability and measures of reliability. (For more information about these sources, see *Methodology*.)

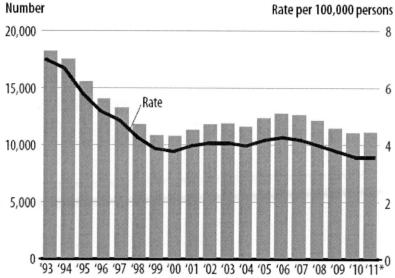

Note: Excludes homicides due to legal intervention and operations of war. See appendix table 1 for numbers and rates.

* Preliminary estimates retrieved from Hoyert DL, Xu JQ. (2012) Deaths: Preliminary data for 2011. *National Vital Statistics Reports*, 61(6).

Source: Centers for Disease Control and Prevention, National Center for Injury Prevention and Control. Web-based Injury Statistics Query and Reporting System (WISQARS), 1993–2010. Retrieved March 2013 from www.cdc.gov/ncipc/wisqars.

Figure 1. Firearm homicides, 1993–2011.

Table 1. Criminal firearm violence, 1993–2011

| Year | Total fatal and nonfatal firearm violence | Number | | | Rate of nonfatal firearm victimization[c] | Percent | |
		Firearm homicides	Nonfatal firearm victimizations[a]	Nonfatal firearm incidents[b]		All violence involving firearms	All firearm violence that was homicide
1993	1,548,000	18,253	1,529,700	1,222,700	7.3	9.2%	1.2%
1994	1,585,700	17,527	1,568,200	1,287,200	7.4	9.3	1.1
1995	1,208,800	15,551	1,193,200	1,028,900	5.5	7.9	1.3
1996	1,114,800	14,037	1,100,800	939,500	5.1	7.9	1.3
1997	1,037,300	13,252	1,024,100	882,900	4.7	7.7	1.3
1998	847,200	11,798	835,400	673,300	3.8	7.0	1.4
1999	651,700	10,828	640,900	523,600	2.9	6.1	1.7
2000	621,000	10,801	610,200	483,700	2.7	7.3	1.7
2001	574,500	11,348	563,100	507,000	2.5	7.7	2.0
2002	551,800	11,829	540,000	450,800	2.3	7.4	2.1
2003	479,300	11,920	467,300	385,000	2.0	6.2	2.5
2004	468,100	11,624	456,500	405,800	1.9	6.9	2.5
2005	515,900	12,352	503,500	446,400	2.1	7.4	2.4
2006	627,200	12,791	614,400	552,000	2.5	7.4	2.0
2007	567,400	12,632	554,800	448,400	2.2	8.3	2.2
2008	383,500	12,179	371,300	331,600	1.5	6.0	3.2
2009	421,600	11,493	410,100	383,400	1.6	7.4	2.7
2010	426,100	11,078	415,000	378,800	1.6	8.6	2.6
2011[d]	478,400	11,101	467,300	414,600	1.8	8.2	2.3

Note: See appendix table 3 for standard errors.

[a] A victimization refers to a single victim that experienced a criminal incident.

[b] An incident is a specific criminal act involving one or more victims or victimizations.

[c] Per 1,000 persons age 12 or older.

[d] Preliminary homicide estimates retrieved from Hoyert DL, Xu JQ. (2012) Deaths: Preliminary data for 2011. *National Vital Statistics Reports*, 61(6).

Sources: Bureau of Justice Statistics, National Crime Victimization Survey, 1993–2011; and Centers for Disease Control and Prevention, National Center for Injury Prevention and Control, Web-based Injury Statistics Query and Reporting System (WISQARS), 1993–2010. Retrieved March 2013 from www.cdc.gov/ncipc/wisqars.

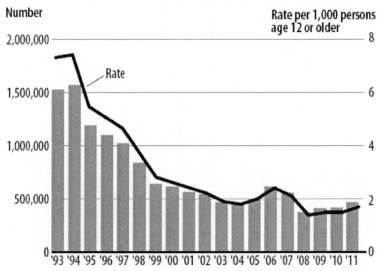

Note: See appendix table 2 for numbers, rates, and standard errors.
Source: Bureau of Justice Statistics, National Crime Victimization Survey, 1993–2011.

Figure 2. Nonfatal firearm victimizations, 1993–2011.

Trend estimates of nonfatal firearm violence are presented as annual 1-year averages or 2-year rolling averages, as noted in each table or figure. For ease of presentation, 2-year estimates are referenced according to the most recent year. For example, estimates reported for 2011 represent the average estimates for 2010 and 2011. Other tables in this report focus on a single 5-year aggregate period from 2007 through 2011. These approaches—using rolling averages and aggregating years—increase the reliability and stability of estimates, which facilitiates comparisons over time and between subgroups.

THE MAJORITY OF FIREARM CRIMES WERE COMMITTED WITH A HANDGUN

From 1993 to 2011, about 60% to 70% of homicides were committed with a firearm (table 2). Over the same period, between 6% and 9% of all nonfatal violent victimizations were committed with a firearm, with about 20% to 30% of robberies and 22% to 32% of aggravated assaults involving a firearm.

Table 2. Percent of violence involving a firearm, by type of crime, 1993–2011

Year	Homicide	Nonfatal violence[a]	Robbery	Aggravated assault
1993	71.2%	9.1%	22.3%	30.7%
1994	71.4	9.2	27.1	31.9
1995	69.0	7.8	27.3	28.0
1996	68.0	7.8	24.6	25.7
1997	68.0	7.6	19.9	27.0
1998	65.9	7.0	20.1	26.5
1999	64.1	6.0	19.2	22.4
2000	64.4	7.2	21.1	26.6
2001[b]	55.9	7.5	29.5	26.0
2002	67.1	7.3	23.4	28.7
2003	67.2	6.1	22.4	22.2
2004	67.0	6.8	19.7	23.6
2005	68.2	7.2	21.8	25.7
2006	68.9	7.3	16.6	24.3
2007	68.8	8.1	20.0	32.6
2008	68.3	5.8	19.6	24.6
2009	68.4	7.2	27.0	23.2
2010	68.1	8.4	24.7	25.4
2011[c]	69.6	8.0	25.7	30.6

Note: See appendix table 4 for standard errors.

[a] Nonfatal violence includes rape, sexual assault, robbery, aggravated and simple assault. A small percentage of rape and sexual assaults involved firearms but are not shown in table due to small sample sizes.

[b] The homicide estimates that occurred as a result of the events of September 11, 2001, are included in the total number of homicides.

[c] Preliminary homicide estimates retrieved from Hoyert DL, Xu JQ. (2012) Deaths: Preliminary data for 2011. *National Vital Statistics Reports*, 61(6).

Sources: Bureau of Justice Statistics, National Crime Victimization Survey, 1993–2011; and Centers for Disease Control and Prevention, National Center for Injury Prevention and Control, Web-based Injury Statistics Query and Reporting System (WISQARS), 1993–2010. Retrieved March 2013 from www.cdc.gov/ncipc/wisqars.

Handguns accounted for the majority of both homicide and nonfatal firearm violence (table 3). A handgun was used in about 83% of all firearm homicides in 1994, compared to 73% in 2011. Other types of firearms, such as shotguns and rifles, accounted for the remainder of firearm homicides. For nonfatal firearm violence, about 9 in 10 were committed with a handgun, and this remained stable from 1994 to 2011.

Table 3. Criminal firearm violence, by type of firearm, 1994–2011

Year	Homicide				Nonfatal violence					
	Handgun		Other firearm*		Handgun		Other firearm*		Gun type unknown	
	Annual number	Percent	Annual number	Percent	Average Annual Number	Percent	Average Annual Number	Percent	Average Annual Number	Percent
1994	13,510	82.7%	2,830	17.3%	1,387,100	89.5%	150,200	9.7%	11,700!	0.8%!
1995	12,090	81.9	2,670	18.1	1,240,200	89.8	132,800	9.6	7,700!	0.6!
1996	10,800	81.1	2,510	18.9	999,600	87.1	141,000	12.3	6,400!	0.6!
1997	9,750	78.8	2,630	21.2	894,200	84.2	159,800	15.0	8,400!	0.8!
1998	8,870	80.4	2,160	19.6	783,400	84.3	141,100	15.2	5,300!	0.6!
1999	8,010	78.8	2,150	21.2	659,600	89.4	74,100	10.0	4,500!	0.6!
2000	8,020	78.6	2,190	21.4	555,800	88.8	65,300	10.4	4,500!	0.7!
2001	7,820	77.9	2,220	22.1	506,600	86.3	65,900	11.2	14,100!	2.4!
2002	8,230	75.8	2,620	24.2	471,600	85.5	63,200	11.5	16,700!	3.0!
2003	8,890	80.3	2,180	19.7	436,100	86.6	53,200	10.6	14,400!	2.9!
2004	8,330	78.0	2,350	22.0	391,700	84.8	53,400	11.6	16,900!	3.7!
2005	8,550	75.1	2,840	24.9	410,600	85.5	56,200	11.7	13,200!	2.8!
2006	9,060	77.0	2,700	23.0	497,400	89.0	47,600	8.5	14,000!	2.5!
2007	8,570	73.6	3,080	26.4	509,700	87.2	65,600	11.2	9,300!	1.6!
2008	7,930	71.8	3,120	28.2	400,700	86.5	57,400	12.4	5,000!	1.1!
2009	7,370	71.3	2,970	28.7	348,700	89.2	37,600	9.6	4,400!	1.1!
2010	6,920	69.6	3,030	30.4	382,100	92.6	26,700	6.5	3,800!	0.9!
2011	7,230	72.9	2,690	27.1	389,400	88.3	49,700	11.3	2,100!	0.5!

Note: Nonfatal violence data based on 2-year rolling averages beginning in 1993. Homicide data are presented as annual estimates. See appendix table 5 for standard errors.

* Includes rifle, shotgun, and other types of firearms.

! Interpret with caution. Estimate based on 10 or fewer sample cases, or coefficient of variation is greater than 50%.

Sources: Bureau of Justice Statistics, National Crime Victimization Survey, 1993–2011; and FBI, Supplementary Homicide Reports, 1994–2011.

MALES, BLACKS, AND PERSONS AGES 18 TO 24 WERE MOST LIKELY TO BE VICTIMS OF FIREARM VIOLENCE

Sex

In 2010, the rate of firearm homicide for males was 6.2 per 100,000, compared to 1.1 for females (figure 3). Firearm homicide for males declined by 49% (from 12.0 per 100,000 males in 1993 to 6.2 in 2010), compared to a 51% decline for females (from 2.3 per 100,000 females in 1993 to 1.1 in 2010). The majority of the decline for both males and females occurred in the first part of the period (1993 to 2000). Over the more recent 10-year period from 2001 to 2010, the decline in firearm homicide for both males and females slowed, resulting in about a 10% decline each.

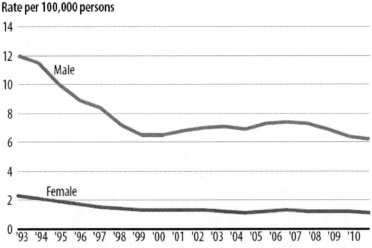

Note: See appendix table 6 for numbers and rates.

Source: Centers for Disease Control and Prevention, National Center for Injury Prevention and Control, Web-based Injury Statistics Query and Reporting System (WISQARS), 1993–2010. Retrieved March 2013 from www.cdc.gov/ncipc/wisqars.

Figure 3. Firearm homicides, by sex, 1993–2010.

In 2011, the rate of nonfatal firearm violence for males (1.9 per 1,000 males) was not significantly different than the rate for females (1.6 per 1,000) (figure 4). From 1994 to 2011, the rate of nonfatal firearm violence for males declined 81%, from 10.1 to 1.9 per 1,000 males. During the same period, the rate of nonfatal firearm violence against females dropped 67%, from 4.7 to 1.6 per 1,000 females. As with fatal firearm violence, the majority of the decline occurred in the first part of the period. From 2002 to 2011, the rate of nonfatal firearm violence for males declined 35%, while there was no no statistical change in the rate for females.

Rate per 1,000 persons age 12 or older

Note: Data based on 2-year rolling averages beginning in 1993. See appendix table 7 for rates and standard errors.

Source: Bureau of Justice Statistics, National Crime Victimization Survey, 1993–2011.

Figure 4. Nonfatal firearm violence, by sex, 1994–2011.

Race/Hispanic Origin

In 2010, the rate of firearm homicide for blacks was 14.6 per 100,000, compared to 1.9 for whites, 2.7 for American Indians and Alaska Natives, and 1.0 for Asians and Pacific Islanders (figure 5). From 1993 to 2010, the rate of firearm homicides for blacks declined by 51%, down from 30.1 per 100,000 blacks, compared to a 48% decline for whites and a 43% decline for American Indians and Alaska Natives. Asian and Pacific Islanders declined 79% over the same period, from 4.6 to 1.0 per 100,000. Although blacks experienced a decline similar to whites and American Indians and Alaska Natives, the rate of firearm homicide for blacks was 5 to 6 times higher than every other racial group in 2010. As with other demographic groups, the majority of the decline occurred in the first part of the period and slowed from 2001 to 2010.

The rate of firearm homicide for both Hispanics and non- Hispanics was about 4 per 100,000 each in 2010 (figure 6). However, the Hispanic rate had a larger and more consistent decline over time. The Hispanic rate declined 54% from 1993 to 2001 and declined 34% since 2001. In comparison, the non-Hispanic rate declined more slowly, down 42% from 1993 to 2001 and down 5% since 2001.

In 2011, non-Hispanic blacks (2.8 per 1,000) and Hispanics (2.2 per 1,000) had higher rates of nonfatal firearm violence than non-Hispanic whites (1.4 per 1,000) (figure 7). The rate of nonfatal firearm violence for Hispanics was not statistically different from the rate for blacks. From 1994 to 2011, the rates of nonfatal firearm violence for blacks and Hispanics both declined by 83%, compared to 74% for whites.

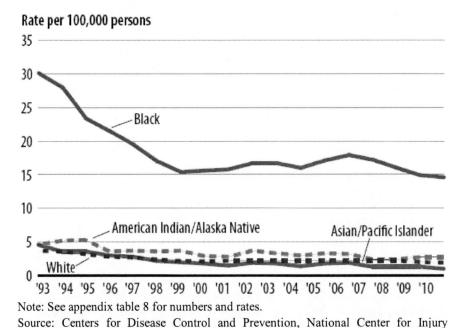

Note: See appendix table 8 for numbers and rates.

Source: Centers for Disease Control and Prevention, National Center for Injury Prevention and Control, Web-based Injury Statistics Query and Reporting System (WISQARS), 1993–2010. Retrieved March 2013 from www.cdc.gov/ncipc/wisqars.

Figure 5. Firearm homicides, by race, 1993–2010.

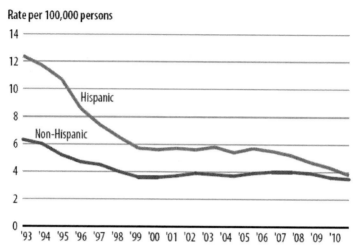

Note: See appendix table 9 for numbers and rates.

Source: Bureau of Justice Statistics, Centers for Disease Control and Prevention, National Center for Injury Prevention and Control, Web-based Injury Statistics Query and Reporting System (WISQARS), 1993–2010. Retrieved March 2013 from www.cdc.gov/ncipc/wisqars.

Figure 6. Firearm homicides, by Hispanic origin, 1993–2010.

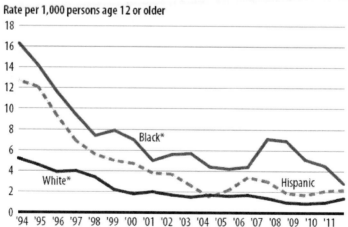

Note: Data based on 2-year rolling averages beginning in 1993. See appendix table 10 for rates and standard errors.

* Excludes persons of Hispanic or Latino origin.

Source: Bureau of Justice Statistics, National Crime Victimization Survey, 1993–2011.

Figure 7. Nonfatal firearm violence, by race and Hispanic origin, 1994–2011.

Age

In 2010, the rate of firearm homicide was 10.7 per 100,000 for persons ages 18 to 24, compared to 8.1 for persons ages 25 to 34 and 0.3 for persons age 11 or younger (table 4). Firearm homicide against persons ages 18 to 34 accounted for about 30% of all firearm homicides in 2010. From 1993 to 2010, the rate of homicides for persons ages 18 to 24 declined 51%, compared to a 35% decline for persons ages 25 to 34 and 50% for persons age 11 or younger.

In 2011, persons ages 18 to 24 had the highest rate of nonfatal firearm violence (5.2 per 1,000). From 1994 to 2011, the rates of nonfatal firearm violence declined for persons ages 18 to 49, with each group declining between 72% and 77%. The rate for persons ages 12 to 17 declined 88%, from 11.4 to 1.4 per 1,000.

PERSONS LIVING IN URBAN AREAS HAD THE HIGHEST RATES OF NONFATAL FIREARM VIOLENCE

Region

In 2010, the South had the highest rate of firearm homicides at 4.4 per 100,000 persons, compared to 3.4 in the Midwest, 3.0 in the West, and 2.8 in the Northeast (figure 8).

From 1993 to 2010, the rate of firearm homicides in the South declined by 49%, compared to a 50% decline in the Northeast, a 37% decline in the Midwest, and a 59% decline in the West.

In 2011, residents in the South (1.9 per 1,000) had higher rates of nonfatal firearm violence than those in the Northeast (1.3 per 1,000) (figure 9). Residents in the South (1.9 per 1,000), Midwest (1.7 per 1,000), and West (1.8 per 1,000) had statistically similar rates of nonfatal firearm violence.

Urban-Rural Location

The publicly available National Vital Statistics System fatal data files do not contain information about the incident's urban-rural location or population size. This information is limited to nonfatal firearm victimizations. Urban residents generally experienced the highest rate of nonfatal firearm violence (figure 10). In 2011, the rate of nonfatal firearm violence for residents in urban areas was 2.5 per 1,000, compared to 1.4 per 1,000 for suburban residents and 1.2 for rural residents. From 1994 to 2011, the rates of nonfatal firearm violence for all three locations declined between 76% and 78%.

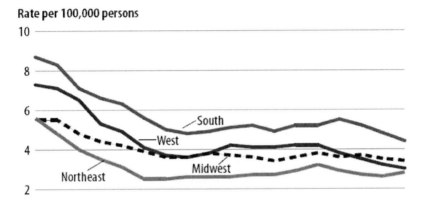

Note: See appendix table 13 for numbers and rates.
Source: Centers for Disease Control and Prevention, National Center for Injury Prevention and Control. Web-based Injury Statistics Query and Reporting System (WISQARS), 1993–2010. Retrieved March 2013 from www.cdc.gov/ncipc/wisqars).

Figure 8. Firearm homicides, by region, 1993–2011.

Population Size

In 2011, higher rates of nonfatal violence occurred in areas with a population of more than 250,000 residents than in areas with a population under 250,000 (table 5). From 1997 to 2011, the rates of nonfatal firearm violence for populations between 250,000 and 499,999 and 1 million residents or more declined between 57% and 62%, compared to a 37% decline for residents living in populations between 500,000 and 999,999 residents.

Table 4. Fatal and nonfatal firearm violence, by age, 1993–2011

Year	Firearm homicide rate per 100,000 persons						Nonfatal firearm violence rate per 1,000 persons age 12 or older				
	11 or younger	12–17	18–24	25–34	35–49	50 or older	12–17	18–24	25–34	35–49	50 or older
1993	0.5	8.0	21.9	12.4	6.7	2.2	~	~	~	~	~
1994	0.4	7.8	21.2	12.0	6.3	2.1	11.4	18.1	8.7	6.3	1.6
1995	0.4	7.0	18.6	10.6	5.3	2.0	9.8	16.1	7.7	5.5	1.6
1996	0.4	5.6	17.2	9.4	4.9	1.8	7.6	12.3	6.8	4.8	1.4
1997	0.4	4.8	16.3	9.0	4.6	1.6	7.1	12.8	5.4	4.5	1.2
1998	0.3	3.7	14.4	7.9	4.2	1.5	5.7	12.4	4.5	3.8	1.0
1999	0.3	3.6	12.4	7.6	3.7	1.4	4.7	8.9	4.6	2.6	0.7
2000	0.2	2.9	12.4	7.7	3.8	1.4	3.2	7.0	3.6	2.5	1.0
2001	0.3	2.8	12.9	8.4	3.9	1.3	2.2	6.8	3.1	2.4	1.0
2002	0.3	2.9	13.0	8.8	4.0	1.4	2.4	7.3	3.1	1.8	0.8
2003	0.3	2.7	13.3	9.0	4.0	1.3	2.8	6.3	2.7	1.6	0.7
2004	0.2	3.0	11.9	8.9	3.9	1.4	1.9	3.9	2.5	2.1	0.8
2005	0.2	3.1	12.9	9.6	4.1	1.3	1.2	4.4	3.1	1.8	1.0
2006	0.3	3.6	13.6	9.6	4.1	1.4	2.3	5.6	3.4	1.8	1.0
2007	0.3	3.5	13.1	9.5	4.2	1.3	4.3	4.6	3.0	2.2	0.9
2008	0.3	3.3	12.1	9.0	4.1	1.3	3.5	3.2	2.7	1.6	0.7
2009	0.3	2.9	11.1	8.1	3.9	1.4	0.9	3.9	2.3	1.5	0.6
2010	0.3	2.8	10.7	8.1	3.6	1.4	0.6!	5.8	2.0	1.3	0.6
2011	...	...	...	...	...	...	1.4	5.2	2.2	1.4	0.7

Note: Nonfatal firearm violence data based on 2-year rolling averages beginning in 1993. Homicide data are annual estimates. See appendix table 11 for firearm homicide numbers and appendix table 12 for nonfatal firearm violence standard errors.

~ Not applicable.

... Not available.

! Interpret with caution. Estimate based on 10 or fewer sample cases, or coefficient of variation is greater than 50%.

Source: Bureau of Justice Statistics, National Crime Victimization Survey, 1993–2011; and Centers for Disease Control and Prevention, National Center for Injury Prevention and Control. Web-based Injury Statistics Query and Reporting System (WISQARS), 1993–2010. Retrieved March 2013 from www.cdc.gov/ncipc/wisqars.

Table 5. Nonfatal firearm violence, by population size, 1997–2011

Year	Rate per 1,000 persons age 12 or older					
	Not a place*	Less than 100,000	100,000– 249,999	250,000– 499,999	500,000– 999,999	1 million or more
1997	3.9	3.8	7.0	10.3	7.3	7.3
1998	3.0	3.9	4.8	7.0	9.2	5.7
1999	1.9	3.1	3.1	5.5	9.0	6.4
2000	1.5	2.2	3.9	6.5	6.3	5.6
2001	1.4	2.1	4.1	6.1	5.5	5.1
2002	1.2	2.3	2.8	3.9	4.9	5.3
2003	1.4	2.0	2.8	3.3	5.1	3.6
2004	1.4	1.4	3.0	4.1	5.5	2.7
2005	1.2	1.6	2.9	3.6	4.5	4.6
2006	1.6	2.1	2.6	2.6	3.8	4.9
2007	1.5	2.6	2.7	2.4	5.4	2.1
2008	0.8	2.1	2.1	3.2	4.9	1.4
2009	0.9	1.1	2.2	3.0	4.0	3.5
2010	0.9	1.2	1.8	2.8	5.1	4.0
2011	1.4	1.2	1.3	3.9	4.6	3.2

Note: Data based on 2-year rolling averages beginning in 1996. Population size information was not available from 1993 to 1995. See appendix table 16 for rates and standard errors.

*A concentration of population that is not either legally bounded as an incorporated place having an active government or delineated for statistical purposes as a census designated place with definite geographic boundaries, such as a city, town, or village.

Source: Bureau of Justice Statistics, National Crime Victimization Survey, 1996–2011.

ABOUT 11% OF NONFATAL VIOLENCE COMMITTED BY A STRANGER INVOLVED A FIREARM

Intimate partners suffered about 4.7 million nonfatal violent victimizations in the 5-year period from 2007 through 2011, and the offender used a firearm in about 4% of these victimizations (about 195,700 incidents) (table 6). Similar to intimate partner violent victimizations, offenders who were either a relative or known to the victim (e.g., a friend or acquaintance) used a firearm in about 4% to 7% of these total victimizations. In comparison, persons victimized by strangers experienced about 11 million violent victimizations, and the offender used a firearm in 11% of these victimizations.[2]

Rate per 1,000 persons age 12 or older

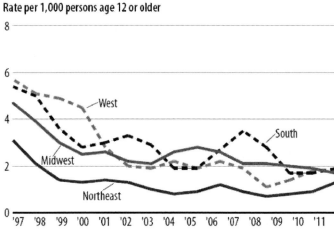

Note: Data based on 2-year rolling averages beginning in 1996. Region information was not available from 1993 to 1995. See appendix table 14 for rates and standard errors.

Source: Bureau of Justice Statistics, National Crime Victimization Survey, 1996–2011.

Figure 9. Nonfatal firearm violence, by region, 1997–2011.

Rate per 1,000 persons age 12 or older

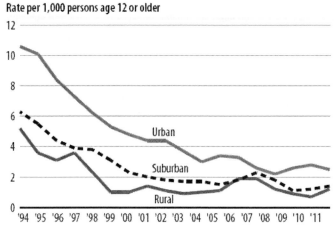

Note: Data based on 2-year rolling averages beginning in 1993. See appendix table 15 for rates and standard errors.

Source: Bureau of Justice Statistics, National Crime Victimization Survey, 1993–2011.

Figure 10. Nonfatal firearm violence, by urban-rural location, 1994–2011.

Table 6. Nonfatal firearm and nonfirearm violence, by victim-offender relationship, 2007–2011

Relationship to victim	Total nonfatal violence	Firearm violence		Nonfirearm violence	
		Number	Percent of total violence	Number	Percent of total violence
Total	29,611,300	2,218,500	7.5%	27,392,800	92.5%
Nonstranger	15,715,900	738,000	4.7	14,977,900	95.3
Intimate[a]	4,673,600	195,700	4.2	4,477,900	95.8
Other relative	2,157,700	158,100	7.3	1,999,500	92.7
Friend/acquaintance	8,884,600	384,100	4.3	8,500,500	95.7
Stranger	10,983,100	1,177,900	10.7	9,805,200	89.3
Unknown[b]	2,912,300	302,600	10.4	2,609,600	89.6

Note: Detail may not sum to total due to rounding. See appendix table 17 for standard errors.

[a] Includes current or former spouses, boyfriends, or girlfriends.

[b] Includes relationships unknown and number of offenders unknown.

Source: Bureau of Justice Statistics, National Crime Victimization Survey, 2007–2011.

Table 7. Nonfatal firearm and nonfirearm violence, by location of crime, 2007–2011

Location	Total nonfatal violence		Firearm violence		Nonfirearm violence	
	Number	Percent	Number	Percent	Number	Percent
Total	29,618,300	100%	2,218,500	100%	27,399,800	100%
Victims home or lodging	6,491,400	21.9	427,600	19.3	6,063,800	22.1
Near victim's home	4,804,700	16.2	504,500	22.7	4,300,200	15.7
In, at, or near a friend, neighbor, or relative's home	2,175,900	7.3	132,600	6.0	2,043,300	7.5
Commercial place	2,878,600	9.7	195,400	8.8	2,683,200	9.8
Parking lot or garage	1,688,400	5.7	340,600	15.4	1,347,900	4.9
School*	3,931,100	13.3	12,600 !	0.6 !	3,918,500	14.3
Open area, on street, or public transportation	4,636,900	15.7	508,400	22.9	4,128,500	15.1
Other location	3,011,200	10.2	96,800	4.4	2,914,400	10.6

! Interpret with caution. Estimate based on 10 or fewer sample cases, or coefficient of variation is greater than 50%. See appendix table 18 for standard errors.

* Includes inside a school building or on school property.
Source: Bureau of Justice Statistics, National Crime Victimization Survey, 2007–2011.

In 2007-11, the majority of nonfatal firearm violence occurred in or around the victim's home (42%) or in an open area, on the street, or while on public transportation (23%) (table 7). Less than 1% of all nonfatal firearm violence occurred in schools.

Table 8. School-associated homicides of youth ages 5 to 18, by location and school years, 1992–93 to 2009–10

School year	Homicides of youth ages 5 to 18		Percent of all homicides of youth at school
	Total homicides[a]	Homicides at school[b,c]	
1992–93	2,719	34	1.3%
1993–94	2,911	29	1.0
1994–95	2,691	28	1.0
1995–96	2,548	32	1.3
1996–97	2,210	28	1.3
1997–98	2,104	34	1.6
1998–99	1,791	33	1.8
1999–00	1,566	14	0.9
2000–01	1,501	14	0.9
2001–02	1,494	16	1.1
2002–03	1,538	18	1.2
2003–04	1,459	23	1.6
2004–05	1,545	22	1.4
2005–06	1,687	21	1.2
2006–07	1,796	32	1.8
2007–08	1,740	21	1.2
2008–09	1,579	17	1.1
2009–10	...	17	...

Note: At school includes on school property, on the way to or from regular sessions at school, and while attending or traveling to or from a school-sponsored event.
... Not available.
[a] Youth ages 5 to 18 from July 1, 1992, through June 30, 2009.
[b] Youth ages 5 to 18 from July 1, 1992, through June 30, 2010.
[c] The data from school year 1999–00 through 2009–10 are subject to change until interviews with school and law enforcement officials have been completed. The

details learned during the interviews can occasionally change the classification of a case.

Sources: Table 1.1 from Robers, S., Zhang, J., and Truman, J. (2012). *Indicators of School Crime and Safety: 2011* (NCES 2012-002/NCJ 236021). National Center for Education Statistics, U.S. Department of Education, and Bureau of Justice Statistics, Office of Justice Programs, U.S. Department of Justice. Homicide data are from: Centers for Disease Control and Prevention (CDC), 1992–2010 School-Associated Violent Deaths Surveillance Study (SAVD); FBI and Supplementary Homicide Reports (SHR), 1992–2009.

SCHOOL-RELATED HOMICIDES OF YOUTH AGES 5 TO 18 ACCOUNTED FOR LESS THAN 2% OF ALL YOUTH HOMICIDES

The number of homicides at schools declined over time, from an average of 29 per year in the 1990s (school year 1992-93 to 1999-00) to an average of 20 per year in the 2000s (school year 2000-01 to 2009-10) (table 8). Generally, homicides in schools comprised less than 2% of all homicides of youth ages 5 to 18. During the 2000s, an average of about 1,600 homicides of youth ages 5 to 18 occurred per year. The majority of homicides against youth both at school and away from school were committed with a firearm.

IN 2007-11, ABOUT 23% OF ALL NONFATAL FIREARM VICTIMS WERE INJURED

In 2007-11, about 23% of all nonfatal firearm victims were physically injured during the victimization (table 9). About 7% suffered serious injuries (e.g., a gunshot wound, broken bone, or internal injuries), while 16% suffered minor injuries (e.g., bruises or cuts). Of the nonfatal firearm victims who were injured, 72% received some type of care, with about 82% receiving care in a hospital or medical office.

The victim reported that the offender had fired the weapon in 7% of all nonfatal firearm victimizations. The victim suffered a gunshot wound in 28% of these victimizations (not shown in table).

Table 9. Nonfatal firearm and nonfirearm violence, by injury and treatment received, 2007–2011

Injury and treatment	Total nonfatal violence		Firearm violence		Nonfirearm violence	
	Number	Percent	Number	Percent	Number	Percent
Injury	29,618,300	100%	2,218,500	100%	27,399,800	100%
Not injured	22,187,500	74.9	1,707,800	77.0	20,479,700	74.7
Injured	7,430,800	25.1	510,700	23.0	6,920,100	25.3
Serious[a]	1,249,300	4.2	148,300	6.7	1,147,000	4.2
Gun shot	46,000	0.2	46,000	2.1	~	~
Minor[b]	5,742,700	19.4	357,100	16.1	5,385,700	19.7
Rape without other injuries	374,300	1.3	5,400 !	0.2 !	368,900	1.3
Treatment for injury[c]	7,430,800	100%	510,700	100%	6,920,100	100%
No treatment	4,304,300	57.9	140,700	27.5	4,163,600	60.2
Any treatment	3,103,500	41.8	370,000	72.5	2,733,500	39.5
Treatment setting[d]	3,103,500	100%	370,000	100%	2,733,500	100%
At the scene/ home of victim, neighbor, or friend/location	1,078,000	34.7	68,000	18.4	1,010,000	36.9
In doctor's office/hospital emergency room/overnight at hospital	2,025,600	65.3	302,000	81.6	1,723,500	63.1

Note: See appendix table 19 for standard errors.
! Interpret with caution. Estimate based on 10 or fewer sample cases, or coefficient of variation is greater than 50%.
~Not applicable.
[a] Includes injuries such as gun shots, knife wounds, internal injuries, unconsciousness, and broken bones.
[b] Includes bruises, cuts, and other minor injuries.
[c] Includes only victims who were injured.
[d] Includes only victims who were injured and received treatment.
Source: Bureau of Justice Statistics, National Crime Victimization Survey, 2007–2011.

THE MAJORITY OF FIREARM VIOLENCE IS REPORTED TO THE POLICE

In 2007-11, about 61% of nonfatal firearm violence was reported to the police, compared to 46% of nonfirearm violence (table 10). Among the nonfatal firearm victimizations that went unreported in 2007-11, the most common reasons victims gave for not reporting the crime was fear of reprisal (31%) and that the police could not or would not do anything to help (27%).

IN 2007-11, ABOUT 1% OF NONFATAL VIOLENT CRIME VICTIMS USED A FIREARM IN SELF DEFENSE

In 2007-11, there were 235,700 victimizations where the victim used a firearm to threaten or attack an offender (table 11). This amounted to approximately 1% of all nonfatal violent victimizations in the 5-year period. The percentage of nonfatal violent victimizations involving firearm use in self defense remained stable at under 2% from 1993 to 2011 (not shown in table). In 2007-11, about 44% of victims of nonfatal violent crime offered no resistance, 1% attacked or threatened the offender with another type of weapon, 22% attacked or threatened without a weapon (e.g., hit or kicked), and 26% used nonconfrontational methods (e.g., yelling, running, hiding, or arguing).

In instances where the victim was armed with a firearm, the offender was also armed with a gun in 32% of the victimizations, compared to 63% of victimizations where the offender was armed with a lesser weapon, such as a knife, or unarmed (not shown in table). A small number of property crime victims also used a firearm in self defense (103,000 victims or about 0.1% of all property victimizations); however, the majority of victims (86%) were not present during the incident. No information was available on the number of homicide victims that attempted to defend themselves with a firearm or by other means.

METHODOLOGY

Estimates in this report are based primarily on data from the Bureau of Justice Statistics' (BJS) National Crime Victimization Survey (NCVS) and the

National Center for Health Statistics' (NCHS) Centers for Disease Control and Prevention Center for Disease Control's Web-based Injury Statistics Query and Reporting System (WISQARS).

Additional estimates come from the School-Associated Violent Deaths Surveillance Study (SAVD), the National Electronic Injury Surveillance System All Injury Program (NEISS-AIP) data, the FBI's Supplemental Homicide Reports (SHR), the Survey of Inmates in State Correctional Facilities (SISCF), and the Survey of Inmates in Federal Correctional Facilities (SIFCF).

Table 10. Nonfatal firearm and nonfirearm violence reported and not reported to police, 2007–2011

	Total nonfatal violence	Firearm violence	Nonfirearm violence
Total	100%	100%	100%
Reported	46.9%	61.5%	45.7%
Not reported	51.7%	37.6%	52.9%
Reason not reported	100%	100%	100%
Dealt with it another way	35.0	12.1	36.4
Not important enough to respondent	18.4	6.2	19.1
Police could not or would not help	16.7	27.1	16.1
Fear of reprisal	6.5	31.3	5.1
Did not want to get offender in trouble advised not to report	5.1	4.3!	5.1
Other/unknown/not one most important reason	18.2	19.0	18.2

Note: Detail may not sum to total due to rounding. Reasons for not reporting represent the reason the victim stated was most important. See appendix table 21 for standard errors.

!Interpret with caution. Estimate based on 10 or fewer sample cases, or coefficient of variation is greater than 50%.

Source: Bureau of Justice Statistics, National Crime Victimization Survey, 2007–2011.

NONFATAL SHOOTING VICTIMS

According to the NCVS, an average of about 22,000 nonfatal shooting victims occurred annually from 1993 to 2002 (not shown in table). From 2002 to 2011, the number of victims declined by about half to 12,900 per year. In the 5-year aggregate period from 2007-11, a total of 46,000 nonfatal firearm victims were wounded with a firearm and another 58,483 were victims of a firearm homicide. The total firearm nonfatal gunshot injuries and homicides accounted for 5% of all firearm violent crimes in 2007-11.

Number of injuries

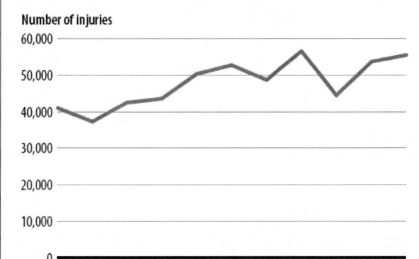

Note: See appendix table 20 for numbers and standard errors.
! Interpret with caution. Estimate based on fewer than 20 NEISS cases (based on unweighted data), national estimates less than 1,200 (based on weighted data), or the coefficient of variation (CV) of the estimate greater than 30%.
Source: Consumer Product Safety Commission, National Electronic Injury Surveillance System All Injury Program (NEISS-AIP), 2001–2011. Accessed from the National Center for Injury Prevention and Control, CDC.

re 11. Nonfatal firearm injuries, 2001–2011.

Data on nonfatal injury are also available in the National Electronic Injury Surveillance System All Injury Program (NEISS-AIP), which is operated by the U.S. Consumer Product Safety Commission (CPSC).

According to these data, an average of 47,870 nonfatal assault injuries resulted from a firearm from 2001 to 2011 (figure 11). In 2007-11, the average number of nonfatal injuries from a firearm increased slightly to 51,810.

The differences noted between the NCVS and NEISS- AIP firearm injury estimates are due in part to a variety of technical issues. Both estimates are generated from samples and are subject to sampling error. The NCVS is a residential household survey that does not include the homeless, persons in institutional settings such as jails, prisons, mental health facilities, and certain other group quarters. Therefore, NCVS may miss injuries that involve persons who are homeless, victims who require lengthy stays in a hospital, and offenders who are incarcerated or placed in other institutional settings after the incident.

Table 11. Self-protective behaviors, by type of crime, 2007–2011

Self-protective behavior	Violent crime		Property crime	
	Number	**Percent**	**Number**	**Percent**
Total	29,618,300	100%	84,495,500	100%
Offered no resistance	12,987,300	43.8	10,162,000	12.0
Threatened or attacked with a firearm	235,700	0.8	103,000	0.1
Threatened or attacked with other weapon	391,100	1.3	38,200	--
Threatened or attacked without a weapon	6,552,900	22.1	421,300	0.5
Nonconfrontational tactics[a]	7,768,700	26.2	1,187,100	1.4
Other	1,641,300	5.5	223,400	0.3
Unknown	41,300	0.1	12,200 !	--
Victim was not present[b]	~	~	72,348,200	85.6

Note: See appendix table 22 for standard errors.

! Interpret with caution. Estimate based on 10 or fewer sample cases, or coefficient of variation is greater than 50%.

~ Not applicable.

-- Less than 0.05%.

[a] Includes yelling, running, or arguing.

[b] Includes property crime where the victim was not present.

Source: Bureau of Justice Statistics, National Crime Victimization Survey, 2007–2011.

FIREARM USE BY OFFENDERS

In 2004, an estimated 16% of state prison inmates and 18% of federal inmates reported that they used, carried, or possessed a firearm when they committed the crime for which they were serving a prison sentence (table 12). This represented a slight change from 1997, where an estimated 18% of state prison inmates and 16% of federal inmates reported having a firearm when they committed the crime for their current sentence. During the offense that brought them to prison, 13% of state inmates and 16% of federal inmates carried a handgun. In addition, about 1% had a rifle and another 2% had a shotgun. Of inmates armed with a firearm during the offense, about 7% of state inmates and 8% of federal inmates were armed with either a single shot firearm or a conventional semiautomatic, and 2% of state inmates and 3% of federal inmates were armed with a military-style semiautomatic or fully automatic firearm (table 13).

In 2004, among state prison inmates who possessed a gun at the time of offense, fewer than 2% bought their firearm at a flea market or gun show, about 10% purchased it from a retail store or pawnshop, 37% obtained it from family or friends, and another 40% obtained it from an illegal source (table 14). This was similar to the percentage distribution in 1997.

Table 12. Possession of firearms by state and federal prison inmates at time of offense, by type of firearm, 1997 and 2004

Type of firearm	1997		2004	
	State	Federal	State	Federal
Total	100%	100%	100%	100%
Firearm	18.3%	15.8%	15.8%	17.8%
Handgun	15.1	13.6	13.3	15.5
Rifle	1.3	1.4	1.3	1.5
Shotgun	2.3	2.1	1.7	2.0
Other	0.4	0.5	0.1	0.1
No firearm	81.7%	84.2%	84.2%	82.2%

Note: Includes only inmates with a current conviction. Estimates may differ from previously published BJS reports. To account for differences in the 1997 and 2004 inmate survey questionnaires, the analytical methodology used in 1997 was revised to ensure comparability with the 2004 survey. Detail may not sum to total as inmates may have had possessed more than one firearm.

Source: Bureau of Justice Statistics, Survey of Inmates in State and Federal Correctional Facilities, 1997 and 2004.

Table 13. Possession of firearms by state and federal prison inmates at time of offense, by specific type of firearm, 1997 and 2004

Specific type of firearm	1997		2004	
	State	Federal	State	Federal
Single shot	9.9%	7.6%	7.5%	8.2%
Conventional semiautomatic	7.8	8.3	6.6	7.9
Military-style semiautomatic or fully automatic	1.5	1.7	2.0	3.2
Other	0.1	0.2	0.1	0.1

Note: Includes only inmates with a current conviction. Estimates may differ from previously published BJS reports. To account for differences in the 1997 and 2004 inmate survey questionnaires, the analytical methodology used in 1997 was revised to ensure comparability with the 2004 survey.

Source: Bureau of Justice Statistics, Survey of Inmates in State and Federal Correctional Facilities, 1997 and 2004.

Table 14. Source of firearms possessed by state prison inmates at time of offense, 1997 and 2004

Source of firearm	Percent of state prison inmates	
	1997	2004
Total	100%	100%
Purchased or traded from—	14.0%	11.3%
Retail store	8.2	7.3
Pawnshop	4.0	2.6
Flea market	1.0	0.6
Gun show	0.8	0.8
Family or friend	40.1%	37.4%
Purchased or traded	12.6	12.2
Rented or borrowed	18.9	14.1
Other	8.5	11.1
Street/illegal source	37.3%	40.0%
Theft or burglary	9.1	7.5
Drug dealer/off street	20.3	25.2
Fence/black market	8.0	7.4
Other	8.7%	11.2%

Note: Includes only inmates with a current conviction. Estimates may differ from previously published BJS reports. To account for differences in the 1997 and 2004 inmate survey questionnaires, the analytical methodology used in 1997 was revised to ensure comparability with the 2004 survey.

Source: Bureau of Justice Statistics, Survey of Inmates in State and Federal Correctional Facilities, 1997 and 2004.

METHODOLOGY

Estimates in this report are based primarily on data from the Bureau of Justice Statistics' (BJS) National Crime Victimization Survey (NCVS) and the National Center for Health Statistics' (NCHS) Centers for Disease Control and Prevention Center for Disease Control's Web-based Injury Statistics Query and Reporting System (WISQARS). Additional estimates come from the School-Associated Violent Deaths Surveillance Study (SAVD), the National Electronic Injury Surveillance System All Injury Program (NEISS-AIP) data, the FBI's Supplemental Homicide Reports (SHR), the Survey of Inmates in State Correctional Facilities (SISCF), and the Survey of Inmates in Federal Correctional Facilities (SIFCF).

The National Crime Victimization Survey (NCVS)

The NCVS is an annual data collection conducted by the U.S. Census Bureau for BJS. The NCVS is a self-report survey in which interviewed persons are asked about the number and characteristics of victimizations experienced during the prior 6 months. The NCVS collects information on nonfatal personal crimes (rape or sexual assault, robbery, aggravated assault, simple assault, and personal larceny) and household property crimes (burglary, motor vehicle theft, and other theft) both reported and not reported to police. In addition to providing annual level and change estimates on criminal victimization, the NCVS is the primary source of information on the nature of criminal victimization incidents. Survey respondents provide information about themselves (such as age, sex, race and ethnicity, marital status, education level, and income) and if they experienced a victimization. For crime victims, data are collected about each victimization incident, including information about the offender (such as age, race and ethnicity, sex, and victim- offender relationship), characteristics of the crime (including time and place of occurrence, use of weapons, nature of injury, and economic consequences), whether the crime was reported to police, reasons why the crime was or was not reported, and experiences with the criminal justice system.

The NCVS is administered to persons age 12 or older from a nationally representative sample of households in the United States. In 2011, about 143,120 persons age 12 or older from 79,800 households across the country were interviewed during the year. Once selected, households remain in the sample for 3 years, and eligible persons in these households are interviewed every 6 months for a total of seven interviews. New households rotate into the sample on an ongoing basis to replace outgoing households that have been in sample for the 3-year period. The sample includes persons living in group quarters (such as dormitories, rooming houses, and religious group dwellings) and excludes persons living in military barracks and institutional settings (such as correctional or hospital facilities) and the homeless. (For more information, see the *Survey Methodology for Criminal Victimization in the United States, 2008*, NCJ 231173, BJS website, May 2011.)

The 79,800 households that participated in the NCVS in 2011 represent a 90% household response rate. The person level response rate—the percentage of persons age 12 or older in participating households who completed an NCVS interview—was 88% in 2011.

For this report, prior to applying the weights to the data, all victimizations that occurred outside of the U.S. were excluded. From 1993 to 2011, less than 1% of the unweighted violent victimizations occurred outside of the U.S. and was excluded from the analyses.

Weighting Adjustments for Estimating Personal Victimization

Estimates in this report use data primarily from the 1993 to 2011 NCVS data files weighted to produce annual estimates for persons age 12 or older living in U.S. households. Because the NCVS relies on a sample rather than a census of the entire U.S. population, weights are designed to inflate sample point estimates to known population totals and to compensate for survey nonresponse and other aspects of the sample design.

The NCVS data files include both household and person weights. The household weight is commonly used to calculate estimates of property crimes, such as motor vehicle theft or burglary, which are identified with the household. Person weights provide an estimate of the population represented by each person in the sample. Person weights are most frequently used to compute estimates of crime victimizations of persons in the total population. Both household and person weights, after proper adjustment, are also used to form the denominator in calculations of crime rates.

The victimization weights used in this analysis account for the number of persons present during an incident and for repeat victims of series incidents. The weight counts series incidents as the actual number of incidents reported by the victim, up to a maximum of ten incidents. Series victimizations are victimizations that are similar in type but occur with such frequency that a victim is unable to recall each individual event or to describe each event in detail. Survey procedures allow NCVS interviewers to identify and classify these similar victimizations as series victimizations and collect detailed information on only the most recent incident in the series. In 2011, about 2% of all victimizations were series incidents. Weighting series incidents as the number of incidents up to a maximum of ten produces more reliable estimates of crime levels, while the cap at ten minimizes the effect of extreme outliers on the rates. Additional information on the series enumeration is detailed in *Methods for Counting High Frequency Repeat Victimizations in the National Crime Victimization Survey*, NCJ 237308, BJS website, April 2012.

Standard Error Computations

When national estimates are derived from a sample, as is the case with the NCVS, caution must be taken when comparing one estimate to another estimate or when comparing estimates over time. Although one estimate may be larger than another, estimates based on a sample have some degree of sampling error. The sampling error of an estimate depends on several factors, including the amount of variation in the responses, the size of the sample, and the size of the subgroup for which the estimate is computed. When the sampling error around the estimates is taken into consideration, the estimates that appear different may, in fact, not be statistically different.

One measure of the sampling error associated with an estimate is the standard error. The standard error can vary from one estimate to the next. In general, for a given metric, an estimate with a smaller standard error provides a more reliable approximation of the true value than an estimate with a larger standard error. Estimates with relatively large standard errors are associated with less precision and reliability and should be interpreted with caution.

In order to generate standard errors around estimates from the NCVS, the Census Bureau produces generalized variance function (GVF) parameters for BJS. The GVFs take into account aspects of the NCVS complex sample design and represent the curve fitted to a selection of individual standard errors based on the Jackknife Repeated Replication technique. The GVF parameters were used to generate standard errors for each point estimate (such as counts, percentages, and rates) in the report. For average annual estimates, standard errors were based on the ratio of the sums of victimizations and respondents across years.

In this report, BJS conducted tests to determine whether differences in estimated numbers and percentages were statistically significant once sampling error was taken into account. Using statistical programs developed specifically for the NCVS, all comparisons in the text were tested for significance. The primary test procedure used was Student's t-statistic, which tests the difference between two sample estimates. To ensure that the observed differences between estimates were larger than might be expected due to sampling variation, the significance level was set at the 95% confidence level.

Data users can use the estimates and the standard errors of the estimates provided in this report to generate a confidence interval around the estimate as a measure of the margin of error. The following example illustrates how standard errors can be used to generate confidence intervals:

> According to the NCVS, in 2011, the rate of nonfatal firearm violence was 1.8 per 1,000 (see table 1). Using the GVFs, BJS determined that the estimate has a standard error of 0.2 (see appendix table 3). A confidence interval around the estimate was generated by multiplying the standard errors by ±1.96 (the t-score of a normal, two- tailed distribution that excludes 2.5% at either end of the distribution). Thus, the confidence interval around the 1.8 estimate from 2011 is 1.8 ± 0.2 (0.2 X 1.96) or (1.4 to 2.2). In other words, if different samples using the same procedures were taken from the U.S. population in 2011, 95% of the time the rate of nonfatal firearm violence was between 1.4 and 2.2 per 1,000.

In this report, BJS also calculated a coefficient of variation (CV) for all estimates, representing the ratio of the standard error to the estimate. CVs provide a measure of reliability and a means to compare the precision of estimates across measures with differing levels or metrics. If the CV was greater than 50%, or the unweighted sample had 10 or fewer cases, the estimate would have been noted with a "!" symbol (interpret data with caution; estimate is based on 10 or fewer sample cases, or the coefficient of variation exceeds 50%).

Many of the variables examined in this report may be related to one another and to other variables not included in the analyses. Complex relationships among variables were not fully explored in this report and warrant more extensive analysis. Readers are cautioned not to draw causal inferences based on the results presented.

Methodological Changes to the NCVS in 2006

Methodological changes implemented in 2006 may have affected the crime estimates for that year to such an extent that they are not comparable to estimates from other years. Evaluation of 2007 and later data from the NCVS conducted by BJS and the Census Bureau found a high degree of confidence that estimates for 2007, 2008, 2009, and 2010 are consistent with and comparable to estimates for 2005 and previous years. The reports, *Criminal Victimization, 2006*, NCJ 219413, December 2007; *Criminal Victimization, 2007*, NCJ 224390, December 2008; *Criminal Victimization, 2008*, NCJ 227777, September 2009; *Criminal Victimization, 2009*, NCJ 231327, October 2010; *Criminal Victimization, 2010*, NCJ 235508, September 2011; and *Criminal Victimization, 2011*, NCJ 239437, October 2012, are available on the BJS website.

Although caution is warranted when comparing data from 2006 to other years, the aggregation of multiple years of data in this report diminishes the potential variation between 2006 and other years. In general, findings do not change significantly if data for 2006 are excluded from the analyses.

Web-Based Injury Statistics Query and Reporting System Fatal (WISQARS^{TM} Fatal)

WISQARS Fatal provides mortality data related to injury. The mortality data reported in WISQARS Fatal come from death certificate data reported to the CDC's National Center for Health Statistics (NCHS). Data include causes of death reported by attending physicians, medical examiners, and coroners. It also includes demographic information about decedents reported by funeral directors, who obtain that information from family members and other informants. NCHS collects, compiles, verifies, and prepares these data for release to the public. The data provide information about what types of injuries are leading causes of deaths, how common they are, and who they affect. These data are intended for a broad audience—the public, the media, public health practitioners and researchers, and public health officials—to increase their knowledge of injury.

WISQARS Fatal mortality reports provide tables of the total numbers of injury-related deaths and the death rates per 100,000 U.S. population. The reports list deaths according to cause (mechanism) and intent (manner) of injury by state, race, Hispanic origin, sex, and age groupings. Data in this report are provided for homicides by firearm from 1993 to 2010, including some preliminary 2011 estimates. The injury mortality data were classified based on the International Classification of Diseases (ICD)-10 classification system from 1999 and later, and the ICD-9 system for 1998 and earlier. The comparability study showed that the comparability for homicide and firearm homicide between the two systems was very high; therefore, data are shown from both periods.[3]

National Electronic Injury Surveillance System All Injury Program (NEISS-AIP)

The NEISS-AIP is operated by the U.S. Consumer Product Safety Commission (CPSC). It is a collaborative effort by the National Center for Injury Prevention and Control (NCIPC) and CPSC. The NEISS is a national probability sample of hospitals in the U.S. and its territories. Data are collected about all types and external causes of nonfatal injuries and poisonings treated in U.S. hospital emergency departments, whether or not they are associated with consumer products. This report uses the estimates on nonfatal assault injuries from a firearm. This excludes injuries that were unintentional, by legal intervention, or self-harm.

School-Associated Violent Deaths Surveillance Study (SAVD)

The SAVD is an epidemiological study developed by the Centers for Disease Control and Prevention in conjunction with the U.S. Department of Education and the U.S. Department of Justice. SAVD seeks to describe the epidemiology of school-associated violent deaths, identify common features of these deaths, estimate the rate of school-associated violent death in the United States, and identify potential risk factors for these deaths. The surveillance system includes descriptive data on all school- associated violent deaths in the United States, including all homicides, suicides, or legal intervention in which the fatal injury occurred on the campus of a functioning elementary or secondary school; while the victim was on the way to or from regular sessions at such a school; or while attending or on the way to or from an official school-sponsored event. Victims of such incidents include nonstudents, as well as students and staff members. SAVD includes descriptive information about the school, event, victim(s), and offender(s). The SAVD Surveillance System has collected data from July 1, 1992, through the present.

SAVD uses a four-step process to identify and collect data on school-associated violent deaths. Cases are initially identified through a search of the LexisNexis newspaper and media database. Then law enforcement officials are contacted to confirm the details of the case and to determine if the event meets the case definition. Once a case is confirmed, a law enforcement official and a school official are interviewed regarding details about the school, event, victim(s), and offender(s). A copy of the full law enforcement report is also sought for each case. The information obtained on schools includes school demographics, attendance/absentee rates, suspensions/expulsions and mobility, school history of weapon-carrying incidents, security measures, violence prevention activities, school response to the event, and school policies about weapon carrying. Event information includes the location of injury, the context of injury (e.g., while classes were being held or during break), motives for injury, method of injury, and school and community events happening around the time period. Information obtained on victim(s) and offender(s) includes demographics, circumstances of the event (date/time, alcohol or drug use, and number of persons involved), types and origins of weapons, criminal history, psychological risk factors, school- related problems, extracurricular activities, and family history, including structure and stressors.

For several reasons, all data from 1999 to the present are flagged as preliminary. For some recent data, the interviews with school and law enforcement officials to verify case details have not been completed. The details learned during the interviews can occasionally change the classification of a case. Also, new cases may be identified because of the expansion of the scope of the media files used for case identification. Sometimes other cases not identified during earlier data years using the independent case finding efforts (which focus on nonmedia sources of information) will be discovered. Also, other cases may occasionally be identified while the law enforcement and school interviews are being conducted to verify known cases.

The FBI's Uniform Crime Reporting (UCR) Program, Supplementary Homicide Reports (SHR)

The FBI's SHR were used for information about gun type used in firearm homicides. The UCR program collects and publishes criminal offense, arrest, and law enforcement personnel statistics. Under the UCR program, law enforcement agencies submit information to the FBI monthly. Offense information is collected on the eight Part I offenses: homicide, forcible rape, robbery, aggravated assault, burglary, larceny-theft, motor vehicle theft, and arson. The UCR program collects data on only those crimes that come to the attention of law enforcement.

Homicide incident information—through SHR data—is submitted with details on location, victim, and offender characteristics. Homicide is defined as murder and non- negligent manslaughter, which is the willful killing of one human being by another. The analyses excludes deaths caused by negligence, suicide, or accident; justifiable homicides; and attempts to murder. Deaths from the terrorist attacks of September 11, 2001, are not included in any of the analyses.

Not all agencies that report offense information to the FBI also submit supplemental data on homicides. About 90 percent of homicides are included in the SHR. However, adjustments can be made to the weights to correct for missing victim reports.

Estimates from the SHR used in this report were generated by BJS using a weight developed by BJS that reconciles the counts of SHR homicide victims with those in the UCR for the 1992 through 2011 data years.

Surveys of Inmates in State and Federal Correctional Facilities (SISCF and SIFCF)

The SISCF and the SIFCF have provided nationally representative data on state prison inmates and sentenced federal inmates held in federally owned and operated facilities.

The SISCF was conducted in 1974, 1979, 1986, 1991, 1997, and 2004, and the SIFCF in 1991, 1997, and 2004. The 2004 SISCF was conducted for BJS by the U.S. Census Bureau, which also conducted the SIFCF for BJS and the Federal Bureau of Prisons. Both surveys provide information about current offense and criminal history, family background and personal characteristics, prior drug and alcohol use and treatment, gun possession, and prison treatment, programs, and services. The surveys are the only national source of detailed information on criminal offenders, particularly special populations such as drug and alcohol users and offenders who have mental health problems.

Systematic random sampling was used to select the inmates, and the 2004 surveys of state and federal inmates were administered through CAPI. In 2004, 14,499 state prisoners in 287 state prisons and 3,686 federal prisoners in 39 federal prisons were interviewed.

Appendix Table 1. Numbers and rates for figure 1: Firearm homicides, 1993–2011

Year	Number	Rate per 100,000 persons
1993	18,253	7.0
1994	17,527	6.7
1995	15,551	5.8
1996	14,037	5.2
1997	13,252	4.9
1998	11,798	4.3
1999	10,828	3.9
2000	10,801	3.8
2001	11,348	4.0
2002	11,829	4.1
2003	11,920	4.1
2004	11,624	4.0
2005	12,352	4.2
2006	12,791	4.3
2007	12,632	4.2
2008	12,179	4.0
2009	11,493	3.8
2010	11,078	3.6
2011	11,101	3.6

Source: Centers for Disease Control and Prevention, National Center for Injury Prevention and Control. Web-based Injury Statistics Query and Reporting System (WISQARS), 1993–2010. Retrieved March 2013 from www.cdc.gov/ncipc/wisqars.

Appendix Table 2. Numbers, rates, and standard errors for figure 2: Nonfatal firearm victimizations, 1993–2011

	Number	Standard error	Rate per 1,000 persons age 12 or older	Standard error
1993	1,529,700	104,582	7.3	0.5
1994	1,568,200	83,431	7.4	0.4
1995	1,193,200	70,572	5.5	0.3
1996	1,100,800	68,653	5.1	0.3
1997	1,024,100	72,643	4.7	0.3

	Number	Standard error	Rate per 1,000 persons age 12 or older	Standard error
1998	835,400	69,401	3.8	0.3
1999	640,900	54,713	2.9	0.2
2000	610,200	55,220	2.7	0.2
2001	563,100	53,309	2.5	0.2
2002	540,000	50,299	2.3	0.2
2003	467,300	47,783	2.0	0.2
2004	456,500	47,513	1.9	0.2
2005	503,500	55,594	2.1	0.2
2006	614,400	61,310	2.5	0.2
2007	554,800	55,886	2.2	0.2
2008	371,300	45,794	1.5	0.2
2009	410,100	48,765	1.6	0.2
2010	415,000	47,172	1.6	0.2
2011	467,300	53,197	1.8	0.2

Source: Bureau of Justice Statistics, National Crime Victimization Survey, 1993–2011.

Appendix Table 3. Standard errors for table 1: Criminal firearm violence, 1993–2011

Year	Total fatal and nonfatal firearm violence	Number		Rate of nonfatal firearm victimization	Percent of all violence involving firearms
		Nonfatal firearm victimizations	Nonfatal firearm incidents		
1993	105,349	104,582	91,169	0.5	0.6%
1994	84,005	83,431	73,911	0.4	0.4
1995	71,131	70,572	64,501	0.3	0.4
1996	69,183	68,653	62,377	0.3	0.5
1997	73,220	72,643	66,331	0.3	0.5
1998	70,022	69,401	60,556	0.3	0.5
1999	55,268	54,713	48,457	0.2	0.5
2000	55,810	55,220	48,015	0.2	0.6
2001	53,967	53,309	49,987	0.2	0.7

Appendix Table 3. (Continued)

| Year | Total fatal and nonfatal firearm violence | Number | | Rate of nonfatal firearm victimization | Percent of all violence involving firearms |
		Nonfatal firearm victimizations	Nonfatal firearm incidents		
2002	50,946	50,299	45,234	0.2	0.6
2003	48,494	47,783	42,668	0.2	0.6
2004	48,200	47,513	44,433	0.2	0.7
2005	56,378	55,594	51,864	0.2	0.8
2006	62,038	61,310	57,669	0.2	0.7
2007	56,652	55,886	49,166	0.2	0.8
2008	46,637	45,794	42,966	0.2	0.7
2009	49,561	48,765	46,881	0.2	0.8
2010	47,913	47,172	44,695	0.2	0.9
2011	53,942	53,197	49,563	0.2	0.8

~Not applicable.

Source: Bureau of Justice Statistics, National Crime Victimization Survey, 1993–2011.

Appendix Table 4. Standard errors for table 2: Percent of violence involving a firearm, by type of crime, 1993–2011

Year	Nonfatal violence	Robbery	Aggravated assault
1993	0.6%	2.2%	1.9%
1994	0.4	1.9	1.5
1995	0.4	2.1	1.5
1996	0.4	2.0	1.5
1997	0.5	2.2	1.7
1998	0.5	2.5	1.9
1999	0.5	2.3	1.8
2000	0.6	2.6	2.2
2001	0.6	3.4	2.3
2002	0.6	3.2	2.5
2003	0.6	3.1	2.3

Year	Nonfatal violence	Robbery	Aggravated assault
2004	0.7	3.2	2.4
2005	0.8	3.3	2.8
2006	0.7	2.7	2.4
2007	0.8	2.9	2.9
2008	0.7	3.3	3.1
2009	0.8	3.8	2.9
2010	0.9	3.7	3.1
2011	0.8	4.0	3.2

Source: Bureau of Justice Statistics, National Crime Victimization Survey, 1993–2011.

Appendix Table 5:Standard errors for table 3: Criminal firearm violence, by type of firearm, 1994–2011

Year	Nonfatal violence					
	Handgun		Other firearm		Gun type unknown	
	Number	Percent	Number	Percent	Number	Percent
1994	94,313	1.8%	26,713	1.6%	6,951	0.4%
1995	77,109	1.6	21,832	1.5	4,899	0.4
1996	66,253	1.9	21,995	1.8	4,366	0.4
1997	68,335	2.3	25,950	2.2	5,534	0.5
1998	68,151	2.6	25,521	2.5	4,522	0.5
1999	63,909	2.5	18,379	2.3	4,189	0.6
2000	57,439	2.8	17,323	2.6	4,260	0.7
2001	53,625	3.1	17,115	2.7	7,586	1.3
2002	48,977	3.1	16,006	2.7	7,929	1.4
2003	46,655	3.2	14,670	2.7	7,392	1.4
2004	45,846	3.6	15,535	3.1	8,509	1.8
2005	50,621	3.8	17,269	3.3	8,153	1.7
2006	56,341	3.1	15,872	2.7	8,415	1.5
2007	56,630	3.2	18,308	2.9	6,598	1.1
2008	48,199	3.6	16,622	3.3	4,666	1.0
2009	47,110	3.7	14,157	3.4	4,688	1.2
2010	50,636	3.1	11,837	2.7	4,313	1.0
2011	43,185	3.1	13,868	2.9	2,676	0.6

Source: Bureau of Justice Statistics, National Crime Victimization Survey, 1993–2011.

Appendix Table 6. Numbers and rates for figure 3:
Firearm homicides, by sex,
1993–2010

Year	Number		Rate per 100,000 persons	
	Male	Female	Male	Female
1993	15,228	3,025	12.0	2.3
1994	14,766	2,761	11.5	2.1
1995	13,021	2,530	10.0	1.9
1996	11,735	2,302	8.9	1.7
1997	11,147	2,105	8.4	1.5
1998	9,771	2,027	7.2	1.4
1999	8,944	1,884	6.5	1.3
2000	9,006	1,795	6.5	1.3
2001	9,532	1,816	6.8	1.3
2002	9,899	1,930	7.0	1.3
2003	10,126	1,794	7.1	1.2
2004	9,921	1,703	6.9	1.1
2005	10,561	1,791	7.3	1.2
2006	10,886	1,905	7.4	1.3
2007	10,767	1,865	7.3	1.2
2008	10,361	1,818	6.9	1.2
2009	9,615	1,878	6.4	1.2
2010	9,340	1,738	6.2	1.1

Source: Centers for Disease Control and Prevention, National Center for Injury Prevention and Control.
Web-based Injury Statistics Query and Reporting System (WISQARS), 1993–2010. Retrieved March 2013 from www.cdc.gov/ncipc/ wisqars.

Appendix Table 7. Rates and standard errors for figure 4:
Nonfatal firearm violence, by sex,
1994–2011

Year	Male		Female	
	Rate*	Standard error	Rate*	Standard error
1994	10.1	0.6	4.7	0.4
1995	9.3	0.5	3.7	0.3
1996	7.6	0.4	3.1	0.2
1997	6.4	0.4	3.5	0.3
1998	5.5	0.4	3.0	0.3
1999	4.4	0.4	2.3	0.2
2000	3.7	0.3	1.9	0.2
2001	3.5	0.3	1.7	0.2
2002	2.9	0.3	1.9	0.2
2003	2.7	0.2	1.6	0.2
2004	2.5	0.2	1.4	0.2
2005	2.5	0.3	1.4	0.2
2006	2.8	0.3	1.8	0.2
2007	2.8	0.3	1.9	0.2
2008	2.2	0.2	1.5	0.2
2009	2.0	0.2	1.1	0.2
2010	2.0	0.2	1.2	0.2
2011	1.9	0.2	1.6	0.2

* Per 1,000 persons age 12 or older.
Source: Bureau of Justice Statistics, National Crime Victimization Survey, 1993–2011.

Appendix Table 8. Numbers and rates for figure 5: Firearm homicides, by race, 1993–2010

Year	Number				Rate per 100,000 persons			
	White	Black	American Indian/Alaska Native	Asian/Pacific Islander	White	Black	American Indian/Alaska Native	Asian/Pacific Islander
1993	7,918	9,824	106	405	3.7	30.1	4.6	4.6
1994	7,774	9,302	123	328	3.6	28.0	5.2	3.6
1995	7,144	7,935	130	342	3.2	23.4	5.3	3.6
1996	6,240	7,403	90	304	2.8	21.5	3.6	3.0
1997	6,025	6,841	96	290	2.7	19.5	3.7	2.8
1998	5,412	6,053	99	234	2.4	17.0	3.6	2.2
1999	4,918	5,577	104	229	2.2	15.4	3.7	2.0
2000	4,806	5,699	86	210	2.1	15.6	2.9	1.8
2001	5,188	5,885	87	188	2.2	15.8	2.8	1.5
2002	5,185	6,285	117	242	2.2	16.7	3.7	1.9
2003	5,173	6,397	109	241	2.2	16.7	3.3	1.8
2004	5,119	6,201	104	200	2.2	16.0	3.0	1.4
2005	5,266	6,703	117	266	2.2	17.1	3.3	1.8
2006	5,279	7,113	119	280	2.2	17.9	3.2	1.9
2007	5,380	6,960	91	201	2.2	17.2	2.4	1.3
2008	5,305	6,569	97	208	2.2	16.0	2.4	1.3
2009	4,950	6,216	112	215	2.0	14.9	2.7	1.3
2010	4,647	6,151	113	167	1.9	14.6	2.7	1.0

Source: Centers for Disease Control and Prevention, National Center for Injury Prevention and Control. Web-based Injury Statistics Query and Reporting System (WISQARS), 1993–2010. Retrieved March 2013 from www.cdc.gov/ncipc/ wisqars.

Appendix Table 9. Numbers and rates for figure 6: Firearm homicides, by Hispanic origin, 1993–2010

Year	Number		Rate per 100,000 persons	
	Hispanic	Non-Hispanic	Hispanic	Non-Hispanic
1993	3,192	14,597	12.4	6.3
1994	3,149	14,065	11.7	6.0
1995	3,008	12,260	10.7	5.2
1996	2,529	11,229	8.6	4.7
1997	2,298	10,868	7.4	4.5
1998	2,090	9,620	6.5	4.0
1999	1,939	8,821	5.7	3.6
2000	1,958	8,767	5.6	3.6
2001	2,123	9,134	5.7	3.7
2002	2,168	9,575	5.6	3.9
2003	2,316	9,536	5.8	3.8
2004	2,241	9,323	5.4	3.7
2005	2,453	9,835	5.7	3.9
2006	2,472	10,260	5.5	4.0
2007	2,385	10,193	5.2	4.0
2008	2,260	9,882	4.7	3.9
2009	2,115	9,275	4.3	3.6
2010	1,919	9,082	3.8	3.5

Source: Centers for Disease Control and Prevention, National Center for Injury Prevention and Control. Web-based Injury Statistics Query and Reporting System (WISQARS), 1993–2010. Retrieved March 2013 from www.cdc.gov/ncipc/ wisqars.

Appendix Table 10. Rates and standard errors for figure 7: Nonfatal firearm violence, by race and Hispanic origin, 1994–2011

Year	White		Black		Hispanic		American Indian/ Alaska Native		Asian/Pacific Islander		Two or more races	
	Rate*	Standard error	Rate*	Standard error	Rate*	Standard error	Rate*	Standard error	Rate*	Standard error	Rate*	Standard error
1994	5.2	0.3	16.3	1.3	12.7	1.4	15.3!	5.3	10.3	2.0	~	~
1995	4.6	0.3	14.2	1.1	12.1	1.1	16.3	4.9	4.9	1.1	~	~
1996	3.9	0.2	11.6	0.9	9.3	0.9	13.3!	4.4	3.4	0.9	~	~
1997	4.0	0.3	9.4	0.9	6.9	0.8	3.7!	2.6	2.0	0.7	~	~
1998	3.4	0.3	7.4	0.8	5.6	0.8	20.9!	6.6	3.9	1.0	~	~
1999	2.2	0.2	7.9	0.9	5.0	0.8	25.1!	7.5	4.0	1.1	~	~
2000	1.8	0.2	7.0	0.8	4.7	0.7	4.8!	3.2	1.9	0.7	~	~
2001	2.0	0.2	5.0	0.7	3.8	0.6	1.1!	1.5	1.5!	0.6	~	~
2002	1.7	0.2	5.6	0.7	3.7	0.6	1.1!	1.4	0.9!	0.4	~	~
2003	1.5	0.2	5.7	0.7	2.6	0.4	--	~	1.0!	0.5	~	~
2004	1.7	0.2	4.4	0.6	1.5	0.3	--	~	1.1!	0.5	0.9!	1.1
2005	1.6	0.2	4.2	0.7	2.2	0.4	--	~	1.2!	0.5	2.8!	2.0
2006	1.7	0.2	4.4	0.7	3.4	0.6	1.8!	1.9	2.1!	0.7	4.0!	2.2
2007	1.4	0.2	7.1	0.9	3.0	0.5	3.3!	2.4	1.7!	0.6	4.7!	2.1
2008	1.0	0.1	6.9	0.8	1.9	0.4	3.2!	2.3	1.0!	0.5	2.7!	1.5
2009	0.9	0.1	5.1	0.7	1.7	0.4	2.9!	2.3	0.9!	0.4	1.4!	1.2
2010	1.0	0.1	4.5	0.7	2.1	0.4	9.2!	4.2	0.3!	0.2	5.7!	2.5
2011	1.4	0.1	2.8	0.4	2.2	0.4	8.6!	3.4	0.6!	0.3	7.6!	2.3

* Per 1,000 persons age 12 or older.

! Interpret with caution. Estimate based on 10 or fewer sample cases, or coefficient of variation is greater than 50%.

~ Not applicable.

- Less than 0.05.

Source: Bureau of Justice Statistics, National Crime Victimization Survey, 1993–2011.

Appendix Table 11. Numbers for table 4: Firearm homicides, by age, 1993–2011

Year	11 or younger	12–17	18–24	25–34	35–49	50 or older
1993	240	1,735	5,673	5,295	3,808	1,476
1994	176	1,736	5,435	5,059	3,700	1,399
1995	183	1,597	4,726	4,448	3,222	1,351
1996	178	1,295	4,334	3,918	3,030	1,266
1997	174	1,134	4,148	3,706	2,905	1,168
1998	157	888	3,753	3,231	2,669	1,082
1999	142	859	3,319	3,048	2,419	1,026
2000	110	709	3,371	3,074	2,488	1,037
2001	150	685	3,611	3,308	2,530	1,053
2002	151	721	3,708	3,465	2,646	1,125
2003	121	684	3,840	3,540	2,624	1,093
2004	105	763	3,485	3,503	2,533	1,214
2005	111	810	3,808	3,780	2,689	1,145
2006	142	940	4,030	3,767	2,688	1,216
2007	140	898	3,895	3,751	2,737	1,202
2008	140	844	3,662	3,612	2,655	1,264
2009	142	745	3,398	3,300	2,538	1,364
2010	127	708	3,273	3,331	2,294	1,340

Source: Centers for Disease Control and Prevention, National Center for Injury Prevention and Control. Web-based Injury Statistics Query and Reporting System (WISQARS), 1993–2010. Retrieved March 2013 from www.cdc.gov/ncipc/ wisqars.

Appendix Table 12. Standard errors for table 4: Nonfatal firearm violence, by age, 1994–2011

Year	12-17	18-24	25-34	35-49	50 or older
1994	1.2	1.4	0.8	0.6	0.2
1995	0.9	1.2	0.6	0.4	0.2
1996	0.8	1.0	0.6	0.4	0.2
1997	0.8	1.1	0.6	0.4	0.2
1998	0.8	1.1	0.5	0.4	0.2
1999	0.7	1.0	0.6	0.3	0.2
2000	0.6	0.8	0.5	0.3	0.2
2001	0.5	0.8	0.4	0.3	0.2
2002	0.5	0.8	0.4	0.3	0.1
2003	0.5	0.7	0.4	0.2	0.1
2004	0.4	0.6	0.4	0.3	0.2
2005	0.4	0.7	0.5	0.3	0.2
2006	0.5	0.8	0.5	0.3	0.2
2007	0.7	0.7	0.5	0.3	0.2
2008	0.6	0.5	0.4	0.3	0.1
2009	0.3	0.6	0.4	0.3	0.1
2010	0.2	0.8	0.4	0.2	0.1
2011	0.3	0.6	0.3	0.2	0.1

* Rate per 1,000 persons age 12 or older.

! Interpret with caution. Estimate based on 10 or fewer sample cases, or coefficient of variation is greater than 50%.

Source: Bureau of Justice Statistics, National Crime Victimization Survey, 1993–2011

Appendix Table 13. Numbers and rates for figure 8: Firearm homicides, by region, 1993–2011

Year	Number				Rate per 100,000 persons			
	Northeast	South	Midwest	West	Northeast	South	Midwest	West
1993	2,918	7,863	3,365	4,107	5.6	8.7	5.5	7.3
1994	2,489	7,577	3,391	4,070	4.8	8.3	5.5	7.1
1995	2,100	6,659	2,980	3,812	4.0	7.1	4.8	6.5
1996	1,838	6,248	2,791	3,160	3.5	6.6	4.4	5.3
1997	1,641	6,020	2,661	2,930	3.1	6.3	4.2	4.9
1998	1,347	5,434	2,490	2,527	2.5	5.6	3.9	4.1
1999	1,327	4,905	2,319	2,277	2.5	5.0	3.6	3.7
2000	1,391	4,846	2,284	2,280	2.6	4.8	3.6	3.6
2001	1,407	4,989	2,477	2,475	2.6	4.9	3.8	3.8
2002	1,406	5,292	2,381	2,750	2.6	5.1	3.7	4.2
2003	1,489	5,395	2,324	2,712	2.7	5.2	3.6	4.1
2004	1,485	5,164	2,212	2,763	2.7	4.9	3.4	4.1
2005	1,554	5,536	2,387	2,875	2.9	5.2	3.6	4.2
2006	1,715	5,701	2,505	2,870	3.2	5.2	3.8	4.2
2007	1,577	6,055	2,354	2,646	2.9	5.5	3.6	3.8
2008	1,506	5,778	2,439	2,456	2.7	5.2	3.7	3.5
2009	1,440	5,438	2,359	2,256	2.6	4.8	3.5	3.2
2010	1,552	5,082	2,296	2,148	2.8	4.4	3.4	3.0

Source: Centers for Disease Control and Prevention, National Center for Injury Prevention and Control. Web-based Injury Statistics Query and Reporting System (WISQARS), 1993–2010. Retrieved March 2013 from www.cdc.gov/ncipc/ wisqars.

Appendix Table 14. Rates and standard errors for figure 9: Nonfatal firearm violence, by region, 1997–2011

Year	Northeast		Midwest		South		West	
	Rate*	Standard error	Rate*	Standard error	Rate*	Standard error	Rate*	Standard error
1997	3.1	0.4	4.7	0.5	5.4	0.4	5.7	0.5
1998	2.1	0.3	3.9	0.4	5.0	0.4	5.1	0.5
1999	1.4	0.3	3.0	0.4	3.6	0.4	4.9	0.5
2000	1.3	0.3	2.5	0.3	2.8	0.3	4.5	0.5
2001	1.4	0.3	2.6	0.4	3.0	0.3	2.8	0.4
2002	1.3	0.3	2.2	0.3	3.3	0.3	2.0	0.3
2003	1.0	0.2	2.1	0.3	2.9	0.3	1.9	0.3
2004	0.8	0.2	2.6	0.3	1.9	0.2	2.2	0.3
2005	0.9	0.2	2.8	0.4	1.9	0.3	1.9	0.3
2006	1.2	0.3	2.6	0.4	2.7	0.3	2.2	0.3
2007	0.9	0.2	2.1	0.3	3.5	0.4	1.9	0.3
2008	0.7	0.2	2.1	0.3	2.8	0.3	1.1	0.2
2009	0.8	0.2	2.0	0.3	1.7	0.2	1.4	0.3
2010	0.9	0.2	1.9	0.3	1.7	0.2	1.8	0.3
2011	1.3	0.2	1.7	0.3	1.9	0.2	1.8	0.3

* Rate per 1,000 persons age 12 or older.

Source: Bureau of Justice Statistics, National Crime Victimization Survey, 1996–2011.

Appendix Table 15. Rates and standard errors for figure 10: Nonfatal firearm violence, by urban-rural location, 1994–2011

Year	Urban		Suburban		Rural	
	Rate*	Standard error	Rate*	Standard error	Rate*	Standard error
1994	10.6	0.7	6.3	0.4	5.2	0.5
1995	10.1	0.6	5.5	0.4	3.6	0.4
1996	8.4	0.5	4.4	0.3	3.1	0.4
1997	7.3	0.5	3.9	0.3	3.6	0.4
1998	6.2	0.5	3.8	0.3	2.3	0.3
1999	5.3	0.5	3.1	0.3	1.0	0.2
2000	4.8	0.5	2.3	0.2	1.0	0.2
2001	4.4	0.4	2.0	0.2	1.4	0.3
2002	4.4	0.4	1.8	0.2	1.1	0.2
2003	3.7	0.4	1.7	0.2	0.9	0.2
2004	3.0	0.3	1.7	0.2	1.0	0.2
2005	3.4	0.4	1.5	0.2	1.1	0.3
2006	3.3	0.4	1.8	0.2	1.9	0.4
2007	2.6	0.3	2.3	0.2	1.9	0.3
2008	2.2	0.3	1.8	0.2	1.2	0.3
2009	2.6	0.3	1.1	0.2	0.9	0.2
2010	2.8	0.3	1.2	0.2	0.7	0.2
2011	2.5	0.3	1.4	0.2	1.2	0.2

* Rate per 1,000 persons age 12 or older.

Source: Bureau of Justice Statistics, National Crime Victimization Survey, 1993–2011.

Appendix Table 16. Rates and standard errors for table 5: Nonfatal firearm violence, by population size, 1997–2011

Year	Not a place		Under 100,000		100,000–249,999		250,000–499,999		500,000–999,999		1 million or more	
	Rate*	Standard error	Rate*	Standard error	Rate*	Standard error	Rate*	Standard error	Rate*	Standard error	Rate*	Standard error
1997	3.9	0.4	3.8	0.3	7.0	0.9	10.3	1.3	7.3	1.3	7.3	1.0
1998	3.0	0.3	3.9	0.3	4.8	0.8	7.0	1.1	9.2	1.6	5.7	0.9
1999	1.9	0.3	3.1	0.3	3.1	0.6	5.5	1.0	9.0	1.6	6.4	1.0
2000	1.5	0.2	2.2	0.2	3.9	0.7	6.5	1.1	6.3	1.3	5.6	0.9
2001	1.4	0.2	2.1	0.2	4.1	0.7	6.1	1.1	5.5	1.2	5.1	0.9
2002	1.2	0.2	2.3	0.2	2.8	0.6	3.9	0.8	4.9	1.1	5.3	0.8
2003	1.4	0.2	2.0	0.2	2.8	0.5	3.3	0.7	5.1	1.1	3.6	0.7
2004	1.4	0.2	1.4	0.2	3.0	0.6	4.1	0.9	5.5	1.2	2.7	0.6
2005	1.2	0.2	1.6	0.2	2.9	0.6	3.6	0.9	4.5	1.2	4.6	0.9
2006	1.6	0.2	2.1	0.2	2.6	0.6	2.6	0.8	3.8	1.0	4.9	0.9
2007	1.5	0.2	2.6	0.3	2.7	0.5	2.4	0.7	5.4	1.1	2.1	0.5
2008	0.8	0.2	2.1	0.2	2.1	0.5	3.2	0.8	4.9	1.0	1.4	0.4
2009	0.9	0.2	1.1	0.2	2.2	0.5	3.0	0.8	4.0	1.0	3.5	0.7
2010	0.9	0.2	1.2	0.2	1.8	0.5	2.8	0.8	5.1	1.1	4.0	0.8
2011	1.4	0.2	1.2	0.2	1.3	0.3	3.9	0.8	4.6	0.9	3.2	0.6

* Rate per 1,000 persons age 12 or older.

Source: Bureau of Justice Statistics, National Crime Victimization Survey, 1996–2011.

Appendix Table 17. Standard errors for table 6: Nonfatal firearm and nonfirearm violence, by victim-offender relationship, 2007–2011

Relationship to victim	Total nonfatal violence	Firearm violence		Nonfirearm violence	
		Number	Percent of total violence	Number	Percent of total violence
Total	520,018	107,331	0.3%	495,683	0.4%
Nonstranger	351,653	56,980	0.3	341,349	0.4
Intimate	167,301	27,453	0.6	163,040	0.6
Other relative	105,593	24,480	1.1	100,985	1.2
Friend/acquaintance	247,394	39,620	0.4	240,775	0.5
Stranger	281,855	74,319	0.6	262,843	0.7
Unknown	126,046	34,768	1.1	118,113	1.2

Source: Bureau of Justice Statistics, National Crime Victimization Survey, 2007–2011.

Appendix Table 18. Standard errors for table 7: Nonfatal firearm and nonfirearm violence, by location of crime, 2007–2011

Location	Total nonfatal violence		Firearm violence		Nonfirearm violence	
	Number	Percent	Total number	Percent	Total number	Percent
Total	520,094	~	107,331	~	495,761	~
Victims home or lodging	204,185	0.6%	42,032	1.6%	195,889	0.6%
Near victim's home	170,118	0.5	46,062	1.8	159,113	0.5
In, at, or near a friend, neighbor, or relative's home	106,117	0.3	22,283	1.0	102,275	0.3

Appendix Table 18. (Continued)

Location	Total nonfatal violence		Firearm violence		Nonfirearm violence	
	Number	Percent	Total number	Percent	Total number	Percent
Commercial place	125,178	0.4	27,429	1.2	120,070	0.4
Parking lot or garage	91,497	0.3	37,086	1.5	80,309	0.3
School	150,761	0.5	6,544	0.3	150,471	0.5
Open area, on street, or public transportation	166,506	0.5	46,260	1.8	155,261	0.5
Other location	128,572	0.4	18,853	0.8	126,101	0.4

~ Not applicable.
Source: Bureau of Justice Statistics, National Crime Victimization Survey, 2007–2011.

Appendix Table 19. Standard errors for table 9: Nonfatal firearm and nonfirearm violence, by injury and treatment received, 2007–2011

Injury and treatment	Total nonfatal violence		Firearm violence		Nonfirearm violence	
	Number	Percent	Total number	Percent	Total number	Percent
Injury	520,094	~	107,331	~	495,761	~
Not injured	435,239	0.7%	92,106	1.8%	414,216	0.7%
Injured	221,742	0.6	46,376	1.8	212,304	0.6
Serious injuries	76,874	0.2	23,654	1.0	73,196	0.3
Gun shot	12,758	--	12,758	0.6	~	~
Minor injuries	189,519	0.5	38,061	1.5	182,281	0.6
Rape without other injuries	39,058	0.1	4,232	0.2	38,750	0.1
Treatment for injury	221,742	~	46,376	~	212,304~	
No treatment	159,205	1.3%	22,999	3.7%	156,054	1.3%

Appendix Table 19. (Continued)

Injury and treatment	Total nonfatal violence		Firearm violence		Nonfirearm violence	
	Number	Percent	Total number	Percent	Total number	Percent
Any treatment	130,902	1.2	38,813	3.8	121,399	1.3
Treatment setting	130,902	~	38,813	~	121,399~	
At the scene/home of victim, neighbor, or friend/other location	70,643	1.7%	15,653	3.8%	68,065	1.9%
In doctor's office, hospital emergency room, or overnight at hospital	101,753	1.8	34,730	3.8	92,599	1.9

-- Less than 0.05%.

~ Not applicable.

Source: Bureau of Justice Statistics, National Crime Victimization Survey, 2007–2011.

Appendix Table 20. Numbers and standard errors for figure 11: Nonfatal firearm injuries, 2001–2011

Year	Number	Standard error
2001	41,044	10,287
2002	37,321	9,282
2003	42,505	11,558
2004	43,592	11,764
2005	50,320	14,431
2006	52,748	15,027
2007	48,676!	15,139
2008	56,626	16,648
2009	44,466	11,767
2010	53,738	15,769
2011	55,544	15,671

! Interpret with caution. Estimate based on fewer than 20 NEISS cases (based on unweighted data), national estimates less than 1,200 (based on weighted data), or the coefficient of variation (CV) of the estimate greater than 30%.

Source: Consumer Product Safety Commission, National Electronic Injury Surveillance System All Injury Program (NEISS-AIP), 2001–2011, accessed from the National Center for Injury Prevention and Control, CDC.

Appendix Table 21. Standard errors for table 10: Nonfatal firearm and nonfirearm violence reported and not reported to police, 2007–2011

	Total nonfatal violence	Firearm violence	Nonfirearm violence
Total	~	~	~
Reported	0.7%	2.1%	0.7%
Not reported	0.7	2.1	0.8
Reason not reported	~	~	~
Dealt with it another way	0.9%	2.1%	0.9%
Not important enough to respondent	0.7	1.6	0.7
Police could not or would not do anything to help	0.7	3.0	0.7
Fear of reprisal	0.4	3.1	0.4
Did not want to get offender in trouble with law, or advised not to report	0.4	1.3	0.4
Other, unknown, or not one most important reason	0.7	2.6	0.7

~ Not applicable.

Source: Bureau of Justice Statistics, National Crime Victimization Survey, 2007–2011.

Appendix Table 22. Standard errors for table 11: Self-protective behaviors, by type of crime, 2007–2011

Self-protective behavior	Violent crime		Property crime	
	Total number	Percent	Total number	Percent
Total	520,094	~	619,179	~
Offered no resistance	312,558	0.7%	295,645	0.3%
Threatened or attacked with a firearm	30,347	0.1	24,437	--
Threatened or attacked with other weapon	40,012	0.1	14,630	--
Threatened or attacked without a weapon	205,362	0.6	51,411	0.1
Nonconfrontational tactics	227,856	0.6	90,178	0.1
Other reaction	90,004	0.3	36,683	--
Unknown reaction	12,068	--	8,176	--
Victim was not present	~	~	641,196	0.4

~ Not applicable.
- - Less than 0.05%.
Source: Bureau of Justice Statistics, National Crime Victimization Survey, 2007–2011.

End Notes

[1] Many percentages and counts presented in this report are based on nonfatal firearm victimizations. Since firearm homicides accounted for about 2% of all firearm victimizations, when firearm homicides are included in the total firearm estimates, the findings do not change significantly.

[2] The fatal data from the National Vital Statistics System does not have victim-offender relationship information. The SHR victim-offender relationship data are not shown due to the large amount of missing data.

[3] National Center for Health Statistics. (2001). Comparability of cause of death between ICD-9 and ICD-10: Preliminary estimates. Retrieved from http://www.cdc.gov/nchs/data/nvsr/nvsr49/nvsr49_02.pdf.

INDEX

C

D

Q

P

R